Dancing To War

by

Elfi Hornby

The First Word Publishing
305 Lind, Ave SW #9
Renton, WA 98055
425-254-8575
dejonfw@yahoo.com

ISBN No. 0-9708590-2-3

This book is dedicated to
the memory of my brother,
and to the many brothers who fought
on the Russian front in World War II

ACKNOWLEDGMENTS

My lasting gratitude to my family and friends
for their encouragement and support
in writing this book.

Very special thanks to:

My husband, Jim, who gave me the tools
My son Robert, who sponsored the design.
Corkey Holloway, computer First Aid.
Joan Tornow and the Sound Writers
for their valuable critique.
My editor, Radhika Kumar, for her diligence
and thoughtful suggestions.
My publisher, Dejon, for his patience.

Index

INTRODUCTION

In victory or defeat, war is about death, suffering and destruction. It is the taker of youth, the taker of dreams.

I am a survivor of World War II, the cruelest, the deadliest, and the most destructive war in all of history. However, long before the first shot was fired, my family and I lived in the shadow of its cause, under Hitler's dictatorship. These were lean and anxious years for us. My father's opposing political conviction kept us on the fringes of poverty. But my mother had a dream and spent nights bent over intricate needlework in exchange for my dancing lessons. She wanted me to have what was denied her, a life in the theater. I was four years old when I enrolled in dance school. By the time I was six, I was on stage. At age ten, I gave solo concerts all around Bavaria's ritzy alpine resorts until I reached my teens.

Meanwhile, the war had started. After serving the mandatory '*Pflichtjahr*,' (a year of involuntary service on a farm or in a household for most young men and women) I landed a job dancing in a new revue at the *Deutsche Theater* in Munich, my home town. It was that or getting drafted into a munitions factory.

When the show closed in Munich, I traveled with it to Berlin, dancing at the famous *Wintergarten*. The war escalated. Most major cities came under heavy air attacks. Theaters shut down. Again, scrambling to avoid being stuck in a munitions factory, I signed with the Molkow Ballet, a traveling company, affiliated with the Berlin Opera where Egon Molkow had been first soloist and ballet master. Because I was only fifteen, government regulations required that I sign on as an apprentice. When my parents signed a three-year contract, they had also signed away their parental rights and did not suspect that they had delivered me into the hands of an exploitive, unscrupulous director. They expected that I would continue training under him, readying for my State exam, so that I could resume my career as soon as the war was over.

I traveled with the Molkow Ballet through many parts of Germany and German occupied zones, offering a variety program from classical to folk dance, often supplemented by guest soloists such as singers and instrumentalists. In the company of eight to ten other girls, all under the ages of twenty-one, this was mostly fun.

By the end of 1942, the war had converged on Germany. Many of its cities now lay in ashes, and the German army experienced its first major, devastating defeat. 1943 dawned under a cloud of doom. On the second day of January, I left with the Molkow Ballet on a new tour through eastern Germany. We counted ourselves lucky to get out of the range of Allied bombers. What happened next was incomprehensible. This is where my story begins.

The Molkow Ballet with Karlemann(center top),
Molkow(center front) and Bus

Erika and Elfi

Hannimusch

Hilde Molkow

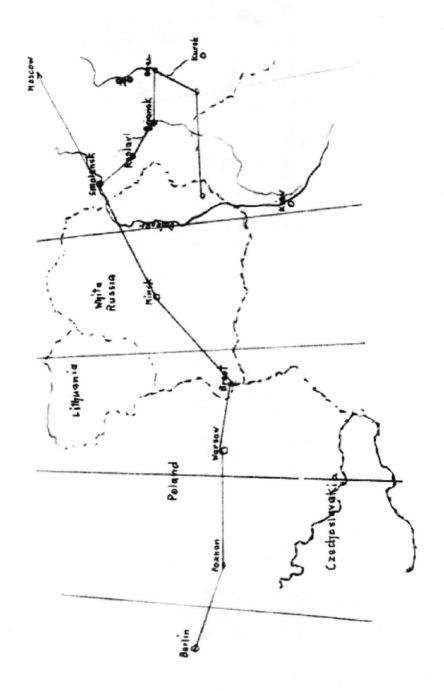

I

Drafted

An eerie, dead darkness shrouded the city of Poznan, Poland on that early January morning in 1943. Unlit streets remained deserted. Blacked-out buildings gave no hint of life within. Only occasional gusts of wind whooshing around corners, rattling a loose shutter or door, broke the dark, ghostly silence, and momentarily cleared the air of soot and smoke. It seemed as if Poznan and all that dwelled within it had fallen into a coma or under some evil spell.

My colleagues and I sat shivering on our trunks and suitcases in the back of a canvas-topped truck, waiting for the driver to take us to the railway station. Cold and miserable inside and out, our usually animated group had slipped into brooding silence. Suddenly sucked into the eye of a vicious storm, a bloody, merciless war, we pondered our helpless, hopeless situation and our chances of survival.

There were eleven of us: eight girls, dancers, between the ages of sixteen and twenty-one; Hannimusch, a matronly singer and our accompanist; Egon Molkow, our director, ballet-and-taskmaster; and his wife, Hilde, mother hen and go-between. I was sixteen, the youngest in the group.

Our small, traveling dance company had recently left

Berlin to begin a new tour through eastern Germany. Relieved to escape the nightly bombing raids on the city, we grudgingly accepted the tedium of wartime travel, from late and overcrowded trains and broken-down buses, to unheated hotels and theaters. At least, we were no longer in the line of fire.

We had spent less than two weeks on the road when our troupe received a summons to appear and audition before the German Military High Command in Poznan, Poland. It superceded all prior commitments and put us on the next train to Poznan. We knew that the military on occasion drafted shows for the sole purpose of entertaining its troops, and speculated with some excitement that we might be sent to France, Belgium, or to some other safe zone.

In a whirlwind of events, within only three days after arriving in Poznan, we had auditioned, were approved and processed like draftees, were given a number and handed our orders--a six-month assignment to the Russian front.

The Russian front!!! Our first reaction was, "No! This can't be happening. Not to us! They would not...they could not send us girls, adolescents to the front, into the bloodiest of all battle zones! To Russia...in the deep of winter? No! We are dancers, not soldiers."

The Russian Front!!! Orders every soldier feared. Orders often given out as a punishment. Too many of our men who had been sent there, never returned. The lucky ones got wounded. It was like a death sentence.

Also, the timing could not have been worse. The German army had just suffered its biggest, bloodiest defeat of the entire war at Stalingrad, which left it crippled and its front lines virtually defenseless. Our soldiers complained bitterly about shortages, from winter clothing, to supplies, to ammunition and equipment. Now they faced a stronger-than-ever Russian army, preparing to launch a new major offensive, and had nothing left to stop it. Morale among them had plummeted to its lowest point.

What could they want with girls, at a time like this?

Our orders listed Smolensk as our immediate destination. On a map at headquarters, it showed Smolensk to be only twenty some miles behind the lines, protruding

14

into enemy territory like a burr. A severe winter freeze had temporarily stalled the fighting there, but once the weather eased, we would be caught in the thick of it. We felt like sacrificial lambs sent to appease the God of war.

During the short, bumpy ride through the narrow, cobbled streets of Poznan to the railway station, my mind raced down a road of gloomy scenarios. Six months from now, where would I be? Dead? Wounded? Or worse-- captured by the Russians? We had heard stories about another troupe like ours that had been captured and was later found raped, tortured to death and mutilated. Would I live to see my seventeenth birthday? I thought of home and my parents. It would break their hearts when they found out. They have had no say, and would not even know about my fate until they received my letter. That could take from one to two weeks.

Dry, voiceless sobs shuddered up my throat.

The truck stopped. With flashlight in hand, the driver came around to the back and lifted us down. Laden down with bags and bundles, we trudged behind our director, Herr Molkow, through a tunnel made of rocks and sand- bags to a massive door which opened onto the enormous, empty lobby of Poznan's railway station. Our entrance stirred up a drone of ghostly echoes. Molkow waited until everyone was accounted for, then ordered us to stay there while he oversaw the transfer of our baggage.

Left standing in the middle of this immense, empty space, our group appeared lost and abandoned. Our voices drowned in the reverberations of Molkow's foot- steps that multiplied to sound like an army, marching. The echoes hung in the chilly air long after he had disap- peared into the shadowy recesses of the depot.

I scanned the dimly lit space for a bench, a counter or shelf, anything where I could set down my load. Nothing. Grimy outlines on the inlaid marble floor still indicated where such furnishings used to stand, but the place was gutted, plundered. Scrap lumber boarded up broken ticket and concession windows. Holes in the stone walls with wires sticking out suggested an earlier presence of light fixtures. A low-wattage bulb dangling on a long, thin wire from high above a domed ceiling cast a dim, shad- owy light, the only light inside the station. It was also the only sign that the station was still in operation.

My eyes lingered on the still undamaged, ornately sculpted border that banded the cupola and two supporting marble pillars. It spoke of Poland's better days, of a time described in dusty old romance novels I had read.

The straps and handles of my bags and bundles cut into my arms and hands. Reluctantly, I set them on the dirty floor to allow the blood to flow back into my freezing, tingling fingers. Inge and Erika did the same. The three of us usually hung out together. Inge was from Hamburg, a quiet, shy, wispy, frizzy-haired dreamer with eyes like a fawn's, only months older than myself. Erika, already seventeen, was my roommate and best friend. Square and solid in build and character, with a no-nonsense attitude, she was my anchor; my source of stability and advice. In many ways, she and I were opposites. She was orderly; I was disorganized. She respected and obeyed rules; I questioned and challenged them. She was level headed; I was impulsive. I was her source of entertainment and adventure, and she made sure that I did not step off the deep end. We were a good combination. We needed and depended on each other.

All three of us had signed on with the Molkow Ballet under a government required apprenticeship contract. As minors, we had to attend and graduate from a State-approved program for artists that included more than just dance training. In Berlin, between tours, we had to take courses in art history, music theory, and had to study the ideology of the *Nationalsozialismus* (Nazi Party), memorizing the names and titles of its leaders. Our director, Egon Molkow, former soloist and Ballet Master at the State Opera in Berlin, was in charge of our dance training. It seemed a privilege to study under him. He had quite a name in theater circles, doing choreography for stage and movies, and directing many political and public extravaganzas. Erika, Inge and I lived with him in a grand villa in Grunewald, Berlin, with movie stars as neighbors. We received our room and board, plus pocket money--sixty Reichsmark per month. In turn, he got well-trained dancers to work in his show.

What looked so promising at the beginning, eventually turned into bitter disappointment. Molkow showed no interest in us; not personally, not professionally. He taught us what the show required, and that was it. For anything else, he put his wife, Hilde, in charge.

While we stood there, waiting, the cold from the surrounding marble and stone penetrated skin and bones and turned our breath to steam. Erika fidgeted with a long, hand-knitted shawl that kept slipping off her head, and she and I kept tapping our feet to keep our toes from freezing. Inge stood stiff like a statue with shoulders drawn up and a blank expression on her thin, pale face. Her eyes were red from crying. None of us had much to say that morning.

Ever since we had learned of our assignment, our emotions had run the gamut from disbelief, panic, outrage, despair, to morbid resignation. We had hardly slept, but had cried a lot. Not until we climbed on that truck did I lose hope that our orders would be changed. "After all, we were just girls, not soldiers. It had to be a mistake," we kept reassuring one another. That hope now gone, I felt empty and betrayed.

As the minutes dragged on, it struck me as strange that we had not seen nor heard anyone else come or go. I was about to ask if, perhaps, we had come to the wrong station when Molkow reappeared.

"Follow me," his deep voice thundered through the hall as he charged toward a large, double door opposite the one through which we had entered. He opened it and, to our astonishment, we stared at a platform jam-packed with German troops and their gear. Dim blue lights here and there allowed just enough visibility to distinguish shapes. In single file we trailed behind our chief, groped and stumbled over and through a tangle of limbs and resting bodies, bumped into mounds of gear, knocked over pyramids of rifles, drew curses, mumbled apologies, until we finally reached the far end of the station where we found our baggage stacked. Knife-sharp, icy gusts of wind tore at our clothing and pelted us with gritty snow whipped up from between acres of track beds. With a sudden spurt of energy, we girls stacked trunks and suitcases against the wind and huddled behind them, wrapped in blankets given to us by the military. Molkow declined his wife's invitation to join us. Instead, he flipped up his coat collar, tightened down his black homburg and started to pace back and forth, alternately flapping his arms and blowing into his gloved fists. His face, partly hidden by large horn-rimmed glasses, remained typically tight-lipped and impenetrable.

Hilde shrugged her shoulders at him, opened her purse and pulled out a gold cigarette case and lighter. Without taking off her leather gloves, she inserted a cigarette into a long-stemmed holder and lit up. Her already sunken cheeks hollowed even further as she drew the smoke deep into her lungs, held it there, and having satisfied that initial craving, let it slowly curl from her nostrils. She passed the case to Ulla, her younger sister, only about half her age and the main soloist of our group. Ulla helped herself, and with a nod from Hilde, passed it on to Betty, Uschi, and Emmy, all eighteen or older.

"May I have one, too? Please?" I begged Hilde, knowing that she did yield on occasion. "Just a drag or two?"

"You know what'll happen if Egon catches you." Her eyes flashed me a warning then glanced up at her still pacing husband. Molkow did not allow us minors to smoke. We could drink, but we could not smoke. Nevertheless, we did so anyway, behind his back. Smoking had become a crutch. It comforted me when I was cold, hungry or afraid. I was all of these things just then. Unfortunately, this time, Hilde stood firm.

Before long Hannimusch, who sat beside me on one of our wooden show trunks, nudged and signaled me to look behind her. One of the girls--it was Uschi, the oldest, smallest and brainiest in our group--passed me a cigarette. I crouched down, drew a couple of deep puffs, then handed it back. Hannimusch, single, in her mid forties, about the same age as Hilde, was our ally. When we girls pulled one of our youthful shenanigans, she usually had a hand in it, too, which often saved us from Molkow's brutal temper. She laughed with us, she cried with us, and we comforted one another in matters of the heart.

Time passed quietly and slowly. Erika, without removing her wool mittens, awkwardly scribbled a few last good-byes on plain, pre-stamped postcards. Inge and Uschi, resting against one another, fell asleep. Everyone else seemed lost in thought. Mine again wandered homeward. I was worried how my parents, especially my father, would react to the news that I had been sent to the Russian front. First my brother, who had volunteered to join his buddies on the front, now me. I feared that my father would burst out cursing the "damned Nazis and their war," and land in Dachau, a concentration camp near Munich. For years, he had been walking a tightrope for refusing to join the Party and for speaking out against it. Every time the doorbell rang early in the morning, my mother panicked, thinking the Gestapo had come to take him away, fearing that we would never see him again. I was more concerned for his safety than for my own.

The wind had settled down. It started to get light. Suddenly children's voices drifted into the station from across the tracks and interrupted my thoughts. I stood up and saw a gang of young scavengers picking the rails clean of anything usable from lumps of coal to cigarette butts. Their noisy scramble entertained the men who tossed them money, food, or whatever else they could spare. However, when some of the older kids tried to sneak off with packs and rifles, the soldiers chased them out of the station.

During an earlier tour through Poland, we had encountered other such juvenile marauders and often wondered to whom, if anybody, these children belonged. Some were as young as four or five and were already quite adept at begging, stealing, wheeling and dealing. At first, our hearts had filled with pity, but then we started missing things. These children pilfered anything within their grasp. A number of times we had to chase them down to get back what they had stolen. Since then, we had learned to keep a close and wary eye on them.

After this short interlude, the station fell quiet again. The wait for the train dragged on. It was already more than an hour late. Every few minutes Herr Molkow checked his watch and muttered to himself. Finally, from an overhead loudspeaker blared a garbled announcement. Soldiers scrambled to their feet and grabbed their packs and rifles. The announcement was repeated. "Train from Brest..." Grumbling, the men settled down again. Suddenly we heard a man shout orders, "Get back,

19

men...get back...make way." I climbed atop the trunk to see what the commotion was about and saw litter-carrying medics clear a path through the crowd, then line up stretchers along the edge of the platform next to the tracks. Minutes later the steel rails hummed. A train marked with Red Cross signs and banners puffed in and screeched to a halt in a cloud of hissing steam. Doors flung open and the first wounded emerged. They walked, limped and hobbled--with canes, on crutches, in casts and bandages--through the crowd toward the depot's exit. Most of them wore brave grins on their haggard faces and waved to the cheering troops in the station. A tall young fellow not far from us cupped his hands over his mouth and shouted, "Hey, you Heinies, it's about time you made room for us up front. We'll show you how to win this war."

"It's all yours," one of the veterans stopped to reply and waved his crutch in the air. "For us the war is over, thank God! We are going home."

The good-natured heckling between the wounded and their cocky replacements continued. But after the first litters were lifted from the train, a hush fell over the crowd. Stretcher after stretcher with moaning, mutilated bodies in blood-soaked dressings passed through the station. Some appeared lifeless, wrapped in white gauze like mummies. Others had stumps of limbs propped up.

"Poor devils," Hannimusch sighed and sat down, wiping her eyes. "God help us!" she added with a shiver, "Where they come from, that's where we have to go."

I, too, had seen enough. It was one thing to watch such scenes on a movie screen accompanied by heroic commentary, and quite another to witness them first hand. "That could be us coming home on stretchers," I said to Erika. "They are marching and we are dancing to war."

A stench of iodine and rotting flesh permeated the air. Back in our huddle, we buried our noses in shawls and coat sleeves. Even Molkow quit pacing and faced downwind. Shortly after the hospital train left the station the arrival of another train was announced.

"This is it," Molkow shouted over the sudden rumble of activity. "Grab your stuff. Let's go!"

A train labored in a few tracks over from the main platform, this time from the opposite direction. It seemed jammed full already. The push was on. Swept along by this driving, shoving mass of men, wedged between smelly uniforms and bulky packs, I lost sight of my group. Some fellows passed their gear overhead and through the windows of the train, then attempted to board it the same way, while the majority swarmed around the doors like bees around a hive. I had dropped back, waiting for the congestion to clear, when I spied Molkow. His black coat flapped in the breeze like the wings of a vulture. He saw me, shook his fist and yelled, "Don't just stand there...get the devil on that train!"

How? Where? I glanced right and left. "What, if I don't get on? Maybe I get sent home?" That hopeful thought lasted a split second, followed by, "Oh, my God! Molkow has my papers, my ID, my ration tickets, my clothes. Without them, I might just as well be dead." Now panic-driven, I squeezed through the throng toward a coach door, managed to get one foot on the first step, then another, and from then on was pushed up-and-onward without effort of my own. The strings and handles of my bags and bundles cut painfully into my hands. I held on to them desperately as they became entangled in the grinding mass of bodies. Barely able to breathe, feeling faint, I fought to stay calm and conscious, knowing that if I sank to the floor, I would be trampled to death before anyone realized I was there.

By the time the train started to move, the men had stacked packs and guns in corners and nooks from floor to ceiling, gradually gaining space to breathe. I advanced into the aisle, which had windows on one side and compartments on the other. I knew I had to find the rest of my troupe, but it seemed impossible. The train picked up speed. Through the swaying, shifting bodies I caught a glimpse of something white farther up the coach. Erika! It had to be. With a great sense of relief, I inched forward in her direction. She saw me finally and waved. Eventually we met by a window.

"*Mensch*, am I glad to see you. I was afraid you didn't get on," she greeted me. We managed a hug. Her worried face broke into a big grin. To look into that familiar freckled face of hers with that broad grin calmed all my fears. What ever happened now, I was not alone. I was with my best friend. And I knew she felt the same way.

"I wish you could see yourself. You look like *vom Wind verweht*," she said.

I knew I did. My coat had twisted around my body that its hem rose to my hip and the row of buttons ended in the back. My hair hung over my face and I had to blow it away from my eyes to be able to see.

"If you think I look messy, go look at yourself," I laughed. Indeed, both of us looked like refugees from a storm.

Finally, we gained enough space to set our bundles down. My fingers were so numb by now that I had to pry them open and wait until life returned to them before I could hold a comb.

The air inside the coach turned gray with smoke. It was uncomfortably warm.

"Shouldn't we start looking for the Molkows?" Erika mentioned with concern.

"Let's wait till everybody has settled down," I told her. "We'll find them soon enough."

Some soldiers continued stacking gear. Others rummaged in their packs. With our backs turned to the men, we gazed out the window at the thinning houses of the city, followed by snow-dusted farmland, squared off by rows of shrubs and trees.

"Looks so peaceful, doesn't it?" Erika said and sighed. I nodded, wishing I were home, wandering through the tranquil woods and meadows that bordered the neighborhood where I lived.

The train swayed and rocked. Bodies bumped against bodies, knocking one another off balance. A fellow behind me lost his footing and slammed me hard against the window. I cried out in pain. His head jerked around, his mouth dropped open, and for seconds he simply stared at me as if he had seen a ghost. "Jesus," he finally found his voice. "Jesus! What do you know? GIRLS! There are GIRLS on this train," he repeated, elbowing a buddy. Till then, everybody had been too concerned getting on the train, keeping track of and stacking their equipment, that nobody had paid us any heed. Suddenly we became the center of attention.

"Hey! What are you doing on this transport? Are you Germans? Are you nurses?" Questions bombarded us from all directions.

"Where are you headed?" The fellow that bumped into me asked.

"To a hospital," I grimaced, rubbing my head and shoulder.

"Sorry," he said, and in the same breath repeated his question, "What are you women doing on a troop train? Where are you going?"

Erika, straight faced, with an exaggerated Saxon dialect, answered dryly. "We finally got tired of the nightly air raids in Berlin and thought we'd take a vacation on the Russian front."

"Ah...come on...really...tell! What are you doing on this transport?" others chimed in.

"The *Fuehrer* sent us to the front to cheer you guys up," I answered.

"I know. You are show people," guessed one of the men.

"Figures," scoffed a pipe-smoking sergeant leaning against the compartment door opposite from us, "We ask for reinforcements, weapons, ammunition, supplies, winter uniforms, and such simple things as socks, long johns, blankets, and what do they send us? GIRLS!"

"Sorry about that," Erika snapped. "We aren't exactly thrilled about it either."

"Don't pay him no mind," the first fellow interceded. "He's already shell-shocked. It's his third year on the front." The young draftees around him laughed. The sergeant, a lean, weathered-looking man in his forties, calmly took the pipe out of his mouth and looked cynically from one to the other. "Greenhorns!" he sneered. "You'll soon find out what it's like out there...holed up in trenches, in below zero temperatures, without long johns and winter uniforms. When your feet freeze so that when you take off your boots, your flesh peels off your bones. Just wait. When you're plowing miles through snow up to your belly because the trucks froze up, or ran out of gas. Oh, yes! Just wait. And when the Russkies come at you and all you have are blanks instead of bullets in your

23

gun. Then...the last thing you'll be thinking of is girls. You'll find out then." He relit his pipe, and with it dangling from his mouth finished by apologizing, "No offense intended, ladies."

Embarrassed silence followed. Erika and I exchanged glances, silently agreeing that, perhaps, it was time to move on and look for the Molkows. We also urgently needed to find a toilet. Normally there was one at the end of every other coach but getting there was not easy. Every step required someone or something to shift or move, because otherwise there was no space to plant one's foot. As we picked our way through the coach, our presence raised quite a stir. When we reached the end of it, there was a toilet all right, but it was stuffed full of gear, its door jammed open, leaving only a narrow path to the stool on which a soldier sat reading a book.

"Let's try for the next one," Erika said. When we reached it, the situation was the same.

"What are we going to do?" Erika whimpered. "I'm about to burst."

"Go on...go...go...go..." I urged her.

We struggled through five coaches, one as jammed full as the other. When we came to the third toilet, it, too, was crammed full and occupied.

"I can't wait any longer," Erika said. Pearls of sweat glistening on her forehead. "This has got to be it."

Desperate action was required. "Hey, fellows..." I addressed the soldiers blocking the door to the toilet, "could you please move? We need to use these facilities." I could feel embarrassment flush my face. At first, the men stared as us, baffled. This was followed by snickers, wisecracks, and finally uproarious laughter. Some did make a feeble attempt to clear the door, but it was hopeless. Suddenly a voice commanded, "*Achtung!* Face front! Eyes left." It cracked through the guffaws like a whip. The soldiers snapped to attention. Those on the floor scrambled to their feet. A human wall two to three bodies deep encircled the toilet's entrance, facing away from it. The fellow barking these commands turned to us. "You ladies may use the facilities now," he said with unexpected chivalry.

"Great!" Erika mumbled, beet-red, rolling her eyes.

"Sing," ordered the commander. A crude tenor started singing, "By a waterfall..." but was quickly overpowered by the leader's voice who chose *"Das kann doch einen Seemann nicht erschuettern..."* a snappy marching tune about fearless seafarers. The facility was now both peek-proof and soundproof. Our modesty thus protected, we did what we had to do. Four choruses later we mumbled an embarrassed "thank you" and fled the scene.

After struggling through three more coaches, we located the Molkows and the rest of our troupe in an officer's coach where Molkow snored by the window in the upholstered comfort of first class. Hilde sat beside him, applying fresh makeup. The deep red color of her wide mouth and the strong, black outline of her large, almond shaped eyes made her face look mask-like and grotesque.

"It's about time you showed up," she greeted us. "Tell me, why is it that you two are always the last ones to show?" She handed us our ration of sandwiches--blood sausage between slices of dry rye bread. "There is a water container in the aisle, if you're thirsty," she advised us.

We grabbed the sandwiches and exited before Molkow woke up and barked at us. He always barked at us. He was our boss, but we did not know him. I had never heard him laugh out loud. He never showed any emotion. He just shouted orders, and when he was drunk, we were afraid of him.

Out in the aisle, Erika opened her sandwich and rumpled her nose. "I am so tired of this diet of bread and blood sausage."

"Bet you, Molkow's got butter, ham and salami on his, on our ration tickets," I grumbled.

"I know. What can we do about it?" Erika shrugged her shoulders, and slapped the two slices of bread together again and took a small bite.

We soon found the rest of our troupe scattered about in the two first-class coaches reserved for officers, and visited back and forth, listening to depressing stories the men had to tell about Russia. Eventually, however, we retreated to the aisle where the air was cooler and less smoky, and where a stack of duffel bags offered soft, comfortable seating. Inge joined us and, from time to time, so did Hannimusch. She could not stand cigar

25

smoke. It bothered her throat and vocal chords. For a while we played cards until we finally succumbed to the hypnotic sway and rhythm of the train. Leaning into one another, we fell asleep.

II

Warsaw

"Next stop--Warsaw!" a conductor announced, entering the coach. He pulled down the blackout shades on the aisle windows and reminded passengers in the compartments to do the same. It was getting dark outside. Without hurry, officers retrieved baggage from racks above the seats, buttoned their uniforms, then sat down again, leaving their overcoats off. "It may be awhile," one said to Hilde, who had sprung into action, hastily gathering her belongings and urging us girls to get ready. Erika, Inge and I had remained in the aisle, peeking out the window from behind the shade, hoping to catch a glimpse of the city, but there was still no sign of it.

Our previous travels had taken us through many parts of Poland but never to Warsaw, the romanticized home of Paderewsky and Chopin. Old books I had read described the city in tantalizing detail, painting a picture in my mind of busy boulevards lined with chestnut trees, elegant sidewalk cafes, high fashion shops, romantic gardens, and gala events where bejeweled ladies dressed in silk and satin danced the Mazurka and Polonaise all night with gallant gentlemen. I had hung on to every word I read. It filled me with a burning desire to see and experience it first hand someday. But what I had seen of Poland so far was mostly poverty and squalor. Several unfortunate experiences had soured me on the entire country.

On our first tour through Poland, everyone in our troupe, including Molkow, had contracted head lice, and we could not get rid of them until we crossed the border into Germany again. The next time, I landed in a Polish hospital, sick with intestinal influenza. I shared a ward with thirty other patients. It reeked of urine, vomit and excrement. In the bathroom, lice marched around the tub's rim as if they were house pets. All patients, even those supposedly under quarantine, shared the same facilities--one toilet, one wash basin, one tub. When I saw a woman use these facilities, who had open, oozing sores all over her face and body, whose nose was partially eaten away from--I was told--advanced syphilis, I fled the place that night with a young Polish girl who was equally appalled and eager to leave.

Poland puzzled me. Every now and then, among the drab, soot-gray city buildings, with dark, dingy rooms and minimum plumbing, along yardless, treeless streets, sometimes piled with garbage on which children played, I glimpsed something stunningly beautiful and extravagant. The most recent example was the railway station in Poznan with its inlaid marble floor, scrolled pillars and sculpted cupola. However, even such treasures had fallen prey to decades of neglect and disrepair. The German press did not miss an opportunity to deride the Poles for these conditions. Without delving into the background and the reasons, we assumed it was a Polish trait. I still had hopes that Warsaw would change our minds.

More than a half-hour had passed since the conductor announced the arrival in Warsaw. The train slowed to a crawl. When it finally did stop, it was pitch dark outside. Erika, Inge and I never did see any sign of the city.

We lined up behind Molkow, who let the officers get off first. "Stay close together," he instructed us. "I don't want to have to look or wait for any of you." As we got off, we stepped out into total darkness, unable to tell whether we were inside a station or a farmer's back yard. Around us commands cracked, whistles blew, dimmed flashlights flicked on and off, and we heard troops assemble and march off toward idling trucks or buses. Molkow assured himself and us that headquarters knew of our arrival and surely had sent someone to pick us up.

We waited...and waited. Before long, we stood alone in the crisp, clear night, alongside the empty, abandoned train, listening to the fading grind of motor cars.

As our eyes adjusted to the night, we saw the outline of a building against the starry sky and headed for it. The pavement under our feet assured us that this was, perhaps, a station after all. We entered a small waiting room. Faint light from a windowed counter and partly open door fell onto the cracked, peeling plaster walls and the crumbly cement floor. Molkow charged like an angry bull into the stationmaster's office, demanding to use his phone to contact headquarters. The rest of us stood around, venting our misgivings about the military. I recalled what the pipe-smoking sergeant on the train had said, "...troops up front need supplies and ammunition, not dancing girls."

A short while later Molkow emerged. Hilde looked at him expectantly. "What's going on?" she asked.

"They're sending a truck," he growled. Hands stuffed into his coat pockets, he stomped outside. We sat down on a short, back-to-back bench standing in the middle of the room, resigned to wait. My enthusiasm and curiosity for Warsaw wilted. Was it all just fiction what I had read?

Later, the long, bumpy ride on the back of an open truck further cooled my romantic expectations. Nor did the hotel promise any pleasant surprises as we entered through a patched door that was about to fall off its hinges. Inside, a storm lamp on a makeshift wooden counter dimly illuminated a spacious lobby with a grand staircase curving upward to either side. The space beneath had been curtained off with army blankets, pinned to a clothesline. From there emerged a short, stout, uniformed figure.

"*Herr Wachtmeister?*" Molkow queried.

"*Jawohl.*"

"I understand we have rooms assigned here...?"

The disheveled sergeant, who looked as if he had just rolled out of bed, ran his fingers through his mussed-up hair and eyed us up and down. He hesitated, and reluctantly handed Molkow a clipboard with a form to fill out.

"This place does not look promising," I overheard Hannimusch say to Hilde. I agreed, but was ready to settle for the bare essentials: a chance to clean up and a bug-free, clean bed.

While Molkow filled out the form, the sergeant helped the truck driver unload our trunks and suitcases, then took the lamp and led us upstairs. We grabbed as much as we could carry and struggled up behind him.

"What is this...? No lights in the building?" Molkow asked. His voice rumbled with irritation like the distant thunder of an approaching storm.

"Lost our electricity," the sergeant replied, "but there are candles in the rooms."

At the end of a dark, narrow hallway he opened a door. "This is for the women. For the men it's round the other way."

"Men? There are no men. Just me." Molkow corrected him. "This is my wife."

The sergeant mumbled something, felt around his pockets for matches, then reached around the door where he lit a candle. He stepped aside to let us enter. Molkow stuck his head in for a quick look, then followed him down the hall with Hilde in tow.

At first glance we saw a long, large room, with a double row of single bunks, twelve in all. Hannimusch lit a few more candles contained in small tin cans, then tested the blanketed beds. "If I were a horse, I'd whinny," she mocked. "Look at that! Straw-stuffed gunnysacks. Not even a sheet." Hannimusch dug her fists into her waist and looked around the room, shaking her head. "We did not always stay in the best places, but this...this...they may as well have stuck us in a barn. "

Erika lifted a blanket between thumb and index finger. "Ugh!" She cringed. "I wonder how many sweaty, stinky bodies have slept in them. I doubt if they have ever been cleaned."

Disgusted, not knowing what to do, we stood around hoping for something, a miracle perhaps, when Molkow's voice boomed up the hall. "...*eine Schweinerei!* Damn it... get that quartermaster...get headquarters on the phone. Who do they think we are?"

It was not often that any of us agreed with Molkow. However, this was one time we all rooted for him. Hannimusch opened the door and cheered him on. "Yeah...go give 'em hell, Egon!"

Hilde, meanwhile, sought refuge with us, complaining that she and Egon were put in a room just like ours with a dozen bunks and that, if troops came through unexpectedly, she would have to move in with us.

"Shows you how much the military values us," Hannimusch commented. "I didn't see any officers being bunked in here. My God, this is Warsaw! What's it going to be like in Russia?"

"Wait till you see the washroom and the toilets," Hilde mentioned, pinching her nose.

"I can imagine."

"No. You can't. Come, look."

With candles in hand we trooped down the hall behind Hilde, but soon could rely on our noses alone to find it. At the door the stench was overwhelming. Against one wall on a tiled floor stood four urinals, two stools, and on the other side hung two small wash basins, all crusted over in various shades of yellow and brown. Out of one faucet came a slow but steady drip.

"I don't think there is any water," Hilde concluded. "That's just the ice melting in the pipes."

Molkow still raved and barked profanities downstairs, apparently getting nowhere. When it became evident that we were stuck in this place for the night, we stormed the sergeant and demanded that he bring us at least a few buckets with water and a washbowl. He was extremely apologetic.

"They should have never assigned you to this place," he said, and promised to try his best to find what we asked for. He came later with a pail and a couple of large tins filled with water.

Erika was so upset about having to sleep in bedding already slept in by countless soldiers that she sank down on a bunk and cried. Inge sat down beside her, about to break into tears also.

Meanwhile, across from me, Hannimusch began to undress. "My girdle is killing me," she explained. She tucked, pulled, wriggled, grunted, huffed and puffed, then with a loud, drawn-out, ecstatic "aahhh..." she let the girdle slide down her legs and massaged her liberated, undulating midriff. Watching her gyrations, I burst

31

out laughing. I laughed and laughed and could not stop. Tears rolled down my cheeks.

"What's so damn funny?" she snarled at me.

"Watching you go through your daily exercise."

She glared at me. My laughter seemed to have offended not only Hannimusch, but everyone in the room. Still, I continued to watch and laugh as she hastily slipped into flannel pajamas, put a wool sweater over that, wool socks on her feet and a shawl around her head. The room was unheated and it was freezing. She then attacked her mattress, punched and shook it with such angry vigor that straw scattered everywhere and the dust made us cough. "Who in hell expects anybody to sleep on this rat's nest?"

My thoughtless behavior in the face of everybody's wretchedness was ill timed. It heaped insult upon injury. "Oh, stuff it." Erika jumped on me. She and Inge would not speak to me anymore all evening. What they did not know, of course, was that had I not laughed I would have screamed or cried. Inside I boiled. The military treated their horses better than us. My anger, however, only masked much deeper emotions. I felt so totally abandoned, so lost, so terribly homesick--feelings I kept carefully hidden, not wanting to destroy my gutsy and dauntless image.

Most of us went to bed fully dressed. Long after the last candle flickered out and I lay rolled up in my own blanket, teeth clenched, I allowed my tears to flow.

I listened to the rustle of straw, as restless sleepers tossed and turned to find a comfortable position on the lumpy mattresses. My thoughts drifted. I was a child again, safe and protected, dreaming about the future. I saw myself as a young woman, a doctor, finding cures to heal the sick and save them from dying.

From about my twelfth year until I left home, I often tagged along with a doctor friend visiting his patients. He coached me to be his assistant, telling me that I had a knack for it. I learned how to bandage wounds, and learned about illnesses and treatments. Then, when a neighbor's boy, a toddler, came down with pneumonia and died, despite the doctor's best efforts to save him, I knew what I really wanted to do with my life. I wanted to find a cure for such devastating illnesses and wrote an essay on the subject in school. My teacher read it and, though she knew I had been groomed to be a dancer, she encouraged me to try. For over a year she tutored me privately, without charge, to prepare me for the entrance exam at the University of Munich.

The war had caused extreme shortages of men in various professions, especially among teachers. To fill these positions, the government offered liberal stipends to young women out of grade school to enter universities. My teacher thought that I would more than qualify, but the government did not. When I filled out the entrance exam questionnaire, I came to the page that listed Party affiliation. "Are you a member of...? Were you ever a member of...? Were your parents members of...?" I went down the list and my answers were all the same. "No. No. No." It did not surprise me when I got my application back from the university, stamped, "Denied." My family and I did not support the government, why should it support us?

That was all right with my mother who had dreams of her own for me. She wanted me to be what she could not, to be in the theater, to be on stage. She had scrimped and saved and sacrificed for my ballet lessons. I reached her goal before I was six years old. By age eleven, I gave solo concerts. I danced because it pleased my parents, and because it pleased my audiences. My own dreams and aspirations were left to wither.

But what did it matter now? With a sigh I buried my regrets over unfulfilled dreams. Trapped between my parents, the political system, and the war, I felt powerless. Like a puppet, I danced as they pulled the strings. But we were all puppets, I concluded. Soldiers marched; we danced. What will be will be. With that, I surrendered to the night.

It seemed as if I had just fallen asleep when a sharp knock on the door woke me up. "Want you downstairs in thirty minutes," I heard Molkow bark. Grunts and groans escaped from the various bunks. Bright sunlight cut through the slits in the cardboard that covered the only window. My body unfurled slowly from its awkward position and I raised my head. Hannimusch with her Persian lamb coat draped around her shoulders, was already sitting up, hugging and resting her chin on her flanneled knees. "God, what did I get myself into?" she lamented. "I could have stayed home. So what, if I would have had to punch a time-card in some factory, at least I could have slept in my own bed." A thoughtful moment later she added with a sigh, "...that is, if I still have a bed." She lived in Cologne, a city that had come under unrelenting, heavy air attacks by allied bombers which had already destroyed over fifty percent of the city.

When most theaters closed in Germany because of the war, a mad scramble ensued to hire on with a traveling company to avoid being put to work in a munitions factory. Those who succeeded considered themselves lucky. So did I. This latest assignment, however, made us realize that even luck had a dark side.

With cold cream and a damp wash cloth we cleaned up the best we could, brushed the wrinkles out of our clothes, combed our hair, and headed downstairs to the lobby where Molkow brooded over a game of solitaire, ignoring our "Good morning!" Hannimusch walked up to him with a fiendish grin. She patted him on the back and needled, "Did you forget to shave this morning, Egon?"

He threw her a dagger of a glance, folded his cards and started counting heads. "Who is missing?"

"Ilse," we answered.

"Where the devil is she?"

"Upstairs, painting her face," Emmy reported.

"That figures. Damn it! Go get her, somebody. She'll take all day."

Just then Ilse came into view, with rouge, lipstick and heavy mascara on her face, her blond hair swept up into a crown of curls. That was Ilse. Hilde was the only other one who bothered with makeup that morning. The rest of us, pale, with dark circles under our eyes, rumpled, and crumpled in spirit, just did not care.

"Where are we going?" Hannimusch asked Hilde.

"To the hospital to get shots."

Outside, bright sunshine and the fresh, almost spring-like air lifted our mood. Before us stretched a narrow cobblestone street, walled in by old, soot-blackened stone and stucco buildings four to five stories high.

Shops on the ground floor as well as most windows had been boarded shut. From a mound of rubble immediately behind the hotel rose the remnants of walls. Bricks, stones and other debris had spilled over the sidewalk and onto the street.

"*Heilige Maria*! That looks like it was part of the hotel!" Hannimusch gasped, pointing to rooms sheered off as if they had been sliced in half with a knife.

"The work of Russians bombers. Happened about a week ago, the Sergeant said," Molkow explained.

"Russian bombers?" we repeated in unison and utter disbelief. Returning veterans always laughed at the Russian Air Force. It was a joke, they said. Pigeons could outfly it and were more likely to hit a target even without aiming. Nobody needed to fear an air raid from the East.

As we went on, we saw building after building bombed and burned out. Most of this damage, we assumed, had been done during heavy fighting and by the *Luftwaffe* when the Germans marched into Warsaw.

Following the directions on a hand-drawn map we came to a main arterial. It was at least five lanes wide with proportionately wide sidewalks. Traffic was light--a few delivery trucks, a horse-drawn cart, bicyclists, and two old women pulling wooden wagons, one heaped with furniture, the other with twigs, branches and scrap wood.

"So little traffic...it feels like Sunday," Hilde commented.

"This used to be what '*Unter den Linden*' is in Berlin," Molkow told her. He knew Warsaw well, having lived and studied there in his youth.

Up and down the street we saw only ruins and hollow facades, much like buildings on a movie set. Wrought-iron balconies and remnants of sculpted masonry still adorned fractured doorways and blown-out windows. On the other side of the street was a park. A broken statue lay at the foot of its dormant fountain. Scattered up and down the street stood totally debarked trunks of trees. White and ghost-like, their jagged limbs reached skyward like the hands and arms of frozen corpses. A wave of sudden recognition forced tears to my eyes. "There were the chestnut trees mentioned in the novels I had read."

Visions of Warsaw stored in my imagination worked like an overlay and for a split second I saw it in all its glamour as described in books--the trees, the shops, the cafes, the gardens, the people. It was gone, forever gone. Damn the war! It devoured everything.

A streetcar came into view and rattled to a stop in front of us. We got on and sat down on the wooden benches that ran the length of the coach beneath the windows. Molkow remained on the platform.

Block after block of bombed out houses, piles of rubble, twisted girders and crumbling walls passed before our eyes. Then, unexpectedly, just around the next bend, we would see a row of buildings miraculously undamaged. "Just like in Cologne," Hannimusch, who sat across from me, commented.

Gradually, the tram filled up. Erika, Inge, Ilse and I relinquished our seats to a couple of older women carrying large bundles of bedding or laundry. They sat down without so much as a nod or thank you. It was then that I noticed how people glared at us with murder in their eyes. Joining Molkow on the platform I whispered to Erika, "Did you notice the looks they gave us?"

"Did I...!" She shuddered. "If they could, they'd cut our throats." Inge, her eyes wide with alarm, ran her index finger up and down the bridge of her nose, a habit and a sure sign that she felt either extremely uncomfortable, embarrassed or afraid. I jabbed her lightly with my elbow and whispered, "Don't let anybody see that you're scared."

Soon, Hannimusch, Hilde and the other girls joined us. "The air is getting a little too thick in there," Hannimusch said, raising her eyebrows. Never before had we encountered such open hostility.

At the next stop, some people got off. One of the women to whom we had given our seat muttered in passing "*Deutsches Schwein* (German pig)."

From then on we kept silent or spoke in whispers. The scene changed. Streets became narrower, houses dingier with man-high garbage piled in front. I drew Erika's attention to huge cobwebs behind some windows. "How can people live in such filth?" She shook her head in disbelief.

"Cleanliness is next to godliness." This was drilled into me since early childhood. It was a national standard. Back home, women prided themselves on making their laundry the whitest, their silver, brass, iron stoves and wood floors the shiniest. On Fridays, every self-respecting housewife scrubbed her place from top to bottom, including the cement steps and walks outside.

The streetcar stopped again, this time at a corner across from a barbed-wire fence patrolled by armed guards. More people got off the tram and a few got on. Behind the fence two men with beards, wearing long black coats and oddly shaped hats, gestured wildly as if arguing. I remembered seeing men dressed just like that years ago in downtown Munich. "They are Jews," my mother had explained when I asked why they dressed and looked so strange.

When the trolley moved again, a tall brick wall running alongside the tracks suddenly cut off our view.

"Where are we?" Hilde asked her husband.

"The ghetto...the Jewish ghetto," he whispered.

The word 'ghetto', though I had heard it often enough, had no meaning for me other than that it was a place where Jews lived. I was curious about it.

What I knew about Jews was what I had heard at home and learned at school.. I never really knew one. Once, months ago, in Berlin, a girl wearing the yellow star, about the same age as myself, approached me on the street and asked me to help her buy a few groceries. She showed me ration tickets with the word "Jude" stamped on them and said that stores refused to take them and sell her anything. I went with her to three stores. The first one was a chain called 'Konsum'. "Sorry, we can't help you," a sales person said and shoved my hand with the ration tickets away. When I asked "Why?" she did not even bother to answer. The man behind the counter in the next store also refused to sell to us. "Sorry, I can't take coupons issued to Jews." When I asked him "why?" he explained, "I have to turn all ration tickets over to the wholesaler to get more supplies. If there is one with 'Jude' on it I get blackballed, get cut off, get nothing, and my customers get nothing."

"Why do these people get ration tickets if nobody can

honor them? What are these people suppose to do? They have to eat."

"Sorry. You have to find a Jewish store," the man said.

By now I was really angry. The Jewish girl was near tears. "I've got to bring home something. We are starving."

At the third store, a Mom and Pop operation, the owner repeated what the man in the second store had said. However, he winked at me to wait. When the customer he was waiting on left, he said, "I can't take your coupons, but ..." His eyes shifted quickly from us to the door and to the street as he put a few things in a paper bag. "Here," he said and handed it to me, "it's the best I can do." When the girl tried to pay him he responded, "No, no. I want nothing, just don't tell anybody where you got this." We left. The girl thanked me and we went our separate ways. That chance meeting was the only time I knowingly had contact with a Jew.

For a long stretch the streetcar rode along that wall. It was so high that only where it was damaged could one catch a glimpse of the other side. I saw a square with many people, mostly men, milling about. They looked nothing like the Jews I had learned about in school, always depicted as fat, cigar-smoking bankers who swindled honest, hard working people out of their land by loaning money, then foreclosing on them when they could not repay on time. They looked nothing like people who conspired to enslave the world. And they looked nothing like the Jewish doctor my mother spoke of, whose kindness, skill and generosity had saved her life and mine when she was pregnant with me. Most of them looked like ordinary working people, war-worn and drab.

The wall, the barbed wire, the armed guards, the strange, hostile attitude of the people on the bus, reminded me of the creepy, uncomfortable feeling I had experienced during an incident that happened months earlier in November 1942, in Auschwitz. We performed at what we were told was a top-secret underground factory. My suitcase, made of cardboard, had become rain-soaked during its transport from the railway station to the factory compound where we stayed. It totally disintegrated.

Desperate to find a new one, I ignored warnings not to stray from our barracks unless accompanied by a guard, and set out to explore the shops in Auschwitz. Erika, sick with fever and flu-like symptoms, could not come with me, so I went by myself. Guards at the main gate let me pass without problems and I walked down a street along an electrified, barbed wire fence that enclosed the compound. The street was deserted except for a pair of young children who climbed around on a pile of rubbish in front of a building. When they saw me coming they stopped, stared at me with big, dark, frightened eyes, then ran quickly into the house. I came to a row of little shops, most of them locked up, and asked in those still open where I could buy a suitcase. My very appearance seemed to create confusion and suspicion and I did not know why. People shut the door in my face. Finally, I found a shop that had what I was looking for. When I entered, a little girl, four or five years old stood by a counter. I smiled at her and said "Hello." A door behind the counter opened, a man came out, quickly grabbed and pushed the child out of sight and shut the door behind her. He looked me up and down as if asking himself, "Where did she come from, who is she, what does she want?" I explained. He, like all the others I had approached, spoke and understood German quite well. At first he said he could not help me, he had no suitcases for sale though I saw some on the shelves. I pleaded, telling him I was a dancer on tour, performing for the workers at the factory, pointing in the direction of the barbed wire fence. Remembering belatedly that I should not have mentioned 'factory', I corrected myself, "that place behind the wire fence." His face, tense with mistrust, gradually relaxed. He positioned a ladder against floor to ceiling shelves, pulled down a suitcase from the very top and set it on the counter in front of me. "Yes...yes...yes! That's exactly what I need," I exclaimed, beaming, and thanked him profusely. He quoted a price. I paid. The little girl came out again from behind the door. I had an apple in my pocket and offered it to her. All my coaxing could not make her take it though she could not take her eyes off it. Finally, I set it on the counter and left, thanking the man again. As I walked back to the compound I had the creepy feeling that eyes were watching me from everywhere.

When I reached the gate, guards interrogated and frisked me, demanded my ID, and after a few phone calls to officials, they escorted me back to my barracks. They did not scare me half as much as what Molkow would do to me when he found out that I had broken the rules again.

That night, after our performance before a mixed audience, uniformed and civilian, we were shuttled through the muddy compound, past acres of barracks to a reception at a club house for officials, mostly men forty and older, in SS uniforms. Erika, sicker than ever, had to stay behind. One look at the balding heads and bulging bellies made me wish I had stayed with her. After about an hour, finding nothing of interest there, I said I was feeling sick and wanted to be taken back to the barracks. My reluctant escort was a short, stout SS officer in his fifties, who did not seem happy having to walk with me in the darkness through rain, sleet and mud, past guards with drawn revolvers and rifles, who demanded the password. I felt mighty uncomfortable in his company. When we passed an open space, lit up by several spotlights, I saw a row of men digging a ditch. "My, this must certainly be important work going on here when men have to dig ditches by night and in pouring rain," I said just to break the silence and to relieve my tension. It was past midnight.

"Just a bunch of Jews digging a ditch. When it's deep enough, we line them up and shoot them in," my escort remarked flippantly. I figured, he meant to shock me with his answer, never suspecting that what he said could be the awful truth.

Back at the barracks I told Erika about it. "He must have been really ticked that he had to walk you back in that miserable weather," she chuckled.

God only knows what I would have said and done, if anything, had I known then what I learned years later.

I sensed a sinister, dark connection between riding along this ghetto wall and walking down the street in Auschwitz along that electrified barbwire fence, as if I had come upon a deadly secret.

For the longest time the streetcar did not stop at all. When it finally did, more people got off and again I heard the phrase *'Deutsches Schwein'*. An old man spat on the floor in front of us. Molkow read our moods like a weather forecaster reads a barometer and warned, "Don't you say or do anything foolish. We'll be getting off soon."

Never had we experienced such collective hatred. It was unnerving. People usually responded to us the way we treated them. Seeing the destruction around us explained their attitude somewhat. But I did not blame the pilot who dropped the bombs on our cities; I blamed the governments that gave the orders. They caused the wars, not I, not we. We were people just like them, caught in the middle.

When we got off the trolley at the hospital, we heaved a collective sigh of relief.

There, a friendly German-speaking staff ushered us right away into the dining room for a breakfast of hard rolls with honey and *Ersatz Kaffee* (imitation coffee made from roasted barley). Afterwards we got a chance to wash up, something we appreciated even more than breakfast.

A nurse took us to an examining room, told us to undress and line up for shots and a physical. As we stood there, stark naked, three young male doctors entered, accompanied by a male nurse. The doctors examined us, the male nurse administered the shots. Never had I felt so humiliated and embarrassed. Perspiration poured out of my pores, yet I shivered. My cheeks burned with shame. Erika stood beside me like a red-faced wooden soldier, not looking right or left. She held a slip in front of her. I covered myself with a blouse. The doctors listened front and back to our chests, felt and looked down our throats, looked into our ears, had us cough, bend over, raise our arms. One came up to me and cupped his hand under my breast. "Nice," he said and grinned, bobbing his eyebrows. I did not know how to react. So rattled was I, that I could not have told him my name had he asked me.

The Molkows and Hannimusch had been examined privately. When we met again in a waiting room, Molkow sat slouched in a chair with a wet towel draped across his forehead, his face the color of parchment.

41

"He fainted when he got his second shot," Hilde tattled on him, "and I almost did, too, when I saw the size of the needle," she admitted, still rubbing her skinny arms.

If she expected sympathy, we had none to give. The sting of a needle seemed minor to the humiliation and embarrassment we had suffered.

After Molkow recovered, we kept an appointment at the military headquarters, which required another short ride on the streetcar. We vowed not to utter a single word this time so nobody knew we were German. Most of us blended quite well with the rest of the people. It seemed to work. The Poles still stared at us, but acted less hostile than before. We reached headquarters without incident.

III

Enchantment Under Ground

Government offices all seemed to look alike. In front of a long counter with windows stood lines of bored, blank-faced soldiers, moving up one at a time, and when they finished at one window, got in the back of a long line again in front of another window.

"Makes one feel right at home," Hannimusch remarked out of one corner of her mouth.

Molkow scanned the situation then made a determined dash toward a door with a sign in big letters "*Eintritt Verboten.*" Still stewing over our miserable accommodations, "Off Limits" signs were not about to keep him out.

As we waited, we cast dire predictions for the months ahead. We knew we were at the bottom of the military's priority list. What could we expect when the front lines started to crumble? They would save a tank before they would save us. We were expendable, a nonessential commodity. No one in particular had a personal interest in, or responsibility for our welfare. We were just a number.

We continued bemoaning our fate, when we noticed a familiar face beaming at us from across the room. "It isn't...it couldn't be..." we told ourselves, then broke into a chorus, "Dieter...Dieter..."

"Our guardian angel," Hannimusch sighed and glanced heavenward, then rushed to crush him to her bosom with theatrical flair. Letting go abruptly she added accusingly, "Where have you been when we needed you most?"

Dieter laughed, raised both hands in defense and shook his head. "Never expected to bump into you here. Thought you would be somewhere in France by now, basking in the sun on the Riviera."

"You thought! We wished!" Hilde said.

Our joyous reunion drew the attention of everybody in the room.

"Come on, kids, let's go some place where we can talk," Dieter said and ushered us through doors with the 'Verboten' signs. "Have you kids had lunch?" he asked.

Ah...that was Dieter! Our Dieter! Always looking out for us. He had been in charge of our tours through 1942, when we worked for the *KDF*--Hitler's "Strength through Joy" program. He saw to our every need from transportation to accommodations, food, stage set-up, and even the replacement of show paraphernalia. Unlike Molkow, who looked out for himself, Dieter really cared about us.

"Did I hear you say something about lunch?" Hannimusch sidled up to him, taking his arm. Both were tall in stature and from the back made a stately pair. He looked especially trim and fit in his black uniform and much younger than his thirty years. His face reminded me of Dutch portraits--long, with slightly bulging eyes and a prominent nose--not the most handsome man, but his personality made up for his looks.

"By the way, where is Egon?" Dieter asked Hilde.

"He stormed through that door," Hannimusch pointed, "and is probably wringing somebody's neck."

"We'll find him. Come on."

Behind all the counters and "*verboten*" signs were offices connected to offices. From one of them droned Molkow's voice. "See, I told you, we'd find him," Dieter chuckled. "I'll get him as soon as I get you set up."

He walked us into a dining room, arranged some polished wood tables and chairs so all of us could sit together, then had a quiet talk with an orderly. We had barely sat down when the orderly brought baskets heaped with fresh buns and butter and placed them on the table before us.

Erika's eyes grew round and big. "I think, that is

44

REAL butter," she gasped, "I hardly remember what it tastes like." We never even got to see the little bit of butter issued to us on the monthly ration tickets. For that matter, we never saw our ration tickets, except when Molkow sent us to the store to get him something.

It was torture having to wait until we could dig in. Dieter went to fetch Molkow and, upon their return, he signaled the orderly to serve the food--plates piled high with beef Stroganoff on a bed of noodles.

Erika kicked me under the table. "Watch Hilde," she murmured. Sitting kitty-corner from us, Hilde, quite unladylike, shoveled the food into her mouth as fast as she could while her eyes already scanned the table for more. As skinny as she was, she ate a lot. I did a quick imitation of her hollow cheeks and big hungry eyes. Erika, Inge and I broke into giggles and we fought them all through the meal.

"So, what are you doing in Warsaw?" Molkow asked Dieter.

"Got transferred to run a radio station here," he answered. "By the way, just had an idea...! Would you kids like to do an interview over the airwaves?"

We looked at one another. This was a first and everybody seemed a little shy.

"Ah...come on. There's nothing to it. It'll give those poor chaps up front something to look forward to. How about it?" He nudged Egon. "What do you say, old man? Is it a deal?"

Molkow managed a crooked smile.

"By the way, where are you staying?"

Instantly, all conversation ceased. Molkow's face changed color. Some of us pretended to choke on our food.

"OHHH...! I get it! Sorry I asked," Dieter chuckled. "It's that bad, huh?"

Then our indignation gushed forth like water from an opened sluice.

"Tell you what..." Dieter interrupted, "you kids dress up this evening and I'll take you to a place where you will forget all about it. I'll show you Warsaw by night."

"Sure! Do you want us to bring candles?" Hannimusch mocked. She thought, as we all did, that he was

45

joking.

"No-no-no, kids. I'm not joshing you." He leaned forward, lowered his voice and said, "there are places, I swear, where you forget that there is a war, where you can have anything you want to eat or drink...and then some. Of course, it's a little expensive, but..." he straightened up, looked at Molkow, slapped him on the back and said, "...we'll treat, won't we, Egon?"

Molkow jerked back in his seat and sputtered objections. His already flushed face turned a few shades darker.

"Come now, Egon," Dieter grinned mischievously, "spring a little. You make plenty off those kids and you won't be spending any of it in Russia, I guarantee you. You can afford it, you old miser."

Before Molkow could protest, Dieter rose from his chair. Suddenly, his attention shifted to a round, gold swastika pin in Molkow's lapel.

"You fox..." Dieter fingered it, "I didn't know you belonged to the elite."

Molkow squirmed, obviously annoyed, opened his mouth to reply but changed his mind. With a smirk Dieter let go of Molkow's jacket. "It's all set then," he confirmed and slapped him on the back again.

"Well, kids, got to run. I'll arrange for a car to take you back to the hotel," he said and waved good-bye to us.

It was fascinating to watch how Dieter's magic could disarm even Molkow, who was not usually swayed by charm. However, knowing Molkow, it was more likely Dieter's influence and power, and knowing all the right people in the right places, to which Molkow capitulated.

"Oh, my God...!" A new thought stirred panic in my soul. "He said 'dress up!' What'll I wear...?" My wardrobe was disastrously sparse because I had outgrown everything just at a time when nothing new could be bought anymore, even with ration tickets. I could not find a store that had material or clothes in stock. To keep clad, I knitted gauze bandages into sweaters and braided straw into shoes.

"What'll I wear?" That was suddenly the topic of the hour.

Back at the hotel we tore through our suitcases,

spread everything out, then consulted and swapped items with one another. The room soon reminded me of a department store's year-end sale, way back when. Time flew. We borrowed Hilde's iron, curling iron and spirit burner, fussed and primped and critiqued one another. A knock on the door and there was Dieter already. "Who is coming to the radio station with me?"

It came down to Hannimusch, Ilse, Ulla and me. The others had excuses.

"If you are ready, let's go," Dieter said. "It won't take long."

The radio station was a small, dark room in a drab old building, with a microphone, a turn table, shelves with records, a cone shaped speaker, and a few black boxes with knobs and dials. Dieter grouped us around the mike, put on earphones, checked his watch, then signaled us to be quiet. "Comrades on the front," he began, "heading your way is a surprise straight from home." Borrowing one of Molkow's lines he introduced us as, "Ten girls and one man. It's the popular Molkow Ballet from Berlin, and they'll dance and sing themselves right into your hearts." He motioned for Hannimusch to move closer to the mike. "And here is the singer of the group."

"*Hallo, Jungs!* I am Hannimusch from Cologne."

"Tall, blond and blue-eyed, she's got the voice of an angel and a repertoire that doesn't quit," Dieter added. "What will you sing for them, Hannimusch? Opera?"

"Anything they want to hear. How about '*Es geht alles vorueber*' and '*In der Heimat, in der Heimat, da gibt's ein Wiederseh'n.*'" Hannimusch sang a few bars from each of these songs.

"*Wunderbar!* And now, here are some of the dancers. Ulla, where are you from?"

Ulla leaned toward the mike, "I am from Berlin," she said.

"Ulla is the major soloist. She floats across the stage on tiptoes, swaying and twirling to the lilt of the Blue Danube Waltz. Tell me, Ulla, doesn't it hurt to dance on your toes?"

"Sometimes," Ulla answered hesitantly.

"And what about you. Where are you from?" Dieter motioned to Ilse.

47

"I am Ilse, also from Berlin," she said.

"...*eine Puppe!* She is a doll on stage and off. Blond, blue-eyed, curvy, soft and graceful. She and Ulla dance a classic *pas de deux.*"

It was my turn. Nervous, I thought my voice sounded raspy as I spoke into the mike. "Hello, I am Elfi from Munich."

"This mischievous little imp can dance, I tell you. Wait till you see her in the *czardas* or the *malaguena.* She's got fire in her soul."

Dieter then went on to ask all sorts of silly questions and clowned around until he had us bending with laughter.

"Well, there you have it, comrades. Soon they'll be singing and dancing for you, straight '*in den Himmel hinein*'--(into heaven)." He quoted a line from a popular song.

After he signed off he turned to us with a smile, "See, there was nothing to it, now was there?"

In an adjoining room with a car seat for a couch, Dieter served us *Cointreau* in small liqueur glasses.

"I could have used some of that before we went on the air," Hannimusch told him jokingly and lifted her glass, "Well, here is to you and all the Dieters in the world."

"And to many more such happy encounters," Dieter added. We clinked our glasses and sipped the syrupy liquid.

"Mmmmm...that's good! Where in the world can you still get that stuff?" Hannimusch wanted to know.

"Connections!" Dieter grinned and poured everybody a second glass. He emptied his in one gulp.

An orderly entered, saluting, "*Heil Hitler!* Your car is waiting." Dieter acknowledged him with a wave of his hand. "Good." To us he said, "I'll take you back to the hotel then pick you up a little later for a night on the town."

The drinks went straight to my head. Crammed into the back of a forerunner of the Volkswagen, we prattled and giggled all the way back.

Molkow, who sat in the lobby playing solitaire on the counter again, eyed our giggly group with suspicion as we entered. In our room, Hilde and the others quizzed us to the minutest detail about our radio debut. In a slightly inebriated state we grossly exaggerated the event, especially what we had said about them.

Later Dieter came for us in a commando car. It had no doors or windows, just a canvas top, but it had enough room for all of us to squeeze in. After a short ride through dark, deserted streets, he let us off at a corner and parked the car out of sight.

"So, this is Warsaw by night?" Erika scoffed. "Can't see my hand in front of my eyes."

"Well, kids, here we are," Dieter announced upon returning and opened a door to the building in front of us. With a flashlight in hand, he gestured us inside, one by one. "Hilde...Egon...Ulla. Careful now. There are steps," he warned and led us down dark cellar stairs toward a faint glow of light.

"Ladies and gentlemen, we are now entering the catacombs of Warsaw." Hannimusch announced, imitating a tour guide.

Erika and I were the last to follow, mostly just feeling our way. Suddenly a man's voice behind us demanded, "Password!" My blood momentarily turned to ice. I suppressed a scream.

Dieter answered the man, and we proceeded through a short tunnel and a door held open by a tall, brawny fellow with dark, slicked back hair. Dieter handed him a wad of money. The man counted it then pulled aside a heavy curtain behind him. Our mouths dropped open as we stood on the threshold to another world.

From the vaulted ceiling, supported by square columns, hung magnificent, sparkling crystal chandeliers. Their soft light reflected off white, damask covered tables, and spilled over onto tufted leather chairs and a lush, red carpet. Along one side of the room, tasseled velvet drapes partially hid a series of intimate alcoves with large, romantic paintings on the walls. Waiters in tuxedos and tails moved silently about, serving guests from gleaming silver trays.

We checked our coats, then followed a waiter with a French mustache to a large round table. Walking on the carpet felt like floating on a cloud.

"Sit down," Dieter said, watching our reactions with obvious delight.

I let my body sink into the soft embrace of a round leather chair and wondered if I was dreaming, recalling what I had read about Warsaw. This was it.

More and more people arrived, all dressed to the hilt. Men wore dark suits. Women wore furs, long gowns, jewels, and trailed scents of French perfume. In contrast to them our group looked like the clean-up crew. Across from us rose a small stage with a piano where a small Gypsy band began to tune its instruments. I noticed that no one in the room wore a uniform, not even Dieter. Who are all these people? I wondered.

"Why so quiet, everybody?" Dieter asked.

"I am overwhelmed," Hilde confessed. She spoke for all of us.

In the past, whenever we stayed in Berlin between tours and ran out of ration coupons, Molkow took us to the Theater Club, a hangout for movie stars, where one could still get a meal without coupons. That, too, had been plush, but this was luxury beyond imagination.

"Who are these people in here? Are they Germans? Poles?" Hilde asked what we all wanted to know.

"The less you know, the better," Dieter instructed her.

"This must be black market heaven. What'll happen if this place gets raided? We will all get arrested or shot!" Hannimusch whispered, half-joking, half-serious.

"Don't worry. Just enjoy. We've got Egon with us with his little gold pin," Dieter teased, then added, "This place is frequented by too many big shots to get raided."

"Ja...and the dumb Heinies on the front freeze their toes off and get killed," Hannimusch mumbled. "Crazy world, this is."

Waiters brought champagne in silver ice buckets and set trays with scrumptious hors d'oeuvres--puff pastry filled with caviar, creamed lox and goose liver pate--on the table in front of us. Once all our glasses were filled, Dieter rose to his feet and proposed a toast.

"Yesterday is gone, we don't know what tomorrow brings, therefore, let us live and enjoy this moment."

"To this moment! And to you, Dieter!" Hilde reciprocated, ceremoniously lifting her glass. The rest of us echoed "to Dieter" and clinked glasses.

By this time the musicians had started to play. A

small, dark-haired, dark-eyed fellow wearing a white, full-sleeved shirt with black pants, and a red cummerbund, wandered from table to table, playing the violin. He bowed his instrument to make it sing and laugh and cry as only a Gypsy can. He came around to where Erika and I were sitting. Erika nudged me, raising her eyebrows, knowing how much I loved anything Gypsy.

Dieter, who sat next to Ulla, flirted with her all evening long. At one point he said to her, "I think you have something in your eye. Let me take a closer look." He tilted her head back, holding her face between his hands but instead of examining her eye, he kissed her on the lips. Ulla feigned surprise and indignation, but she was a bad actress. We could tell that she was flattered.

"Clever, isn't he?" I sighed and nudged Erika, feeling just a little jealous. "Don't you wish somebody were kissing us right now? In this atmosphere, I could fall in love with the doorman."

"That wouldn't surprise me one bit," Erika quipped. She knew my flighty heart.

Conversation bubbled like the wine. We did not realize how fast time was passing. Molkow, who had switched from champagne to straight cognac, suddenly rose to his unsteady feet and announced, "Time to leave!" then fell back into his chair. Hilde and Dieter divided the check, counting out paper marks by the hundreds. Molkow, his head bobbing from side to side, but still aware of what was happening, watched Hilde and the money closely, then turned to us and driveled, "Consider this evening an advance on your salary."

"Mangy dog," Erika mumbled.

"Miser," I agreed. "He already gets away with paying us next to nothing. Now he wants it all."

It was long after midnight when we got back to the hotel. Dieter, the sergeant and Hilde had to help Molkow upstairs, then Dieter said good-bye, gallantly kissed everyone's hand and wished us luck.

I sensed that it was good-bye forever, good-bye to him and maybe to life itself.

Shocked back to reality by our lousy accommodations, Hannimusch sighed, "One minute we are sipping champagne from silver goblets, the next we don't have a pot to pee in--literally."

No one seemed to want to change clothes and get ready for bed. Finally, Hannimusch faced the inevitable. "The clock has struck twelve, you Cinderellas. Let's blow out the candles and try to get some sleep," she urged. "We only have a few hours before we must be up and on our way again."

The magic was gone. It was a dream. "Back to your ashes, Cinderellas!"

IV

Where are the Russians?

Overnight the weather changed. Light snow flurries dusted the streets and ruins of Warsaw and increased as we left the city behind us. Finally, the falling snow obscured the passing landscape like heavy lace. Ahead of us lay a long, boring ride to Brest-Litovsk--the Russian border--where we had to change trains one last time before the final and longest leg of our journey to Smolensk. Nestled in two compartments that Dieter managed to reserve for us, we planned to catch up on lost sleep. For awhile we talked, reliving every amazing, delectable detail of the night before. "What a send-off that was!" I thought out loud. But Hannimusch summed it up differently. "Children" she said, "this may well have been 'The Last Hurrah'...'The Last Supper'." It was so typical of Hannimusch to find a little black cloud in an otherwise blue sky and to shock us back into reality. She was right, of course, but why cast a dark shadow over our brief happiness by reminding us of what may be waiting in the wings. I was a little miffed.

The surreal elegance of the night before cruelly emphasized the contrast between what life could have been and what it was. It reminded me of all the things I had dreamed of while growing up. "When I am big, I want to be like the ladies in the resorts where I dance," I told my mother. They all dressed so nice and smelled so good, and could order anything they wished to eat. "You will," she promised. Then came the war. Now, we just tried to survive.

One by one, our sleepy crew succumbed to the lulling sound of the train and we did not wake up until we pulled into Brest-Litovsk. Dozens of western tracks ended abruptly in front of a spiked iron fence with gated check stations, unmanned and open when we arrived. Beyond that rose a city of barracks and tents--a giant processing center for German forces, complete with de-lousing facilities for westbound troops. I had the impression that the world ended here. Just then, Inge drew my attention to a crude cardboard sign hanging on an iron post that read, "*Tor zur Ewigkeit*" (gate to eternity), and scribbled underneath, "*zur Hoelle*" (to hell).

Our entire baggage, five large show trunks, more than a dozen large suitcases, Hannimusch's accordion, and a large assortment of smaller cases, bags and cartons, was loaded onto two large carts which Inge, Erika, Ilse and I had to pull a good three-quarters of a mile over rutted, frozen ground to a check point. From there, we trudged from one barracks to another to have our papers stamped, to exchange marks into scrip, and, finally, to get our rations for the trip. The latter turned out to be the first of a few pleasant surprises. Just like the soldiers on the front, we, too, received combat rations that included such rare items as canned butter, bacon, ham, fruit, candy, cigarettes, and beer. Molkow had everything put into big boxes for distribution later. The second surprise came as we boarded the train. It was a hospital train with empty coaches, equipped with bunk beds, a table and chair and a clean washroom. Best of all, we had one coach all to ourselves.

"Look everybody," Hannimusch cried out with delight, "clean sheets...and pillows...!"

We got into a flap over who would sleep in what bunk. Some wanted an upper, others a lower. Emmy and Ilse got into a real fight over one of the lower berths, each claiming to have gotten there first.

"All right, Emmy," Ilse hissed, fists at her waist. "All right, I'll take the upper. Just don't say I didn't warn you when I get sick and start throwing up."

"For God's sake, what am I running here...a kinder-garten?" Molkow snapped at them. "Shut up and get busy stacking the luggage away."

Emmy finally gave in to Ilse, and by the time every-body had settled down, we were rolling through open country into the impending night. Hilde sorted and handed out a few days of rations, calling us one by one. It was Inge's turn.

"Don't I get any cigarettes?" she asked timidly.

"What do you want with cigarettes? You have no busi-ness smoking," Molkow growled at her from his bunk where he played solitaire again.

"Oh, I don't smoke, but my father...I wanted to send..."

Hilde looked at Egon.

"Damn it!" he barked and slammed his fist down on the bed that the cards flew up and scattered all over. "Damn it! I said no."

"But...but...the other girls..."

"Until you are eighteen I decide what you get, when, and where."

Erika looked at me. I looked at Erika. "He is doing it again!"

Then came my turn. On purpose, I made a special point to ask for my cigarettes.

"You heard Egon." Hilde said loudly and firmly for Molkow's benefit, then slipped me a handful, signaling to keep quiet. Her eyes pleaded with me not to cause a row. Though I was not appeased, I felt sorry for her. Later Erika, Inge, Ilse and I got into a huddle and fumed. "It's not fair. It's just not fair. Molkow takes advantage of us whenever he can. He has butter on his bread; we get mustard or have to eat it dry. He uses our ration tickets for himself as he sees fit. Now he keeps our cigarettes."

"One of these days," I pledged, "I'll have it out with him."

Meanwhile, Hannimusch unpacked her accordion. She began to play and sing, urging us to join in. We pulled the window shades, sampled and shared the deli-cacies, and started to relax. For the moment at least, life was not so bad. Wartime travel--drafty stations, un-heated hotels, damp beds, and growling stomachs--had taught us to appreciate the smallest comforts.

Suddenly the door to our coach opened and a man's face appeared. "May I come in?"

Startled, because some of us were already in pajamas, we did not know what to say.

"Sergeant Menke, medic," he introduced himself, saluting.

"Oh, come on in...what the heck...come on in." Hannimusch called out and waved him in.

He stepped inside, shutting the door behind him. "Just wanted to tell you, if you need something from the kitchen, let me know."

"Kitchen...?" we repeated in unison.

"Well, sort of. On this trip, all we can serve up is coffee, tea or hot water."

"Things are getting better all the time," Hannimusch said and laughed.

"Sergeant, have you made this trip before?" Molkow cut in on our chitchat.

"So often, I've lost count."

"So what time tomorrow, would you say, we will be arriving in Smolensk?"

"Tomorrow? Tomorrow...ha! I wouldn't count on tomorrow," Menke replied and chuckled, "Figure on at least three to four days from now."

"What...?" Molkow postured. "How can that be?"

To keep his footing on the swaying, jostling train, the medic braced himself between the door and the last bunk post and went on to explain that there was only one track between Brest and Smolensk. When trains came from the opposite direction, this one had to pull over at the nearest turnout and wait for them to pass. "We can sit there for hours. Who knows what, when or where, but something usually happens on this run," he said. "A Russian plane might swoop down, get lucky and hit the tracks. Or Russian partisans may blow them up. Like I said, anything can happen on this route."

We looked at him wide-eyed. "That sounds dangerous," Hannimusch said. "What if they blow up the train?"

Realizing that he had frightened us, the medic tried to make light of it. "That just happens once in a great while. It's more likely that we run into a blinding snowstorm

56

and have to wait it out. There isn't much to worry about."

"Tell us about the partisans," we prodded him. We had heard unbelievably gruesome stories and wanted to know if they were true.

"There are enough troops on this train to protect the train and you. You'll be all right," he reassured us, evading our questions. Turning to Hannimusch, he asked, "May I ask you a favor?"

"Please!" she encouraged him.

"Do you know the song about the Boehmerwald?"

"Boehmerwald...Boehmerwald..." Hannimusch searched the vast repertoire in her mind and began to play. "Is this what you mean?"

"*Ja*, that's it."

Menke listened, then hummed along, and finally sang three whole verses of it with full voice and great enthusiasm. His boyish, square, ruddy face beamed. This song took him home to the Boehmerwald, a beautiful wooded mountain range along the Czechoslovak-German border.

Touched by the glow in Menke's eyes, Hannimusch followed with a soft melody to allow him to linger. Polite moments later, Hannimusch asked him, "How long has it been since you were back there, soldier?"

"Three years. It's been three years since I had a furlough, since I saw my family," Menke answered wistfully.

"That's a long time," Hannimusch acknowledged with sympathy. She invited him to sit down and stay a while.

We sang, talked, joked and laughed. Hours passed quickly. Finally Menke left, Hilde went to bed, Molkow snored, but we girls, tired as we were, could not go to sleep. The thought of closing our eyes while we rolled deeper and deeper into dangerous territory with partisans on the prowl absolutely terrified us. In spite of that, sleep eventually overpowered us, one by one.

When I woke up the next morning, Emmy and Erika were sitting cross-legged in front of the window on the bunk adjoining mine, staring out.

"Any sign of Russians yet?" I asked, yawning and stretching.

"Nothing. As long as we've been sitting here, we've seen nothing; no house, no people, no animals, nothing. Just an endless white sheet of land."

I joined them. It was awesome to look out over miles and miles of snow toward the horizon, and see no road, no village or any sign of life. West of the Russian border the country was dotted with hamlets and farms; no sooner did one pass, then another came into view. Here we saw nothing but land and sky. Finally, in the distance appeared what looked like a few little shacks. When Menke brought us coffee a short while later we asked him about that.

"What you saw is probably one of the collective farms," he explained.

"But these huts looked so small...more like sheds for hay. We didn't see any barns or any livestock."

"What few animals they have, often live under the same roof with the people."

"Come on! These huts looked so small, the Russians would have to be pygmies," we argued.

"I am telling you, that probably was a farm."

Convinced we were talking about two different things, we dropped the subject.

During the course of the day, Molkow had us run through some exercises and *barre* work, just to give us something to do. In the aisle between bunks and windows, we did knee bends, kicked and swung our limbs and finished with stretches. It felt good, except that our arms still hurt from the shots. Molkow rarely conducted a class anymore. He left it mostly up to us to keep in shape, which was a great disappointment to me. I had such great expectations to be training under him.

The rest of the time we played games and, of course, I had to lay cards for everybody. Since childhood, I had been around people who dabbled in the occult. People in the theater are a superstitious lot. I picked up a little here and a little there, and just for the fun of it, I laid cards, too. I did not really take it seriously, but there were times when I had cause to wonder, particularly when some of my most outrageous predictions came true. The girls, even Hilde and Molkow asked me to read for them.

As I laid out the cards first for Hilde, then the others, a pattern emerged. "We won't make it to Smolensk," I told them. "Something is going to happen to interrupt our journey."

Nobody laughed or called me crazy; they just wanted more details. "I see danger ahead," I said. When I could give them no specifics they spun their own scenarios of what could happen. It kept the conversation lively way into the night.

On the second day the scenery changed from flat snowy fields to dense forests. Shafts of sunlight cut through broken clouds immersing the frosted evergreens in shimmering silver one minute and brooding shadows the next. The train plodded along, stopped for long intervals in the middle of nowhere, heaved, and crawled on again. Comfortable and content for the moment, we really did not mind.

Suddenly the train braked sharply, knocking us off balance.

"Alarm! Alarm! Everybody out!" someone shouted outside.

We slipped into shoes, grabbed our coats and scrambled outside and down a snowy embankment. Above us we heard the whirring sound of an engine. Following orders, we climbed back up and under the train. Soldiers set up tripods with machine guns and fired at the sky.

Whooom! An explosion momentarily sucked the air out of my lungs. Gravel and dirt rained down around us. Laughter from the troops. "Eh, you Russkie... how many eggs have you got in that crate of yours?" a soldier yelled at the vanishing plane. More laughter. I inched out from under the train to have a look. The waltzing purr of an engine returned and a small plane suddenly dove out of the clouds, met by furious machine gun and rifle fire. It quickly nosed up again and disappeared.

"Incredible...! That's incredible...!" I gasped, excitedly pulling on Erika's arm. "Did you see the pilot's head pop over the side? Can you believe it, I actually saw him grin. I could have counted his teeth!"

"Yes, I saw it...I saw it...! Let go. You are ripping my coat!"

The gunners yanked their machine guns this way and that, firing away, all the while laughing, yelling and waving at the circling plane. When everything turned quiet for a while, we crawled out and joined the soldiers. They cracked one joke after another about 'Ivan and his coffee grinder,' referring to the Russian pilot and his outdated plane. We also examined a small crater way off to one side of the locomotive. Menke walked up to us. "Hope this didn't scare you too much. It really shouldn't. Your chances of getting dropped on by a bird are a hundred times better than getting hit by one of those Russkies. Heck! You could be on crutches and still outrun and out-maneuver these buzzards."

We listened with gaping mouths. That crater did not seem that far off target to me.

"You make it sound like a game," Hannimusch observed.

"It is!" Menke chuckled and tried to explain, "Who can take the Russkies with their rust-buckets seriously? We can pick them off with a rifle. We know their routine. They make two sweeps then, on the third, grab a bomb and drop it over the side. By that time their plane usually looks like Swiss cheese. He is lucky if he can make it back."

"Doesn't anybody get hurt or killed?" Hannimusch questioned.

"Ah...not very often. It's all too predictable."

Once again we heard the purring of the plane's engine and ducked back under the train. Another explosion, much further away than the first. More laughter.

Menke came over to us. "You can relax now and get back inside. He won't be back. He can't carry more than two bombs at the most."

The train had suffered no damage and moved on without further delay.

Another day and night passed. Stop and go, stop and go. We broke out of the woods and rolled again through wide-open terrain. Menke had just brought us hot water for washing up and we waited for our turn in the wash-room when the train suddenly stopped again.

"What now? Another water tower? Another alarm?" We did not even bother to look out anymore. Suddenly, we heard whistles and commands.

"Everybody out! Fall in line! Fall in line!"

Behind mounds of coal along the track, we saw a stone building. "Hey! This must be a station," Hilde alerted her husband.

"The first house in Russia!" we exclaimed excitedly and pressed our noses against the dirty windows for a better look. A group of officers from the Luftwaffe in riding breeches stood in front of a wooden shelter by the tracks, gesturing, saluting, commanding, and pointing out directions with their swagger sticks. Troops from our train, not more than a hundred in number, assembled outside with all their gear and marched off toward the building. Molkow finally ventured out to inquire what this interruption was about. We watched him talk with one of the officers and by his gestures could tell that he was getting upset. When he came back, all he said was, "Pack up! We get off here." In passing he glared at me and hissed, "You witch!"

"Where are we? What's going on?" everybody wanted to know but got no answer.

"Egon! Why do we have to get off here?" Hilde demanded.

"Somewhere up ahead the Russians broke through. That's all I know," he muttered in reply.

"My Lord!" Hilde exclaimed. I had never seen her move so fast as she gathered up all her things and stuffed them into suitcases. "My Lord!" she repeated several times more. "What do we do now? Where do we go?"

Ulla paled, stared and pointed at me. "She said it! Remember? She said that something would happen."

Chills rippled up and down my spine. I kept telling myself, that it was just coincidence, though I was not so sure. Maybe there was more to card reading than I thought. Vacillating between feeling scared and being intrigued, I wondered if it was even right to dabble in such things.

With feverish haste we gathered and packed our belongings, then piled them outside between the train and the coal mounds. "Get the trunks...put them outside and stay with them," Hilde relayed her husband's instructions. Of course, she meant Erika, Inge, and me, plus Ilse, who had only a few months of her apprenticeship left. We were the pack mules. "Hee-haw...hee-haw," I answered. She and the other girls dashed toward the house. The ground was rough and frozen, with patches of ice and snow. A sharp wind whistled around the train throwing coal dust into our faces and eyes. All the soldiers had left. So had the locomotive.

Standing there, watching over our luggage, we got colder by the minute. "Let's go into the house and find out what's going on," I suggested after awhile.

"Molkow's going to kill us if we leave the luggage unguarded," Inge hesitated.

"Well, do you want some Russians to kill us instead?" I snapped back. "I'm going in."

I started walking toward the building. Ilse came with me; Erika and Inge hesitated but changed their minds and ran after us. Just as we reached the house, Hilde and the other girls met us coming out.

"We have to bring all our stuff inside," they informed us. "The trunks and everything."

"We? Who is 'we'?" I growled, already knowing the answer.

Inge, Erika and I made several trips carrying all of Molkows' things plus the heavy show trunks while Ilse positioned herself by the door, holding it open. "Typical!" I muttered and threw her a dirty look as we struggled past her.

The two storied stone building was, as we had figured, a station house. A wooden sign above the door read 'Chatalovka,' written in bold, German letters. After our entire luggage was stacked inside, Erika, Inge and I joined the others around a fire in a gigantic stone fireplace that formed one wall of the building. Opposite the fireplace, across a large, empty space, were two small rooms, one with radio equipment manned by two 'landsers' (soldiers of the German infantry). Molkow breathed down their necks, wanting to get hold of headquarters in Smolensk while they tried to keep abreast of the current situation.

Tense hours passed. Finally, the message came that the Russians had been intercepted and stopped, and later Molkow got word that we had to spend the night at the station, then continue on to Smolensk on another train the following morning.

"That's nice!" Hannimusch flared up. "You mean we are stuck here with Russians on the loose, and only two guys with a rifle each to protect us?"

"Simmer down!" Molkow squashed her concerns. "I'm sure we are in no immediate danger."

The landsers showed us to a dorm on the upper floor. One look and we agreed that the hotel in Warsaw was first class compared to this. Rickety double bunks, nailed together out of scrap lumber with straw-stuffed gunny-sacks, filled up the room. No blankets, no sheets, no pillows. The landsers offered to lend us theirs and apologized for not being able to provide anything better.

We stayed by the fire until we could keep our eyes open no longer, then shuffled upstairs with candles, our overnight cases and blankets, and crawled or climbed into the nearest available bunk. It was unbearably cold. Molkow and Hilde remained with the radiomen downstairs. As I climbed to an upper bunk above Erika's, the rickety structure creaked and swayed so much that I was afraid it would break or topple over at any moment. Erika complained that I caused her to get a face full of dust and straw.

"If you want, I'll gladly trade places with you," I offered.

"Everybody set?" Hannimusch asked after awhile before blowing out her candles. For a few minutes all was quiet, except for the creaking of beds. Suddenly something bit me on my neck, then on my face, and my hands, wherever my skin was exposed.

"What are you doing up there?" Erika griped. "Can't you lie still?"

"I swear this place is full of fleas or bed bugs. I am itching all over," I complained.

"Yeah...me too," Ilse echoed my complaint.

"Me too...me too..." the others joined in.

"Hell! I'm getting out of here," Hannimusch sputtered and relit the candles, "even if I have to stay up all night downstairs by the fire."

Sudden chaos.

Gingerly, I climbed down from my rickety loft and was glad to touch ground when I heard the splintering of wood. In the shadowy light of the candles I caught a glimpse of Emmy, her legs dangling over the side of a swaying bunk. "Watch out, you'll crash!" I cried.

Too late. The bunk broke into pieces and collapsed over Ilse's head, who was not fast enough to get out. Emmy landed on her behind, more startled than hurt. Buried under debris, Ilse's head emerged. It looked like an egg in a nest. Gagging, spitting, coughing, she escaped unhurt. Everybody burst into laughter. "Divine justice!" Emmy called it, and laughed so hard that she could not get on her feet. "That'll teach you. Think about that next time you insist on a lower bunk."

So much for sleep. We spent the rest of the night downstairs around the fire scratching our flea bites and listening intently to intermittent salvos of machine gun fire not very far away. Some of us dozed off now and then, but every time a gust of wind rattled the door, we shot up like a flock of skittish birds.

At the first sign of dawn we sighed with relief, as if daylight was a guarantee of safety. Fear has no rationale, I learned. When we went upstairs to retrieve our suitcases, we discovered a room with a fireplace. Over it hung a large, black iron kettle. Water from a dripping faucet splashed into a stone trough, covering it and the brick floor with a sheet of ice.

"Weird place for a wash room, on the second floor," I remarked.

"If we had something to burn, we could build a fire, heat some water and wash up," Erika answered.

At times, Erika and I needed only to look at one another to know what each was thinking. Without a word, we gathered up the debris from the splintered bunk in the other room, straw sack and all, and in no time had a roaring fire going and a kettle of water heating. Erika undressed and showed me her upper arm where she got the shot. It was very red and swollen. "It really hurts," she complained.

"Put a hot, wet cloth on it," I advised her. "It may take away the swelling."

Ulla's arm looked even worse. Mine still hurt but was not quite as swollen. The fleabites bothered me much worse.

In the middle of our morning toilette Hannimusch called us to a window to watch a spectacular sunrise, like nothing we had ever seen before. A giant orange-red sphere rose from the horizon into a deep red sky. In awe, we took it as some kind of omen.

"The sky looks as if the world's on fire." I said.

"To me, it looks like a sea of blood," Hannimusch remarked in a hushed voice, raising goose bumps on my skin.

"Oh, Hannimusch!" I scolded her.

"Well... that's what it looks like to me," she insisted. "Besides, *Morgen rot, schlecht Wetter Bot'* (morning red, weather bad)," she recited an old saying.

V

The First Casualty

On the final trek to Smolensk we boarded a short, heavily armed train. Soldiers with machine guns stood guard on the roof of the train, others patrolled the inside, warning us to keep away from windows and, in case of gun fire, to duck between the seats. These measures indicated that we could expect trouble ahead. Exhausted, after spending a sleepless, spine-chilling night at the station house, I had hoped for a chance to sit back and relax on this last, short leg of our journey. That was not to happen.

A howling wind swept across the plains that morning, causing spiral updrafts and ripples in the snow. Violent gusts threatened to rock the train off its tracks. It started to snow. By noon, a full-blown blizzard slowed us from a walking to a crawling pace. The dry, powdery snow filtered through the tiniest cracks around windows and doors, accumulating in small fluffy piles inside the coach. We talked and expressed our concern for the soldiers on the roof, having to stand guard in this fierce, freezing weather. I knew I would not last five minutes out there in my flimsy winter coat and threadbare shoes.

Usually, we girls passed the time napping or playing games. On this ride, we fidgeted nervously in our seats, holding patchy conversations about if and when we might get the next hot meal, be able to take a bath, or find a clean bed to sleep in once we arrived in Smolensk.

Left unspoken was the fear that there might not be a next anything.

As the minutes and hours ticked away, Molkow grew steadily more restless and agitated. Finally, he stood up. Bracing himself between the wooden seats and the aisle wall, he looked out through the upper, ice-free parts of the windows.

"At this rate of speed, we'll be lucky to get to Smolensk by midnight," he growled to the next patrol that entered our coach.

"Just be glad to get there at all," the soldier answered. "We are in partisan territory."

Molkow gave the soldier a pausing glance, then stared out at the swirling snow again. "Aha!" he suddenly exclaimed. "Now I know why we are going so slow! We are following one of those hand-powered railcars. What's it doing in front of this train?"

"That handcar is checking for mines," the patrol answered.

He stopped next to where Inge was sitting. She looked up and gasped. "You mean to say that someone could have planted a mine on this track?" she asked, wide-eyed with fright. "How can you find a mine under all this snow?" From her worried expression, I gathered that she already knew the answer.

"When you run over it. That's how," the patrol replied with a sarcastic chuckle.

"But...but...aren't there people operating this handcar? Won't they be blown to bits?"

"At least, they are Russians--partisans--not our guys."

Inge paled. The soldier quickly justified his callous remark. "It's them or us. That's the rule of war, Miss."

Concerned and curious, I stood up to have a look myself, but could see nothing until the train took a curve. Even then, the blowing snow veiled much of my view. I barely saw the shadowy outline of figures on a flatcar, bobbing up and down, pumping what looked like a tee-ter-totter. The prospect of them or us--any of us--being blown up by a mine tightened my muscles and nerves another notch. Every hard bump or loud knock made my stomach flip-flop and my heart jump into my throat.

The terrain changed from open plains to a dense forest, offering, at least, some protection from the storm. A wide strip along both sides of the rails had been cleared of trees. It was littered with the twisted wreckage of burnt-out coaches and freight cars. Nearby, poking out of the snow stood clusters of crude wooden crosses with helmets on them, marking the graves of German soldiers. Images appeared in my mind of the young, cocky enlistees at the Poznan station. How many of them would wind up buried in Russian soil? I worried about my brother, who was somewhere on the Russian front. A ripple ran up my spine and shook my body as if it were trying to shake my brain free of these disturbing thoughts. I took a deep breath and forced myself to think of something else.

The train stopped sharply. Simultaneously, we heard a salvo of shots and ducked between the seats. Minutes turned into an eternity. When the wheels cranked into motion again, the body of a man, a Russian, lay sprawled and motionless in the snow. He had been shot, the patrol told us, because he had jumped off the handcar and tried to escape into the partisan-infested woods.

"I would have tried to escape, too," I said. "He could do that or freeze to death on the handcar, not sure if he gets blown up the next second anyway."

It was a Russian, our enemy. For us he had no face. And like the patrol said, it was them or us. But it was a human life, snuffed out in an instant by bullets. Death seemed shockingly simple. There was not even a trace of blood in the snow.

None of us had seen anybody being killed before. Nerves began to snap. Ulla was the first to fall apart. Trembling and whimpering like a frightened little puppy, she grabbed on to Betty, her best friend, who in turn sought comfort from a higher source. Betty crossed herself and buried her face behind her tightly clasped hands, mumbling, "Don't let me die. Please, God, don't let me die."

I sat between Erika and Inge. Barely breathing, the three of us sat upright and frozen in our seats. I wished I could think of something to do or say to ease this tension. Hilde, who had been sipping on a small bottle of medicine to control her nervous stomach, tried dutifully but not very convincingly to calm us girls. She repeatedly looked at Molkow for support, but he kept on staring out of the frosted windows.

"Other entertainers have been sent to the Russian front, and they came out all right. We will, too," she reminded us.

"Yeah! And what about those that didn't? Those that disappeared and were later found tortured to death?" Hannimusch sniffled into her handkerchief.

The tightness in my muscles had spread to my neck and shoulders. My head felt clamped in a vice. I wished with all my heart, I still had my childhood faith in God, believing that all I needed to do was pray to Him and He would take care of me and make everything all right. Instead, all the church-taught fears I thought I had already conquered reemerged. Warnings rang in my ear. "God punishes those who doubt His word." His word? Or the word of the church? My thoughts oscillated between fear and reason. I turned inward, concentrating, searching for that gut feeling that so often let me know the outcome of a situation way ahead of time. I listened for its voice. And it said, "You'll be all right...don't worry...you'll be all right."

"We'll be all right," I repeated aloud. "We'll be all right." It helped me to relax. The calm confidence in my voice surprised me. It broke and soothed the tension. Erika and Inge leaned back in their seats.

The wind howled again, and the train crept along. Night was falling rapidly. Every few minutes, Molkow asked the patrols, "How much longer? How much further is it to Smolensk?"

"We are there," the patrol finally gave him the answer he wanted to hear. We girls jumped up, embraced one another with great relief and joy, and cried, "We've made it! We've made it!" mindless of what would lie ahead in the days and months that followed.

When we got off the train we stepped straight into Russia's fabled winter. We had to form a chain and lean with our backs into the wind in order to stay on our feet. Fine snow penetrated every fold of our clothes and pricked our skins, swirling down our necks and up our

69

skirts. It blew at us horizontally in icy gusts that sucked our breaths away and froze our nostrils shut. Only able to take a few steps at a time, we inched toward the warm light from the window of a small log house a mere fifty yards away. When we reached it, we were exhausted, out of breath, and chilled to the bone.

In the center of this otherwise empty cabin stood an oil barrel stove, fired up to a red glow. We gathered around it, brushed the snow off our clothes and thawed out. An overhead lamp and the glow from the fire reflected softly off the pealed log walls. It smelled of pine scent. Behind a partition was the switchman's office where somebody cranked a field telephone. Molkow went inside. A short wait later, a bus pulled up and the driver, a tall fellow wearing a lambskin coat over a black uniform, came stomping in.

"Welcome to Smolensk!" he greeted us with a wide smile. With a click of his heels and a brisk nod, he introduced himself. "Karl Heinz Paneck...at your service. I am your chauffeur during your stay here."

Molkow emerged from the office. By habit, he raised his right hand in a Nazi salute, then briefly introduced himself, his wife, Hannimusch and our troupe. "Well, then," he said, "let's get our baggage loaded and go on to where we have to go."

Karl Heinz buttoned his coat, lowered the earflaps on his fur cap and put on fur-lined leather gloves. All the while, his dark eyes wandered appraisingly over our group, from one to the other. Molkow was giving him instructions as to the order in which he wanted our baggage loaded on the bus, when Hannimusch cut in, "Bet, they call you Karlemann?"

The driver's head jerked around. Caught off guard, he stuttered, "I'll be...great God...the last time anybody called me Karlemann was when I said good-bye to my mother. You must be from Hamburg." His face lit up.

"Grew up there," Hannimusch answered with a smug grin. "Still can spot a Hamburger brogue when I hear one. I'm sure, little Inge here can, too. She's genuine Hamburg."

The three shook hands while the rest of us looked on.

Molkow cleared his throat. Karlemann, we called him

70

so from then on, reached for the door. "There will be plenty of time to reminisce later. See you in a little while." His smile, his warmth, his confident posture reminded me of Dieter, who had always taken such good care of us. We were in good hands, I thought.

As soon as the baggage was loaded, we boarded the bus for a short ride to our quarters. The bus fishtailed through heavy snowdrifts, bogged down a few times, but Karlemann managed to keep it going. He apologized for the rough ride, and for not having heat aboard.

"Here we are," he finally announced and pulled up to the door of a two-storied building. "It's called the *'Künstler Heim'* (artists home). I hope you find it reasonably comfortable."

He jumped out, unlocked a heavy double door, stuck his head inside and called, "Katja?" A young Russian girl in a white apron with a white kerchief tied over her hair appeared in the doorway and curtsied as we hurried inside. She looked about my age. Her round face with its high cheekbones and bushy eyebrows above small blue eyes, and her short, stocky build made her distinctive--a definite departure from the western European look.

"Are the rooms ready?" Karlemann asked her in German. She nodded and gestured for us to follow her upstairs.

"You wait here," Molkow told us, "Hilde and I will check it out."

"Naturally," I mumbled, exchanging glances with Erika and Inge.

We stood in a long hallway with a row of windows on one side and a wall with half a dozen doors on the other. The building was heated. Thriving houseplants on rustic benches beneath the windows added a homey touch. So did an old oriental carpet covering the long, warped boards of the clean wood floor. Small iron doors, like oven doors, hung at waist high intervals on the wall and aroused my curiosity. Below these doors stood baskets with firewood and coal. I gathered that it was some kind of heating system. Later, Karlemann confirmed that this was a quite common and efficient way of heating houses in Russia. The fire in these ovens heated the stones of the chimney, and they in turn heated the rooms on either

71

side of it. The stones retained the heat for a long time and spread a comfortable warmth throughout the entire building. It seemed to work wonderfully well.

Having checked out the rooms and selected his, Molkow then assigned us to ours. Erika, Inge and I shared one, Emmy and Ilse another, Betty shared one with Ulla, and Hannimusch with Uschi. The Molkows took the one closest to the bathroom.

Erika, Inge and I usually got the crummiest room. This time, it was far better than we had expected. We were more than happy. It was furnished with three iron bedsteads, a small table under a shaded window, two chairs, and it had a large corner fireplace with wood for burning. Each bed had a horsehair mattress covered with grayish flannel sheets and odds and ends in blankets and quilts. The place reminded me of weekend cabins back home, where one stuffed furniture, beds, and things no longer good enough for the home, but too good to throw away. Everything was clean. For us, it was heaven.

Katja and Karlemann brought our suitcases up. "If you care for some tea and sandwiches, come downstairs to the dining room," Karlemann announced. Tea sounded wonderful since we had had nothing warm in our stomachs for almost two days. Though dead tired, we wanted to wash up before going downstairs. Katja brought pitchers full of hot water up to the bathroom, curtsying every time she entered and left. The bathroom had a large tub. When Erika and I saw it, we danced like children, round and round, chanting, "we can take a bath, we can take a bath." We had not bathed or showered since we left Poznan. Pointing to the tub, we converged on Katja. "Tomorrow? Can we take a bath?" A little overwhelmed, she answered with a shy smile, shrugged her shoulders, and said "*Da.*" Not sure if she understood us, we asked Karlemann, who had waited for us downstairs. He warned us to allow ample time between baths, and to use water sparingly because it had to be heated in pots and pans and carried up.

"We can discuss that tomorrow," he said. "You kids look beat. You need to go to bed."

He was right. We were exhausted.

I could not get over how friendly, kind and good-looking Karlemann was. The black uniform of the National Workers Party complimented his blond hair and deep-set, dark-brown eyes. His smiling, handsome face followed me into my dreams.

Smolensk

Cathedral — The Wall — The Streets

Smolensk

Bridge over Dnieper — City Street — Last Night in Smolensk

VI

Smolensk

A rap at the door startled us awake. "Girls? It's time to get up. GIRLS?" It was Hannimusch. We answered with grunts and groans. I could have slept ten hours more and hated to leave the comfort of my bed.

"Don't go back to sleep now! You hear?"

Erika was the first to get up. "Let's hurry to get to the bathroom before everybody else does," she urged.

I hung my feet over the edge of my bed and sat up. Out of the corner of my eyes, I saw something small and dark dart across the floor but was still too groggy to pay it much attention.

Armed with towel and toiletries, I shuffled behind Erika and Inge down the hall to the bathroom which, of course, was already fully occupied. Ulla was in the process of shampooing Hilde's hair. "Want you to know, we've only got an hour before we have to leave here," Hilde warned us from under a cloud of lather.

My hair hung like a stringy, dark brown mop around my shoulders, too oily to hold curls anymore. It needed washing badly but I wondered if I had enough time.

"Only an hour?" we protested.

"We've got to be in the theater by ten to unpack, iron our costumes, rehearse and get ready for tonight's show."

"*Himmel...Mensch!* They don't give us much time, do they?" Hannimusch griped.

Katja carried up bucket after bucket of hot water to

fill a few inches of the large tub. If we wanted to take a bath at all, it became clear that we would have to double up. Hilde reluctantly allowed her sister, Ulla, to get in the tub with her. When they were done, and before they let the water run out, Hannimusch stared into this milky, scummy pool, hesitated a moment, then said "Oh, what the hell," dropped her robe and climbed in. Erika rumpled her nose, repelled by the mere thought of doing something like that. "Eeek...you come out dirtier than you went in."

I would not have done it either. It took a mere week for us to forget such niceties.

One bathroom for ten women was asking for trouble. Squabbling broke out over who would get the next bowl full of clean, warm water to, at least, take a sponge bath. Even without the bickering, we could not possibly be ready in one hour. Molkow, intolerant of tardiness, worked himself into a foaming rage downstairs. His cursing could be heard throughout the entire building. Finally, he left ahead of us. Karlemann was to come back to pick us up a little later.

Ulla, Erika and Betty compared the swollen sores on their arms where they had gotten the shots. Hilde took one look and gasped, "That's got to be looked at by a doctor. There must be an aid station or hospital somewhere. I'll ask Karlemann."

When we boarded the bus our hair was still wet, rolled up in rag-curlers and wrapped in towel-turbans. Karlemann distributed blankets to put over the frost-coated seats. Once the bus was in motion, my eyes locked onto its large rearview mirror that reflected Karlemann's face and lingered over every inch of it, from his square chin and straight nose to his high forehead. His attention focused on stirring the bus through the wind-blown snow, but he looked every bit as handsome as when he smiled. For an instant he looked up and our eyes met. As if I had touched a hot wire, I felt a shock surge through my body. Afraid to make a fool of myself, I looked away, melted a spot on the frosted window, gazed out, and tried to calm my pounding heart.

In the distance, up on a hill, glistened the golden, onion-shaped spires of a Russian cathedral, overlooking a city that was no more. All that remained of Smolensk, as far as I could see, were chimneys. A forest of chimneys. Silent monuments to the dead, they rose out of snow-covered rubble, pointing at heaven like accusing fingers. Smolensk resembled a graveyard. Street after street, there was not a house left standing.

"Where did all the people go who once inhabited this city?" I wondered.

We passed some ramshackle huts, thrown together out of salvaged lumber and metal, with stovepipes sticking out, buried half way in snow. "Here they are, the people, the survivors," I answered myself. "Is that all that's left of a population of about 60 000?" They had to be the toughest of the tough to make it through this destruction, and now through one of the coldest, meanest winters.

Overnight the wind had died down and an occasional break in the clouds allowed the sun to come through. Attempts had been made to clear a path through major snowdrifts. Still, the bus bottomed out now and then and Karlemann had to rock it back and forth to get it going again. Finally we arrived at a few isolated buildings and stopped in front of one with a big sign, *"Front Theater."*

"That's the place," Karlemann announced.

Not knowing what to expect, we were again pleasantly surprised to find a real theater inside with stage, curtain, backdrops, lights, dressing rooms, and with seating for about three hundred people or more.

A rehearsal was in progress as we entered. Soldiers, partly costumed in skirts, wigs, fake bosoms, hammed up a scene from a Lehar operetta. Singing falsetto, they flounced back and forth, batted their eyelashes and flirtatiously lifted their skirts, exposing pairs of bony, hairy legs. It was hilarious. Even the musicians and stage crew came unraveled with laughter, missing cues and drawing reprimands from the director.

"They are not only funny, they are good," Hannimusch acknowledged after watching for awhile. No wonder! We found out that most of them came from legitimate theaters in Germany, and some of them were quite well known. They were no amateurs. Unfortunately, our presence interrupted this delightful entertainment.

"Hey...are you by any chance from the Molkow Ballet?" the landsers asked us, gathering around.

"Yes. How did you guess?"

"We heard it on the radio for days that you were coming. We heard an interview you gave a while back, before leaving Warsaw," the soldiers informed us.

"Well...well...good old Dieter!" Hannimusch laughed, then struck a pose. "Who thought we would be so famous."

Then the work began.

Molkow talked a landser into pounding nails in the dressing room walls so we could hang up our many costumes. Each of us had at least six changes per show, some of them so frenzied, that everything had to be in place and ready. We had no time to look for or fuss with anything.

I danced in six numbers, starting with a courtly gavotte to open the show. The first half of the program was more classical in style, requiring a lot of toe work. It finished with a lively, exhausting Hungarian number. The second half began with a comical interpretation of the *Berliner Schusterjungen* (the mischievous shoeshine boys of Berlin), and finished with a parody of Prussia's King Frederick's elite regiment. This number was a special hit with our troops, reminding them of some of the first commands they had to learn, like "Attention! Eyes left. Eyes right. About face. Hit the ground!" Of course, we goofed up in an exaggerated way just like new recruits may have done.

The unpacking and sorting took until noon. Hilde set up an ironing table while we checked and double-checked our paraphernalia.

"Hey...I am missing a red boot!" Ilse panicked.

"My waltz skirt...Hilde...look at my waltz skirt!" Ulla cried holding it up, displaying a ten-inch rip in one of its white tulle ruffles. "How could that have happened?"

"Never mind how it happened. Just fix it," Hilde told her. Her voice vibrated with stress.

"Hannimusch? H a n n i m u s c h!" Molkow called from the direction of the stage.

"Ja...ja, I'm coming...I'm coming," she twittered in a good mood.

"Bring the sheet music. We are working with an orchestra tonight."

"Ask him when he plans to hold a lunch break," I yelled after her.

"On stage everybody!" His voice boomed into my ear.

I jumped. Molkow, who seconds before had been on the other side of the stage, suddenly stood behind me.

"First, we rehearse," he said.

Once he was out of sight and earshot again, we girls beseeched Hilde to talk to him, to let us have something to eat before rehearsal. We were starving.

"He'll just get mad."

"If WE ask him, yes. But YOU...?"

"Well," she shrugged her shoulders and said, "you just have to grab a bite on the run. Karlemann is bringing some sandwiches."

The rehearsal was a nightmare. Our muscles did not want to respond. We lacked pep and balance. After two hours of toe work, I had blisters that popped and bled right through my shoes. Ulla felt sick. Her arm hurt more than she could bear. She also started to run a fever. Molkow had me take over her solos in the *pas de deux*, and the lead in the *Blue Danube Waltz*. I now had to dance four solos and eight numbers in all.

It was after three o'clock when we stopped to rest up for the evening performance. Exhausted, weak from hunger, bathed in sweat and aching all over, our morale was at zero.

Karlemann drove us back to the 'Home' where a hot meal awaited us, the first since Warsaw. After we ate, we had some time to relax. I looked at my feet. Swatches of skin hung from the knuckles of my toes, exposing raw flesh. I cleaned away the blood, then wrapped each toe carefully in gauze and cotton. Inge and Erika doctored their blisters also. Theirs were not nearly as bad as mine, because they only danced on toe in two numbers.

"I'm not looking forward to tonight," I confessed.

"It's going to be a catastrophe," Erika predicted, massaging her sore legs.

"Molkow said, it's our fault that we are so out of shape. We should have practiced more," Inge grumbled.

"On the train? He's got some nerve blaming us," I protested. During the year and a half I had been with the Molkow Ballet, Molkow had conducted classes no more then six times. I felt myself sliding backwards technically and was very bitter about that. "He is supposed to train us, not just use us."

Erika and Inge remained silent. They did not disagree, but feared being drawn into a rebellious confrontation.

When the curtain parted that night, the lights, the music and the dark space full of people worked its magic as always. As the applause rose, so did the quality of our performance. There was pain, there were slip-ups, but at the end, a trampling, shouting, all male audience would not let us off the stage. "We did it! We did it!" We congratulated one another. Molkow gave us the signal for an encore, a cute drill routine in our blue, gold and red uniforms.

Backstage, we were mobbed. Every soldier wanted an autograph, wanted to shake our hands, thank and congratulate us for a wonderful show. They wanted to know where each of us was from, and beamed when our hometown was the same as theirs. I began to understand why we were there, what our purpose was.

Invitations poured in from various units to have dinner with one, a few drinks or a party with another. Elated over our success, we felt like celebrating and hoped Molkow would accept one of the invitations for that night. He did.

"We are stopping at headquarters for a drink," he told Karlemann.

It usually took us an hour, taking off makeup, getting dressed and sorting our costumes. That evening we were done in half the time.

At headquarters, a long line of officers waited to welcome us. One by one, they introduced themselves with a handshake and heel click. Not one was below the rank of major. I received many nice compliments about my dancing.

Molkow pulled me aside and introduced me to the General. "This is Elfi, our young soloist." It was tradition for the main soloist to sit with the host. I looked over my shoulder at Ulla, whose place I was taking. She snootily raised her chin and turned her head.

The General, a thin-faced, gray-haired man of medium build, smiled at me benevolently. "Well then, young lady, shall we sit down?" He offered me his arm and led me to the center of a u-shaped table arrangement. Once he and I were seated, everybody else sat down. I should have felt honored to be the General's table partner for the evening. Instead I wished to be with somebody young, handsome and romantic, somebody like Karlemann. I would have gladly left these honors to Ulla.

Aides brought copper trays stacked with open-faced sandwiches and served wine in copper goblets. Some men had brought their own bottles. As soon as everyone had been served, the General stood up, as did the officers, and proposed a toast. He thanked us for a delightful show, praised our bravery in coming to the front, (as if we had a choice) and concluded with a wish for a timely and victorious end to the war. Several other toasts followed, lauding our group for heroism, patriotism and the high caliber of our performance--exaggerations, all of them.

My interest had wandered from these boring formalities to the cleverly improvised furnishings in the room, especially the hammered copper trays, side tables, goblets, plates, cups, and ashtrays.

"Someone around here is very clever," I said to the General between speakers, admiring a goblet. "Who makes these things?"

"A Russian makes them. He hammers them out from shell casings," he explained.

I looked at him puzzled. "Shell casings...? The kind guns discard?" The General nodded. "How interesting! I am so glad to learn that guns serve at least one good and useful purpose," I replied.

He smiled graciously. "Speaking of guns, I hope they did not keep you awake last night," he inquired.

"I did not hear a thing. I was so tired that one could have gone off next to my bed and I would not have heard it." Suddenly it hit me. "Guns!" I looked at him. "How close are we to the front?"

"Twenty--thirty kilometers."

"That's not very far."

Putting his arm around my shoulders, he reassured me, "You need not worry. Nothing much will happen on the front right now. Both sides are waiting out the winter."

"That's comforting to know, especially coming from you."

I felt at ease with the General. He was a nice, kind, caring man, though not very talkative and often seemed lost in thought for which he apologized. At such moments his face looked drawn and old.

He asked me about my home, about Munich and nearby mountain resorts that had been his playground before the war. Recalling scenes and places was a walk back to more pleasant times, a most enjoyable walk down memory lane. It connected two people from opposite ends of the human spectrum--he an older man, a general, a warrior--me, an immature, sixteen-year-old dancer, inexperienced and naïve.

I noticed that he drank very little. Not so his officers. They had begun to sing, louder and louder, repeating one song over and over about "*Die Alten Germanen,*" (about ancient Germans drinking ale). Many had left the table, sitting around in comfortable-looking arm chairs made of willow branches, and on divans made from car seats. Half of our troupe was also not very sober anymore. Emmy and Ilse giggled, weaving from side to side as they headed for the bathroom. Ulla and Betty shared one of the armchairs in a corner. Ulla nibbled on Betty's ear again--"Disgusting," I thought--while their table escorts led another round of "*Die Alten Germanen.*"

About that time, the General excused himself. "Sorry to have to leave, but my day begins early. I enjoyed your company very much and hope to see you again." He kissed my hand, bowed and said, "Good luck, child."

I decided to join Erika and Inge who sat off to one side, shaking with laughter over the antics of a drunken officer, but I changed my mind. My eyes burned from the thick smoke in the room. I felt the need for fresh air. Just as I reached the door, Molkow yelled at me, "Where do you think you are going?" From the way he slurred his words, I could tell that he was very drunk, too. I turned around and saw him lean over the table with his arms outstretched and his head bobbing and swaying between them like that of a cobra. To avoid an embarrassing scene, I walked over to Hilde who was a little glassy-eyed herself, and explained that I needed to go to the bathroom. It gave me the excuse to leave the room.

On the way downstairs, an officer staggered up and blocked my path. I tried to fend him off but he pinned me against the wall with his body while his hands slid inside my dress. I managed to slip out from under him and ran down the rest of the stairs and out the door into the snowy darkness. There, in front of the building stood our bus ready and waiting. I tried the door and found Karlemann wrapped in his fur coat and blanket slumped down in the driver's seat.

He jerked up. "Oh! Is everybody ready to go?" he asked.

"Not quite," I answered. "Sorry. Guess, I woke you up."

"That's all right. But what are you doing out here in the cold?"

"I had to get some fresh air," I told him through chattering teeth.

"Well, here..." he said and pulled me up next to him, "put this blanket around you."

"They are getting pretty drunk in there. I hope we can leave soon," I told him.

I could feel the warmth from his body as he nudged closer to tuck the blanket around me. It filled me with a wondrous glow.

"You smoke?" He pulled a case from inside his coat and offered me a cigarette. I nodded. He took two and lit both of them. The flame from his lighter outlined his handsome features. My heart was racing. I tried to think of something clever to say but my mind went blank and for a long while we just sat there in silence and smoked. A faint rumbling in the distance gave me an excuse to start a conversation.

"Is this thunder coming from the front?"

"Yeah. Every so often, each side has to fire its guns to remind everybody that the war is still on. It's nothing to worry about."

"That's what the General said. I hope you are right."

"By the way, how old are you? You can't be more than fifteen or sixteen."

I was tempted to say that I was eighteen. Karlemann was at least in his late twenties. Instead, I said, "I'll be eighteen soon." A year from now, that was soon. It was not an outright lie. I just stretched the truth a little.

Sounding angry he said, "You kids really don't belong out here in this hell-hole."

"It's not that good or safe at home anymore, either," I reminded him.

"If the war doesn't get you, one of those drunken, two-legged brass wolves will."

"I can take care of myself," I assured him. In reality, I was too scared right then to go back inside, knowing I might run into that drunk officer again--or somebody like him. But I was even more scared of Molkow's violent temper, should he notice my absence. "I have to go back," I suddenly decided. "Why don't you come in with me? Like you said, it's cold out here."

Karlemann shook his head. "Sorry. Officers only."

"Oh, poop!" I could not stand such social barriers. I had to deal with them all my life. My family was poor. My father did not have a title. We did not have the best clothes. And "heaven have mercy" we were linked to the theater. I learned early on that there was a front door and a back door, and for poor people like us, it was often the back door.

I would have liked to linger, but fearing Molkow's reprimand, I excused myself. "Got to go back upstairs. See you later. And thanks for the blanket and cigarette," I said.

Karlemann held on to my hand as I climbed out of the bus. Before he let go he squeezed it and said softly, "Take care, angel."

My feet hardly touched the ground as I flew up the stairs and sailed into the room. It had emptied out. The few remaining officers were too drunk to get on their feet. Molkow was out cold. Hilde proceeded to round everyone up to leave. I rushed toward Erika and squeezed her hand. She looked at me with suspicion. "What's with you? Oh, no! Don't tell me. You are in love again. Who is it this time?" she said and rolled her eyes toward the ceiling as if beseeching heaven to help her.

"I'm not telling," I answered, not ready for her scrutiny.

On the way back, Karlemann had to stop the bus twice; once for Molkow who was heaving up, and once for Emmy for the same reason. "How disgusting," I thought every time that happened. At least Emmy was still on her feet. With the help from Hilde, Molkow crawled from the bus, into the 'Home' and up the stairs to his room on all fours like a doped animal.

Changing into our nightclothes, Erika, Inge and I discussed how pleasantly surprised we were over the warm reception, our comfortable housing and the well equipped theater here in Smolensk. "This is better than back home," Erika commented.

The next day we were allowed to sleep in. We washed and mended our clothes and wrote letters. At lunchtime, Molkow appeared in the dining room with a blinding hangover, snorting and acting like a wounded bull. We stayed out of trouble's way by quietly and quickly eating and exiting. Even Hannimusch kept a silent distance. Hilde was gone. Karlemann had taken her, Ulla, Erika and Betty to the hospital to have the girls' arms looked at, and to get Hilde medicine for her chronic diarrhea.

Back in our room, Inge and I examined the fireplace, toying with the idea of building a fire. As we knelt down, rearranging pieces of charred wood, Inge suddenly let out a heart-piercing scream. "A mouse! I saw a mouse!"

"So, that's what I saw yesterday scurrying across the floor," I remembered. Her scream brought everybody rushing into our room, including Katja.

"What's going on? What's going on?"

"Oh, it's nothing. Just a mouse," I told them. "Inge is scared of a little mouse."

"Mouse...nice mouse...mouse pet," Katja said in broken German. Her eyes scanned the table. "Bread..." she said and pointed to the heel of a loaf left on a plate.

"...little bit bread."

I cut off a little piece and gave it to her. She crumbled it onto the ledge of the fireplace, then put her finger to her mouth and motioned to us to stand still. After a few minutes we saw a little face with a pink nose, pink ears and shiny black eyes peek out from under the wood. It did not seem too afraid of us, even dared to come out all the way to get the bread. When we could not hold our breath and stand still any longer, the mouse fled back into its hiding-place.

"So much for a fire in the fireplace," I said. "We can't save the world, but we can spare a little mouse."

Inge was not fond of rodents, but she would never have killed one, especially this one.

Just as we decided to go back to whatever we were doing, Hilde and the girls returned.

"Well, what's the verdict? Are you going to live or die?" Hannimusch asked jokingly.

"We'll be all right. Ulla just can't dance for a few days," Betty answered.

Ulla pulled down the sleeve of her dress, showing us a thick bandage around her upper arm. It reeked of iodine. "I have to change this every few hours," she explained. "I got an infection, the doctor said."

"Great God! Wait till Egon hears about this," Hannimusch warned. "He is in an especially explosive mood today."

It was not long before Molkow's voice boomed up and down the corridor. "Get your stuff. We are leaving in a half hour for rehearsal."

At the theater, we watched the same group of landsers rehearse again as they had the day before. Backstage Molkow debated whether or not Hilde should stand in for Ulla in some of the numbers. She was no dancer, but the last number, the spoof on the army, required only precision, no particular balletic skill. Hilde could do it, but we were too embarrassed to be seen on stage with her. She was terribly skinny. The audience always snickered when she appeared because her legs looked like sticks in boots. What a relief when Molkow decided to change formations instead. Again, I had to take over Ulla's solos. Anyone not needed on stage for the moment, sat around with our male colleagues, watching and chatting. Inge told me later, very excitedly, that the fellow she talked with was first soloist of the Hamburg Opera Ballet. As she described him, her eyes sparkled as never before.

Our show that night was another hit, bringing still

more invitations from units who begged us just to spend an hour or two with them. But Molkow refused all. I was glad. I felt totally worn out and so did everybody else. The excitement, anticipation, and the hazards and tensions of the past few days had taken their toll. Besides, we had to rise early the next morning because of plans made with Karlemann to show us around the area.

The distant, steady roll of thunder from heavy guns lulled us to sleep that night. It followed me into my dreams. Suddenly, several loud bangs in rapid succession shocked me awake. It sounded like gunshots directly from below our window. Not sure if what I heard was real or imagined, I just lay there and listened. Wondering if Erika and Inge had heard it too, I whispered,

"Are you awake?"

"*Ja...ja...*" they whispered back.

"Did you hear..." Just then I heard a man's voice cry out for help, which stopped me in mid sentence. I heard it again, "Help...comrade...help...help..."

"Someone got shot," Erika murmured.

Then there was silence.

"What do you think we should do?" Inge whimpered.

"You are closest to the door. Open it a crack and listen," I suggested. "Somebody may be up to investigate. Maybe the Molkows...?" Before I could finish, Inge fled to my bed and crawled under the blanket with me.

"No way," she said. "What if there are partisans prowling around? I'm not opening that door. I don't even want to be near it."

I peeked out of the window from behind the blackout shade. Again we heard that faint voice calling for help. I scanned the shadowy, snow-covered ground below but saw nothing move. Erika, meanwhile, had gotten up and stepped out in the hallway. "All is quiet out here. I don't hear anybody," she reported.

"What if somebody is wounded and is dying down there. We've got to do something," Inge fretted.

"Well then, go and wake the Molkows," I told her.

"Me...? Not me! I'm not going anywhere." I knew she was too scared to budge.

I looked out again. This time I saw dim circles of light bounce around near the barracks where Karlemann stayed.

"Somebody is out there with flashlights," I said and poked Inge, adding, "You can go back to your bed now. Whatever happened, it's being taken care of."

"I'm not going to sleep next to the door," she said.

"Oh, don't be such a scared rabbit," I scolded her, knowing quite well that I would not be able to get her out of my bed. Erika and I jammed a chair against the door, just in case, and I slept in Inge's bed for that night.

This incident shook us aware that we were in a war zone, and cautioned us not to become too relaxed or complacent.

The shooting was the topic of conversation from the moment we got up the next morning until Karlemann finally cleared up the mystery and put our fears to rest. "It was a landser," he informed us, "who said that a sniper shot him in the leg. More than likely he shot himself."

"That's stupid," Emmy blurted out.

"Some guys do anything to get out of this hell-hole and out of the war. However, if this guy shot himself, he'll be dead anyway. He'll face execution."

I thought of the Russian who jumped off the rail car. I understood.

On the bus later, as Karlemann took us on a tour of the area, we discussed the ethics of a man wounding himself to get out of the army and the war. Molkow insisted that it is an act of pure cowardice.

"In that case, we have quite a few cowards in the army...and a lot of dead heroes," Karlemann responded. "After a couple of years here on the front, a lot of men crack. Some walk right into the line of fire, knowing they'll get killed, just to get it over with."

"They never show that on the news reels," Hannimusch commented.

I wondered what it would take to make us crack. If I had been that partisan, I would have jumped too. Long before he did.

Smolensk lay dead. Nature had covered it compassionately with a white shroud of snow. The bus rumbled through her ruins, coming to a thick, battle-scarred stone wall with massive round turrets. Karlemann stopped. "This wall used to ring the city and once stood in defense against Napoleon's army. On the other side of it is a moat, but without water now. Before the ground froze we found and dug up old swords, helmets, boots, buttons and parts of uniforms...plus bones and skulls from Napoleon's army and previous wars. Mementos, to take home, to show our grand kids some day." We listened in awe. Karlemann paused, squeezing his chin. "Centuries from now, who knows, somebody will dig up our bones and the steel from our shells and our helmets."

From there, Karlemann drove down toward the Dnieper river, crossing it on a makeshift pontoon bridge. Ice-flows had sheeted up against twisted girders from the original bridge, which stuck out of the water upriver from us, and chunks accumulated against the pontoons. A crew of soldiers worked breaking them up. On the other side, up on a hill, towered the cathedral. From the outside it did not seem badly damaged, though its white walls were pitted with shell marks. The appalling damage was on the inside, and not caused by the war. "The work of retreating Russian troops,", Karlemann pointed out.

Intricate mosaics and murals that had once graced the walls of several alcoves were deliberately hacked to pieces and their gilded tiles gouged out. "I was told that some Russians thought that the tiles were pure gold and pried them out, thinking it would make them rich." The most vicious act of destruction, however, had been aimed at the mural above the main altar. It was slashed to shreds and smeared over with excrement. "That was done by Bolsheviks, the Russians say." Karlemann explained.

The roof of the cupola, which spanned the center of the church with graceful arches, was badly damaged. Russian civilians together with German troops had made temporary repairs to preserve at least the graceful structure of this church.

Deeply saddened by the devastation all around us, we returned to our quarters in a somber mood. I asked again why an all-powerful God did not stop this war, the killing, the suffering and the destruction of so many beautiful things. Why did he not strike down the people that caused this madness?

VII

Under Fire

We had been in Smolensk less than two weeks when half our cast came down with colds, sore throats and fever. Hannimusch and Molkow walked around with their necks wrapped in towels soaked in a hot vinegar solution, topped with wool scarves. Both feared losing their voices. Every morning, three or four of us sat in the dining room bent over bowls, inhaling the steam from this vinegar mix to clear our stuffy heads, or soaking our bloody feet in it. Our quarters, the bus, the dressing room began to smell like a pickle factory. Doctors from the hospital urged bed rest. When we did not comply, they threw up their hands and just supplied us with pills and salves. In spite of our discomforts and pains, the last thing anyone wanted was to cancel the show and disappoint the hundreds of soldiers who jammed into the theater night after night. Instead, we added a daily matinee. Knowing we could make these fellows forget the war and its miseries for a couple of hours was worth the effort. Anyway, the moment the curtain opened we forgot about our aches and gave it our all.

Inge seemed to have escaped all the physical ailments. Instead, she acted as if she was losing her mind. She wandered around in a daze. It was impossible to hold a conversation with her because, from one minute to the next, she could not remember what was said.

"Inge, Inge," I had to snap my fingers in front of her face just to get her attention. "Where are you? Come back, come back." Inge had never acted aggressively in any way; suddenly she pushed others aside to be the first one off the bus, and the first one to enter the theater when we arrived there, only to mysteriously disappear for a time. This was not like Inge. Erika and I suspected that it had something to do with that dancer from Hamburg. We teased her, but she angrily denied it.

After days of this, one afternoon as the bus pulled up to the theater, I tricked her. "Isn't that Moedl out there, that dancer from Hamburg? Looks like he's moving out," I said to Erika, loud enough so she could hear.

"Where...where?" Inge, already primed to beat everybody out of the bus again, snapped her head around and stretched her neck to see what I saw. "Where? I don't see him." She looked at me, saw me grinning, and knew she had been had. Her face turned a deep red and she sat down with a pout.

Moedl was there, of course, waiting in the dark hallway between stage and dressing room. Now, that she knew her secret was out, she glanced back at Erika and me, smiling sheepishly. Her face and eyes glowed. "Cover for me, in case Molkow starts looking for me," she said and disappeared.

Either before or between the shows a young doctor from the army hospital routinely stopped by to check on us. The swelling on the girls' arms had gone down, colds were letting up, but now he found new reason for concern. He did not like the railing sound in Erika's chest, nor the yellowish tinge in her and Ulla's eyes and complexion. "Better stop by the hospital...all of you...as soon as possible," he said. His visits, however, were not purely professional. I saw sparks fly back and forth between him and Betty whenever their eyes met.

Between the two daily shows, Karlemann brought tea and sandwiches to the dressing room. We only had an hour and a half to eat and rest. Usually a few officers from headquarters stopped by to chat with us. A major with a monocle and a scar across his cheek consistently planted himself next to me, half-leaning, half-sitting on the makeup counter, smoking, and playing with his swagger stick. I had to listen to his long-winded stories about Anna Pavlova, the greatest dancer of her time, who had been a frequent guest at his family's estate. That, of course, also made him an authority on dance. "I have never seen anyone match her *bourree*. She simply floated across the stage. Yours need a little work, but you definitely share some of her ethereal, spiritual qualities," he flattered me.

Erika, in the chair next to me, rolled her eyes, having to turn away with both hands over her mouth to keep from bursting out laughing. Just a few feet away, Karlemann leaned against the doorjamb and watched me squirm with obvious amusement.

As the major went on and on, I searched desperately for an excuse to get rid of him. "Pardon me for interrupting," I finally said, "I need to get myself something to drink." I rose from my chair with my cup in hand and started to walk to the table where a thermos stood.

"Oh, Elfi," Erika said sweetly, intercepting me, "stay there. I'll get it for you." I could have strangled her.

When the major finally did leave, he became the butt of jokes for the evening.

"I thought monocles went out with World War I," Emmy laughed.

"He is your typical Heidelberg graduate, saber scar and all," Hannimusch professed to know. "Some have brains; some have titles; some have monocles."

That night we had nothing scheduled after the show, but Molkow wanted to stop for a drink at the officers' lounge at headquarters where we had a standing invitation.

"We won't be long," he told Karlemann.

I feared running into "Major Scarface," the name we gave the long-winded braggart, but the place was almost empty. An orderly on duty asked us what we wanted to drink.

"Lemonade and a shot of vodka," I said.

"Vodka? Since when do you drink vodka?" Erika questioned.

"Not for me, silly. I'm sneaking it out to Karlemann."

"You'll get into trouble."

"What's unusual about that?" I replied with a grin.

93

Karlemann sat again in his seat, napping. I knocked on the window. He opened the door and helped me up.

"Since you can't come to the well...you know how the saying goes," I said and handed him the drink.

"Oh...! That's very nice of you. Thanks, angel," he said and took the small goblet. With only one hand free, he handed me his blanket. "Here. Wrap this around you before you freeze to death."

"I can't stay," I told him. "Just thought this might make waiting for us in the cold a little more bearable."

"It's all right. I don't mind sitting out here. This old bus and I share many good memories." He ran his hand affectionately along its dash. "We've been to many nice places together before we got drafted and sent out here."

"You mean, this bus is yours?"

"Sure is. My brother and I ran a touring business back home. They drafted us both, buses and all."

"In that case you'll be twice as happy to know that nobody will be throwing up on it tonight. The place upstairs is dead. Nobody's there, which means we won't stay long," I rattled on.

"Not even the major with the scar? Thought he might be sweeping you off your feet by now," Karlemann teased.

"Not likely. He is not my type!"

"Who is your type?"

I felt the blood rush to my face. Good thing it is dark, I thought.

"Don't suppose I am your type either?" Karlemann leaned forward and lifted my chin, his face only inches from mine. I thought for sure he was going to kiss me.

Wanting to appear cool and sophisticated, I searched for some clever, light-hearted reply but drew an absolute blank. Stupid me, all I managed to stammer was, "I'd better go back inside before Molkow comes looking for me."

"Well, then," he straightened up, "here's to you." He emptied the copper goblet in one gulp and handed it back to me. "I'm sure the brass doesn't like it any better than Molkow to see you out here with me," he muttered. But as I turned to leave, he hooked a strand of my hair around his finger. In his usual, gentle tone, he said, "Thanks for the drink, angel, and for your company."

In bed that night, I analyzed every second of those moments with Karlemann and thought of all sorts of clever things I could have said or done. "I wonder what he thinks of me...?" My heart teetered between ecstasy and agony. If only I could talk to someone. I looked over to Erika. Her labored, raspy breathing told me she was asleep. Inge? No! She floated on a cloud of her own, thinking of nothing else but Moedl.

Next day, Karlemann drove our group to an army warehouse to be outfitted with boots and warm clothing. As expected, the army was not equipped to outfit women, but the fellows there tried. The supply chief and his crew looked for the smallest sizes in boots, socks, sweaters and coats among the standard army wear and among items donated by civilians. I tried on a pair of *Knobelbecher* (military work boots), wool trousers, and over that a long lambskin coat that came down to my ankles. Hannimusch took one look at me and burst out laughing. "Hello, coat! Where are you going with that girl?" she said.

"You think I look funny? Go look at yourself," I giggled. She was stuck half way in a pair of army pants, tugging in vain to pull them over her hips.

Uschi, a scant five foot with heels on, had her legs in a pair of boots that came up over her knees. She walked as if she had buckets on her feet. Then she tried on a wool sweater and completely disappeared in it. One looked more ridiculous than the other. It was a riot and we laughed until we hurt. Even Molkow's face twisted into a reluctant grin. However, regardless of appearance, we were sick of freezing on the bus and plowing through knee-high snowdrifts in our street shoes. So, we opted for boots, a pair of trousers, a sweater or vest. I kept the lambskin coat.

Most of us wanted to wear the boots on the trip back to our quarters, but after just a few minutes, they started to hurt our feet. New and stiff, made of tough leather, they were definitely not meant for women's, much less dancers' feet. Molkow and Karlemann offered suggestions on how best to break them in. "Get them thoroughly wet," Karlemann advised, "then wear them until they dry on your feet."

"Do as the landsers do!" Molkow said. "Pee into them, then wear them."

"Disgusting!" Hannimusch protested.

"I'll get you some grease. That helps to soften the leather, too," Karlemann offered.

"Thank you, Karlemann." Hannimusch nodded gratefully. "That I can handle."

I sat in my usual place on the bus, pleasurably nestled in my warm furry coat, with Erika's feverish head in my lap. My eyes were again drawn to the rear view mirror watching Karlemann. I could think of little else but him. My moods went up and down like a roller coaster; up for joy when he looked and smiled at me; down in deepest despair when he did not. When our eyes met, it felt as if my body was on fire. A couple of times I started to confide in Erika but she made comments about Karlemann like, "He is a skirt chaser. He is looking for a bed partner." Besides, Erika was sick, really sick. She was burning up with fever and was too scared to let Hilde know. "She'll make me stay in bed, and I don't want to stay in the house all by myself at night."

"You really should stay in bed," I said to her. "Ulla can take your place in the show. She is feeling better."

"No way," Erika objected.

"At least tell Hilde, or tell the doctor tonight that you have a fever."

"Just get me some aspirins. I'll be fine," she insisted. "And don't you dare say anything to Hilde. You swear?"

"All right...all right."

I understood how she felt. We were a thousand miles from home and family, in a situation where fear never left us, though we seldom talked about it. Performing for our soldiers was our only joy, our only purpose. We could not stop the war, we could not prevent the killing, but we could spread a couple of hours of happiness. It was worth our pain.

Back in our room, I could not wait to take my boots off. But as much as I tugged, pushed and pulled, they remained stuck on my feet. I asked Inge to help me. She straddled my leg and pulled with all her might. I cried out in pain. After considerable effort, bathed in sweat, we succeeded in getting one boot off but not the other. Hilde happened to come by and she, too, tried to help. By now my foot had swelled inside the boot.

"I'll get Egon," Hilde decided, very concerned. "Maybe he can help."

A little while later Molkow sputtered up the hallway. "For Pete's sake! It's like running a nursery...ridiculous... can't get her boots off...got them on without help... ridiculous...." He charged into our room, shoved Inge aside and headed straight for me. I sat on the bed, moaning.

"Stretch out your leg," he barked. "Here is how you take off boots, for heaven's sake." He straddled my leg with his back to me and ordered, "Now push against my back with your other foot." Erika, Inge and I exchanged glances. This was an invitation with great temptations, but I restrained myself to a moderate shove.

"Didn't you hear me? I said...P U S H !" he growled.

Well, I thought, push he wants, so push he gets. I took a deep breath then thrust my foot against his back giving it all the muscle I had. The boot flew off and Molkow sailed across the room, over a chair, head first into the wall. For a moment, we held our breath as we watched him stagger to his feet. Holding his head, he tottered out of the room, cursing. Once out of earshot we exploded with laughter. Hilde scolded us for being so insolent but could not keep a straight face herself. It was not just funny. To me it seemed divine justice and I felt privileged that fate had chosen me to deliver it. The best part: I was blameless. I only did what he told me to do! This incident filled with glee the heart of anyone who still had a score to settle with Molkow. Uschi came and shook my hand and quipped, "Wish I had been in your boots."

On the way to the theater, Karlemann asked Molkow why he was holding a towel to his forehead. "You have a headache?"

"Just watch the road," Molkow snarled. Puzzled, Karlemann looked at us and, reading our faces, he quickly understood not to press the issue.

After the last performance that evening, we went straight to our quarters. I had been in an exceptionally good mood that day, joking, laughing, and teasing Karlemann a lot. As he dropped us off at the home, he snatched my scarf. I chased him around the bus and before I knew what happened he caught me in his arms and kissed me. He kissed me like I had never been kissed before. His breath steamed warm down the collar of my blouse. I thought I was going to melt. For a glorious, dizzy moment, time stood still. I felt weightless.

When my brain kicked in again, I freed myself, ran inside and up the stairs, and straight to the bathroom where I rinsed out my mouth. He had a strange way of kissing, I thought. I was not at all sure now if I liked it, or if it was proper. Somehow, I expected a scarlet letter to appear on my forehead for all the world to see. I slouched to my room like a sinner, hoping no one would see me. It was just a kiss, but what a kiss.

Erika, already undressed, looked up briefly. I wanted in the worst way to tell her what had just happened, but she was half delirious with fever. Again, I implored her to let me tell Hilde. "No. Just hand me the aspirins," she said in weak, breathy voice and sank down on her bed. I held her head up to help her swallow the pills with a little lemonade.

Inge sat on the stone ledge of the fireplace, absent-mindedly crumbling a piece of bread for the mouse. She paid no attention to either of us. Though I really did not want to confide in Inge, who sometimes was a blabbermouth, I was bursting to tell somebody about Karlemann and the kiss.

"Since when do you like mice?" I probed her to see what mood she was in. She shrugged her shoulders.

"I didn't see Moedl at all today. He promised to be at the theater," she said. That told me where her mind was.

"Has he kissed you yet?" I tried to steer the conversation to the topic of my heart.

"He could have left a message."

"What was it like?"

"What was what like?"

"When he kissed you?"

Inge blushed, squirmed a little, then looked at me as if saying, what kind of question is this?

For awhile we said nothing. Then I had to ask, "Did you ever French kiss?"

"Don't be silly," she answered, indignant. After a

short pause, eyeing me with suspicion she asked, "Did you?"

"I don't think I would like it," I said as casually as I could muster and got up. "Besides, I think it's wrong. Don't you?"

"It's an inquiry at the upper level if the lower level is available, my mother always said," Inge replied.

The conversation stalled there. We both got ready for bed and said good night. Erika was asleep. I had no one to turn to with questions and problems of that sort. What I knew about love and love making came from a mix of church lectures on chastity, off color jokes, or romance novels where the first innocent kiss always led right away either to the altar or to shameful banishment. My troubling thoughts eventually surrendered to the night-sounds of drumming, distant guns.

A terrible explosion shook us out of our sleep and out of bed. Erika, Inge and I collided in the middle of the dark room. "What was that?"

"Shhhh...I hear planes," I whispered. Seconds later sirens sounded and the floor trembled under the thunder of guns.

"It's an air raid!" I screamed over the racket.

"Alarm! Alarm! Open the windows and get down here fast," a male voice yelled up the stairs.

I tried the window. It was frozen shut. In the confusion we threw on clothes over our nightwear, slipped into shoes and raced downstairs. A soldier by the door asked repeatedly, "Is that everybody?" When all were accounted for he urged, "Hurry! Hurry! Follow me," and charged ahead. The air whistled between booms. Beams of light wove a brilliant net across the sky as guns discharged from all directions. We scrambled across a snowy field toward a large mound and down a hole into a narrow shaft, reinforced with sturdy timber. Planks ran along the walls for a place to sit. It was cold and dank down there and smelled of damp soil and wet lumber. Heavy detonations shook the earth and loosened bits of dirt between the timbers. Moments later, Karlemann jumped down with an arm full of blankets. "Here, I thought you might need these." We thanked him profusely.

"What's going on out there?" Molkow asked.

"Ivan is bombing the hell out of the railroad yard again," Karlemann replied.

The fellow who had led us to the shelter remained outside, watching everything. "*Mensch...Mensch!* We just got one! *Heilige Maria!* Look at that Russkie spin," he cheered. "There goes another one with its tail on fire. Look! Look!"

Karlemann shot up the bunker steps, Molkow right behind him and so did I. We caught a glimpse of a burning plane seconds before it hit the ground in a fiery explosion.

What a sight! Huge searchlights scanned the sky. Shimmering silver ribbons from anti-aircraft gunfire crisscrossed the darkness, bursting into orange balls. It was light enough outside to read a paper. Another plane trailed yellow smoke and veered from side to side until it exploded in mid air, raining debris to the ground around us. Molkow retreated hastily to the bunker. Something whistled toward and past us. Karlemann threw me to the ground and himself on top of me. "Watch out!" I heard the soldier yell. Not very far from us, something hit the ground. Crash! The impact sent shock waves through the frozen earth. "You shouldn't be up here," Karlemann scolded, helping me to my feet. "That was too close."

He put his arm around my shoulders and drew me close. Both of us stood transfixed by the spectacle, so exciting, so terrifying, so beautiful to watch. To stand there with him, bold and death-defiant, was the ultimate thrill. Had it been my last hour, I would have had no regrets.

"Elfi! Get the hell down here," Molkow boomed up. "This instant!"

I really did not want to. Suddenly it seemed demeaning to cower and tremble in some dark hole, pleading with fate to be spared, to let me live another day. But I had no choice.

"It's about over anyway. I can't hear any planes anymore," I reported on the way down.

Not long after that, the guns quit firing and we returned to our beds, thankful to find everything as we had left it.

"Come back down a little later. I'll wait for you by the door," Karlemann whispered to me before we entered the house. "We can go over to my place."

Avoiding his eyes, I shook my head. "I can't." Still keyed up from the excitement of the air raid, intoxicated from the thrill of defying death with him, I felt vulnerable. I would not be able to resist whatever he asked of me. To die with him was one thing, to bed with him, another. "I really can't," I repeated and ran off, afraid I would change my mind if I lingered.

For a long time that night I lay in bed and tried to sort through my feelings. If only I could talk to Erika. I needed her cool, sober perspective. I listened to her teeth chatter and got up to spread my lamb coat on top of her blankets, pleading, "Let me get Hilde."

"No! No!" she insisted. "Just let me go to sleep."

I felt her burning forehead. "If you are not better by morning, I will have to tell somebody," I warned her. She took another couple of aspirins and fell asleep.

VIII

Feeling Needed.

In spite of the danger of the now almost nightly air raids, in spite of the strenuous, exhausting work and the aches and pains resulting from it, Smolensk grew on us. Nowhere had we found a more appreciative audience or felt more wanted, needed and rewarded. We had stayed there longer than anywhere since our group had started traveling together. Before, there was never enough time between hellos and good-byes to really get to know anybody. Now we saw the same faces on a daily basis, got to know most of the officers at the club, knew whom we could trust and whom to avoid. Friendships developed, deepened. Conversations broadened, including now and then even topics considered taboo, like Hitler's bungling war strategy, and their grave concern about Germany's future. What I overheard, and I caught only snippets of these conversations, raised the hair on my back and caused me to look over my shoulder. What had been on the minds of many of these officers was Stalingrad. I was astonished how their opinions coincided with those of my father's. He used to say, "Hitler will fight to the last man. He'll take all of Germany down with him. Somebody has to stop him, get rid of him before it's too late." As I listened to these comments I was terrified, at the same time fascinated, but I knew enough to keep what I heard to myself.

As friendships blossomed, so did romance. Up to now we had swooned, giggled and fantasized over the handsome, interesting men we met. At best, relationships only progressed to a holding of hands. Molkow, exercising his parental rights over any of us under the age of eighteen, made sure it ended there unless, of course, we held hands with somebody he could profit from, preferably somebody in charge of supplies. "Holy Mary!" it crossed my mind now and then, "if he only knew what's going on behind his back these days!" Inge regularly sneaked away to meet Moedl every chance she got; Betty used medical reasons to spend time alone with Dr. Kurt; Emmy and Ilse engaged in secret little rendezvous with several fellows; and I exchanged passionate kisses with Karlemann. Only Erika, who was feeling better again, had nothing to worry about. She was waiting for 'Mr. Right,' she said, unwilling to become involved with anyone less. So far, no man had measured up to her expectations. Men seemed to sense that and kept a friendly, cordial distance.

Hannimusch's romantic star was tethered to a man in Cologne who could not decide which sex he preferred. She often cried and read his letters to us. He vowed that she was the only woman in his life, then went on swooning over this or that wonderful man he had met. It broke her heart and made us angry. She deserved better than that. We hoped that among her many admirers would be one to make her forget that creep.

We also became very good friends with Katja. When time allowed, we would sit together primping, laughing, dreaming and exchanging confidences. She confessed how scared she had been at first of all Germans because the Russian propaganda depicted us as man-eating monsters. Her father served in the Russian army and, like us, she was caught in the middle of this war with so much life to live and so little hope to live it. We told her how scared we were of the Russians from what we had heard about them, and we laughed. And we all agreed that people would have no trouble getting along if it were not because of wars. "They ought to put all the warring leaders together into one rink and let them fight it out," we concluded.

Our next challenge was to perform for the wounded at the hospital. For Hannimusch or Molkow this was no problem. They could play, sing or tell jokes on a chair if they had to. But how could we adapt dance numbers to the aisles of a hospital ward? Molkow had doubts until I suggested that we could pair up in different costumes, taking turns doing excerpts from various dances. I could not believe it, but he actually accepted my idea. "Get together with Hannimusch and work it out," he said. So I did.

I had Erika and Inge improvise the Gavotte, weave in and out between the rows of beds in their pastel, lace trimmed costumes. Ilse and I decided to dance the waltz, heeding Hilde's warning, "Be careful. Try not to get hung up on something and rip your skirts." With each turn, the long, full, white, lace-layered skirts flared out to fill the aisle. Ulla and Betty paired up in the Spanish number, and Emmy and Uschi had chosen to do the Dutch dance, cavorting about in wooden shoes. For a finish, we all lined up in our blue and red satin uniforms and performed a parody of military drills, which usually had audiences roaring with laughter.

The wards were enormous, filled with wounded in various stages of health, from the almost mended to the most critical and the dying. The stench from blood, ether, ointments, and whatever else caused us to gag on every breath. Before the show, Hannimusch broke into tears. "How can I play and sing when I can't even breathe," she complained. No one had realized how difficult and heart wrenching it would be. At the last moment, we reconsidered whether we should go through with it. However, just then some fellows spotted us and the ward came suddenly alive with enthusiastic applause. These men wanted us to put on a show, no doubt about that. Suddenly our purpose, our mission was never more clear and we were committed.

With the first sound from Hannimusch's accordion the ward grew quiet. Men who could walk or stand, leaned against the walls, others sat up in their beds, still others had to be propped up. Suppressed tears lent an unusual vibrato to Hannimusch's voice, not at all unpleasant. As always, Molkow MC'ed, told a few jokes. We danced and pranced in and out between the beds, smiling, flirting, interacting with the fellows. The glow on their faces was worth a kingdom. Finished with our program, we made the rounds, shaking hands and making small talk. Many of the wounded were not much older than we. One young soldier reached out to me with both hands. "Mama...Mama..." he rasped, "help me, Mama." I took his hands and stroked his matted blond hair.

"Mama. Take me home. Please, take me home." He stared straight at me and through me with his glazed blue eyes. In dying he saw not me, he saw his mother.

"I am here, *Junge*, I am here," I said softly. Tears streamed down my cheeks. "You'll go home soon, very soon." I kissed him on the cheek like a mother would. His grip loosened, the tension drained from his face, his eyes closed and he sank back into his pillow. When I straightened up to move on he looked at peace. I wanted to throw myself over his body and weep but had to go on. There were still others to comfort.

It was getting late. We had to do another show at the theater that evening, but promised the wounded men in parting that we would return soon. On the bus we broke down sobbing.

Our performance that night lacked spirit. We felt drained. I kept seeing and hearing this young fellow calling for his mother. In the middle of a dance number the tears started to flow anew. "Pull yourselves together," Molkow hissed at us from the wings. Hannimusch, for the first time in her career, could not finish a song. She begged the audience's pardon and stepped into the wings to blow her nose and clear her throat. "I can't go on," she said.

"Yes, you can. Get back out there," Molkow commanded and gave her a shove.

Hannimusch took a deep breath, straightened her spine, and walked back out on stage. She apologized to the audience for the interruption, "We visited the wounded this afternoon..." This was as far as she got. Her words drowned in an instant ovation. The men understood, jumped to their feet applauding, trampling, and for the longest time would not settle down.

When the show was over and the curtain closed,

Hannimusch dragged herself into the dressing room and plopped into a chair. "I need a drink tonight. Maybe a couple," she declared.

"Tonight we all do," we agreed.

Molkow had already accepted the doctors' invitation to join them after the show. In the small staff dining room of the hospital we sat around a U-shaped table, talked about the day's events and finally relaxed. Erika and I sipped hot tea with rum. She thought it would loosen her nagging cough that seemed to linger on. I hoped it would ease my pains--those in my heart and those in my body. My legs burned from the knees to my ankles.

Karlemann was with us that night and sat across from me next to Emmy. She flirted outrageously with him and he seemed to enjoy it. That stung. Erika still did not know about my feelings for him. She commented, "He acts like a cock in hendom. He likes anybody in skirts." Because of similar remarks she had been making all along, I clammed up. It further prevented me to confide in her. I was not sure now if I wanted to, ever.

We ordered another tea. "It makes my chest feel better," Erika said.

Just as the orderly brought the steaming refill, the air raid sirens sounded. No one became very concerned. Recent air raids had not amounted to much. Just then, a landser dashed into the room with a message for our hosts. "Better head for the cellars, everybody. This might be a big one," the chief of staff announced and charged out of the room, followed by the other doctors and staff.

An orderly showed us down winding steps, through a dank, narrow archway into cavern-like rooms that filled up fast with troops and patients who could walk, and Russians in shabby, mud-colored, quilted jackets and fur hats. I could not tell if they were civilians or prisoners and never did find out. The orderly led us into an alcove, away from the throng. Above the din of voices and shuffle of boots, we heard and felt muffled rumblings from above.

"God help us if a bomb hits this place," Hannimusch worried out loud, scanning the wall of humanity in front of us. I knew what she meant--mass panic.

"What about the fellows up there who can't get out of bed, who can't be moved?" I wondered.

"In some way, they might be better off than we. If we get a hit, I would not want to be trapped down here," Hannimusch said.

I thought of the young soldier whose hand I held that afternoon. He no longer had to worry. He was at peace. I almost envied him.

Standing on that hard, stone floor, my legs burned as if on fire. I had done what the doctors suggested, wrapping them in damp compresses at night. In spite of that, the pain had steadily worsened. Like Erika, I swallowed aspirins by the dozen, and after the show, whenever possible, gulped a shot of vodka or brandy. I leaned against the wall to take some weight off my legs. Hannimusch kept a lookout for the rest of our group.

"I see Molkow waving his hat. Maybe we better inch our way over to him to see what he wants," Hannimusch said. She was taller and could see what I could not. I just followed behind her as she weaved through the crowd.

One of the doctors had unlocked a door in the alcove and ushered us into an examining room.

"You can wait the raid out in here. There are cots and chairs in the adjacent room, and the air is a little better in here, too," he said. We entered a whitewashed room with glass enclosed shelves along the walls that held an assortment of bottles, boxes, cans and instruments. In the middle of it stood a black leather-covered examining table.

"Take care of them," the doctor told Karlemann and left.

While everybody else filed into the next room to sit or lie down, Ilse and I hoisted ourselves upon the examining table and studied the various surgical instruments neatly laid out in white enamel trays under glass. The different shapes and sizes of scissors, clamps, and scalpels filled us with horror. At the end of the table hung two saws. Ilse and I looked at one another.

"Are you thinking what I am thinking?" I asked. "What do you think they do with the sawed-off limbs? Do they bury them?"

Ilse grimaced and shrugged her shoulders, "Never

thought about that."

I recalled the wounded veterans at the Poznan station, and the wounded with whom we visited that afternoon. They seemed so happy, in spite of having lost a limb. They had traded limb for life. For them, the war was over. It was their ticket home. For me, a girl, a dancer...? I could not even imagine what it would be like to lose a leg, or an arm.

"I think, it's worse for a woman than a man," I was thinking out loud.

Ilse nodded in agreement. "I want to get married and have a family some day. Men would not even look at us."

We continued looking around the room. One wall had a small window. Fleetingly, it occurred to me that this might be a possible exit in case of an emergency. But I was not worried. The walls were extremely thick. Only a direct hit could penetrate them.

We heard laughter from the adjacent room and decided to join the others there. At that moment, a horrendous blast knocked me down. Glass shattered, the lights went out, and the air was suddenly thick with dust. Screams, cries, scrambled voices added to the instant chaos. I smelled ether and covered my nose and mouth, thinking, "I've got to get out...got to get air...the window...the window..."

How I got out I could not remember, but I found myself staggering through the night, falling, running, falling, feeling woozy and tasting ether with every breath. The sky was lit up again with anti-aircraft fire and the flames from a burning building. I fell again and slid into a crater. Lying there I thought, "My God, this is the end." Behind me, loud, frantic voices and commands filled the lull between explosions. "This is hell...this is hell." Thoughts and pictures flicked through my mind like an unedited, sped-up filmstrip. One second I saw my parents sitting at their kitchen table, next I heard Hannimusch saying, "...you got to play the odds..." Then I saw myself standing beside the dying soldier, hearing him call to me. No...that was not the soldier. Someone else was calling my name. I tried to answer but no sound came out of my mouth. Everything turned black.

I felt myself being lifted, carried and put down on

something cold and hard. "Elfi...Elfi...talk to me." Somebody patted my cheek. "Elfi...Elfi." Slowly I became aware, first of how terribly cold I felt, then of the pandemonium raging around me, as if the earth was breaking apart. It took a while before I realized who was holding me. It was Karlemann.

"Great God, girl! Are you all right? Do you hurt any place?" he questioned me. "Can you stand up?"

"Where are we?" I asked, confused. "What happened?" Sheltered in a cavern beneath a stone archway of a snow-covered ruin, Karlemann gently brushed the hair out of my face. "Are you hurting anywhere?" I shook my head. He opened his coat and drew me inside it. Then he told me, shouting to compete with a new wave of bombings, "The hospital got hit."

Vaguely, I recalled the light going out, the glass shattering, the screams...the ether. "Where are the others?" Overtaken with sudden panic I wanted to search for them. Karlemann held me back. In a calm voice he told me that everybody got out. "When you turned up missing, Ilse thought you may have crawled out of the hole where the window was. So I looked for you."

"I don't know...I can't remember."

"Don't worry. I'm just glad to have found you."

Another wave of planes roared in above us dropping their deadly load. Karlemann covered me and ducked. On impulse I threw my arms around his neck and wept. I wept all the stored-up tears. I wept for the young men in the hospital wards, for all those who would die that night. I wept for my own life that was sure to end at any moment. I wept for my parents whom I would never see again.

"It's going to be all right. Don't cry, we'll make it." Karlemann comforted me and kissed away the tears that streamed down my face and neck. The fury around us, the deafening roar of planes, guns and explosions drowned my thoughts, my senses and my fears. For moments, I had the strange sensation as if there were two of me, one looking down on the other. I did not fight off Karlemann's increasingly passionate kisses and caresses. I just let it happen. He asked if I loved him and I heard myself answer "yes" but did not feel a thing. Nothing seemed real. I saw us entombed in this stony cavern like the lovers in the opera *Aida*. I would die in his arms. I heard the pounding of his heart and the panting of his breath. Suddenly I realized that this was all I heard. The night had fallen silent again. No more planes, no more guns, only distant voices. The raid was over. We were alive. I did not know if I should be happy or sad. Death had only been postponed.

All of life's paradoxes, its dos and don'ts and twisted rules reentered my consciousness and so did fear, inhibition, censorship and shame. What was I doing here, reclined on a slab of stone, my dress front open and Karlemann leaning over me, caressing and kissing me. I jerked up and pushed him away. My hands trembled as I buttoned my dress. "Let's go," I said. My voice sounded shallow. I noted the look on Kalemann's face--a mix of bewilderment, hurt, even anger. I ducked past him and out of the archway. The sky was orange with flames leaping at it a short distance away. What was there left to burn? I wondered. Karlemann caught up with me. "What's with you?" he asked.

"I am sorry," I answered. What could I say? I was lost in a conflict of emotions. Only hours ago I had fantasized about what it would be like to melt into his embrace. I did not picture it happening on a stone slab inside a ruin, amidst a violent air attack that may have hurt or killed people we knew. This was not the time and place. Why did I need to explain this to him? I was disappointed and a little angry that he thought it was all right. At the same time I was angry with myself and filled with guilt and shame. All I wanted was to get back to my group, quietly praying that no one was hurt.

In silence we walked toward the shouting voices coming from the direction of the hospital. Our path was scattered with debris and impact-craters, but it was light enough from the fires to see and avoid them. I felt the tension between Karlemann and me, but did not know how to resolve it.

At the hospital men worked frantically to control still smoldering trouble spots and to rescue the wounded from a damaged section. Karlemann headed straight for his bus. We found it covered with debris, windows knocked out, but otherwise still in one piece. Assuming our group was inside the building, we looked there next.

One wing of the hospital had suffered heavy damage but it was not a direct hit. A bomb had plowed into the ground a few feet from the building, ripping open the wall from the ground to the second floor. Inside, hallways were littered with broken glass, fallen mortar and bricks, and lined with wounded on stretchers. In the dining room, where we had relaxed only a short time earlier, we found our group. Erika and I flew into each other's arms and cried. In turn we all hugged one another.

"What happened to you? Where did you disappear to? We feared you were dead," Erika said to me.

"Where have you been?" Molkow interrogated me, looking back and forth between Karlemann and me. Karlemann explained how and where he found me, and that we were waiting out the raid under a ruin. I still could not explain how I got outside and looked to Ilse, who was sitting against the wall, pale, with bandages on her head, arm and hand. "All I remember is that you said "window...window..." she said..

"She was out cold, from the ether," the others filled me in. "It almost knocked us out, too."

"How did you get out?" I wondered.

"The same way we got in. By the door...and just in time." Hannimusch's banter belied how shook up she really was. A breath later, she drew me into her arms. "God, I am glad to see you. We thought you got sucked out through that big hole where the window was," she sniffled.

"I don't remember. I don't remember how I got out," I repeated over and over.

It was long past midnight when Karlemann took us in his damaged bus back to our quarters. He hurriedly dropped us off, then returned to the hospital where he was desperately needed.

Though we were all dead tired, some of us could not go to bed right away. We sat around for hours more and talked. It had been an emotion-racked day. We reminded ourselves how lucky we were to be alive.

Finally, when the lights were out and I was lying in bed, alone with my thoughts, they returned to

Karlemann. He had probably saved my life and I had not even thanked him. I was not sure if I should feel guilt for pushing him away, anger because I had to, or shame for not stopping him sooner.

"When I talk with him tomorrow, everything will be all right," I kept telling myself.

Brother Willy

Elfi with Parents

IX

Coping with Betrayals

The new day brought new problems.

Katja had just set a carafe full of fresh coffee on the dining room table when Dr. Kurt, Betty's heartthrob, walked in. "Morning, kids," he greeted us, took off his cap and plopped down on a chair, looking totally exhausted.

"Morning, Kurt," we chorused.

Hannimusch poured him a cup. "Don't suppose you got any sleep last night?" she asked with motherly concern.

Kurt shook his head. He rubbed his eyes and unshaven face. "We had to evacuate one entire wing of the hospital. Now we've got wounded stacked everywhere." He yawned.

"Did you have many casualties?" Ilse asked, herself one, still wearing bandages.

"We have quite a few injuries. Mostly, we are left with just a big mess," Kurt answered. He waved Ilse over to him. "Let me have a look," and removed the gauze bandage and cotton pads from her head. Crusted with blood and stuck to her hair and scalp, they did not come off easily. After carefully checking her wounds he said, "You can leave them off."

Ilse's cuts, caused by flying glass, were minor, though she had bled a lot. "When can I wash my hair?" she asked. Kurt answered with a faint smile. "Go ahead, but

113

do it very gently or you'll start bleeding again."

"You must be waiting for Betty." Hannimusch assumed.

He glanced at the open door leading to the hallway. "Actually, I came to see Egon."

"Have seen neither Betty nor Molkow so far this morning," she informed him. "Want me to get them?"

Kurt thought for a moment. Then, as if to emphasize the importance of what he was about to say, he leaned forward. "Meant to tell you last night. You must come in for checkups, all of you. It can't be put off. Ulla has jaundice. Some of you may be infected already. We can't let it spread."

"Oh, but I feel much better," Ulla protested.

At that moment, we heard Molkow come down the stairs, coughing, as he did every morning. Kurt rose immediately from his chair and met him in the hallway, where they talked quietly. Minutes later Kurt left, waving to us. "See you later!"

For days I had had an uneasy feeling that something terrible was about to happen. I thought last night's air raid was it. Kurt's visit triggered it anew.

Molkow entered the dining room, held his head with both hands and muttered, "that's all I need...that's all I need."

Hannimusch intercepted him. "What's going on?"

"He wants to put us all under quarantine."

"Under quarantine? Everybody? Why?"

"Jaundice."

"Is that so serious?"

"Evidently." Molkow shrugged his shoulders. "He wants us at the hospital after lunch for a complete physical."

"Today?" Hannimusch gasped. "Don't they have enough to do right now? What about the show?"

"He said this can't wait," Molkow answered. He flexed his jaw muscles and seemed as perplexed as we were.

"What now? What next?" we asked. We were all still in shock from the night before. Now this.

More bad news awaited us when Karlemann came later with our hot lunch. The first thing he said was, "The Tommies bombed the hell out of Hamburg last night.

114

They also hit Berlin pretty hard."

Many of us had family and friends in one or the other place. We fired questions at him.

"Do you know what sections of the cities got hit? Was there a lot of damage? Did they hit the residential areas?"

He shook his head. "I know only what I've heard on the radio. I'll try to find out more from the guys on the switchboard at headquarters," he promised. The ever-present smile on his face had vanished. He seemed un-usually tense, reserved and distant. I expected a nod, a smile, or some kind of special acknowledgement from him that morning; instead, he avoided me.

Molkow paced the floor, running his fingers through his dark, slicked-back hair. "Do you suppose I could get a call through to Berlin?" he asked Karlemann.

"The lines are jammed. Maybe later tonight."

After we ate, Karlemann took us in his patched up bus to the hospital. We got off and viewed the damage. Half of all the windows at the back of the building were blown out. Russians and soldiers worked side by side to repair cracks and a gaping hole in the foundation, and filled in a deep crater in front of it. All around, rocks and debris littered the snowy ground.

Inside, stretchers with wounded lined both sides of the dark, cold hallway. A medic escorted us through to an examining room. We were expected. He told us to un-dress behind a folding screen while he summoned the doctors. Molkow went with him.

Next to the screen stood a x-ray machine, beyond it two examining tables separated by half-drawn curtains. The room was large and unheated.

A short while later two doctors and a male assistant entered and told us to line up for x-rays. Kurt was not with them. We hated these army-style proceedings that left no room for modesty. I doubted that the male doctors and male nurses looked at us strictly in a professional way. The doctors in Poznan certainly had not.

Holding pieces of clothing in front of us, we emerged shivering one by one from behind the screen, then had to stand for several minutes leaning against the ice-cold metallic surface of the x-ray machine while the doctor scanned the image. After that, the assistant stuck a thermometer under our armpit, and we took turns on the examining tables. The doctor poked my stomach, tapped on my back, listened to heart and lungs, looked into my eyes, ears, throat, and finally checked my reflexes. To do that, he grabbed my legs and swung them over the side of the table. I jerked and let out a yelp. He looked at me startled and asked, "Did I hurt you?" Not wanting to prolong the examination, I played it down. "Oh, it's just my shinbone."

"Your shinbone?" Straightening one leg, he applied light pressure up and down the bone with his thumb. The pain made me cringe.

"Does it hurt when you walk?" the doctor asked, examining my other leg. It hurt, but not as much.

"Only when I jump," I lied.

Then he noticed a small lump on my left kneecap, the size of a bird's egg. When he touched it, the pain was so acute that I jerked backward, almost falling off the table. I could not kneel on that leg anymore and had to fake it or switch legs in some of my dance numbers.

"Hmmmm." The doctor frowned. "It's an inflammation of the tissues. This is not good. You have to stay off those legs for a while, or you'll wind up in a cast."

"You mean, I can't dance?" I stammered, mortified. Like Erika, I was afraid of that and therefore never complained too much about my pains.

My face must have reflected my inner panic because he thought for a moment, then modified his instructions. "Well, at least stay off your feet as much as you can and wrap your legs in damp towels at night." I quickly promised to do so. Anything, to stay in the show and to get this examination over with.

Erika was one of the last to finish.

"What took you so long?" I asked.

She showed me a small bottle and made a face. "I have to spit in it when I cough up phlegm. He thinks I have tuberculosis."

"Ah...Erika, you are not the type to get tuberculosis," I assured and hugged her. "You just have a bad cold. It's the first time you've been that sick."

From the hospital we drove straight to the theater. Molkow had slumped into a brooding silence that even his wife could not penetrate. Squinting and moving his lower jaw from side to side, he looked ominous, threatening, to be avoided at any cost.

Among a group of soldiers standing in front of the stage door was Moedl. Good God, I thought, I hope Inge doesn't do something to light Molkow's fuse. Right now, he would rip her apart. I tried to warn her. Too late. Inge had squeezed ahead of everybody to get off the bus and flew into Moedl's arms. "Did you hear about the raid on Hamburg?" I heard her cry. Molkow took note, but said nothing.

In the dressing room he called for our attention. "There will be only six of you from now on. That means we have to change every dance number."

We stared at him, stunned.

"You...you...you...you..." he selected us by pointing, "you do the waltz. You...you...you do the Spanish number."

He ignored our objections that this would leave us no time to change between numbers. He asked the impossible. It also became obvious that Ulla and Erika were left out. Hilde had to take Erika's place in the Bavarian number.

Erika turned white. Her eyes filled with tears.

"It'll be for just a while, until you get better," Hilde consoled her. Molkow glanced briefly at his wife, then said, "She's being sent to the rear, to some sanatorium... she and Ulla."

Our mouths dropped open. We were momentarily speechless. Hannimusch was first to regain her voice. "What a way to break this news, Egon. I've got to hand it to you. You can be a real *Klotz* sometimes." She put an arm around Ulla, who started to cry.

"This is no time for dribbling sentiments," Molkow growled back at her. "We've got a show to do."

I stood by Erika who sank into her chair at the makeup table, buried her face between her arms and wept. Molkow went over the program again to make sure that everybody knew in what number, what place to appear. He scheduled Hannimusch to perform twice to allow added time for costume changes.

Soldiers started to crowd into the theater for the

matinee. "The show must go on," Hannimusch remarked cynically and started to get ready.

"The show must go on. The war must go on. The killing must go on. We march. We dance. We follow orders." I was not saying it, only thinking it.

What a terrible day! While the rest of us put on a show as best we could, Erika and Ulla quietly packed up their personal belongings. Afterwards, quarantine or not, we numbed our senses, aches and pains with a few drinks at headquarters. It did not lift our depression; it only deepened it. Our show would never be the same with only six of us--seven with Hilde filling in. And I would miss Erika.

While we were upstairs drinking, Karlemann was downstairs at the switchboard trying to find out more about the air raids. I had not been able to exchange one word in private with him all day. Both of us avoided eye contact.

By the time we got back to our quarters it was close to midnight. Hannimusch stopped by our room to comfort Inge, who had been crying on and off all day, worried about her family in Hamburg. Erika sat on the bed, staring into space. We did not know when she and Ulla would be leaving. That depended on the availability of suitable transportation. Meanwhile, we were to avoid all physical contact with them. When Hannimusch left, I walked over to Erika and sat down beside her.

"Don't...don't come too close," she said and shrank away from me.

"I don't care," I said. Like a dam breaking, we threw our arms around one another and wept. Inge joined us.

Our tears washed away the tension. We burst into laughter. Mascara had dissolved all over our faces. We looked like coal miners after a day's shift.

The next morning, Erika and I had a chance to talk. I told her about Karlemann. I told her everything.

"He is too old for you," she lectured. "What do you know about him? He could be married and have kids."

Married? That thought had not even crossed my mind. "He would have told me so," I jumped to his defense. Her negative reaction stung. It irritated me. But where was Karlemann? He had not spoken a single word to me, or even looked at me since the night of the attack. Was he angry because I had pushed him away and cut short his amorous pursuit? I was terribly confused, embarrassed, and blamed myself for what had happened that night. A kind word, a gentle touch from him would have gone far to set things right again. It was not forthcoming. What if Erika was right?

Tempers ran short that day. Molkow paced the floor. He reluctantly followed the doctor's advice and canceled all matinees for awhile. The doctors thought we dancers were overworked and needed rest. Molkow considered it pampering. We had mixed feelings, too, thinking of the hundreds of soldiers who would have to be turned away each day. We did not like to disappoint them. Then the events of the last few days--Erika and Ulla's imminent departure, the torture of not knowing the fate of our families and friends in Berlin and Hamburg--weighed heavily on everyone's mind.

After an uninspired performance that night, everyone except the Molkows congregated in our room again. The girls asked me to lay cards. "Come on! Come on!" they begged. I was not in any mood to play the prophet that night.

"I can't see into the future, any more than you can," I told them.

Hannimusch started shuffling the cards then plopped the deck on the table in front of me. "I am supposed to cut three times. Right?" she asked.

I felt the pressure of everybody's eyes on me. What was I going to tell them? They looked at me for answers I could not give. Why did I ever start doing this?

"Come on. Come on," they chorused.

Reluctantly, I laid the cards out, face down, starting with the pattern of a cross. "This is you, in the center. Above you, are your thoughts, your dreams, your fears. To the left is your future; to the right is your past. On the bottom is where you stand."

I had done this so many times, Hannimusch already knew the sequence, but let me proceed without interrupting. I was afraid to turn the first card in the middle. It was a ten of diamonds.

"You will get something of value," I told her, breathing

a sigh of relief. It could have been the ace of spades, the card of tragedy and death. The next card I turned was a seven of hearts.

"Someone thinks of you with affection and will write you a letter," I said.

"What about the future...the future? Hannimusch asked. Everybody's face was crowding in, looking down on the cards with intense expectations. I turned the card on the left.

"Oh, oh! The Jack of spades! What does that mean?" Hannimusch frowned.

"It's the carrier of bad news," I answered.

"That's what we need. More bad news. Haven't we had enough for the day?"

I did not have to turn the next card. Air raid sirens started to wail again as they did almost every night, only this time heavy flak accompanied the warning. Everyone scattered.

"Air raid! Air raid!" someone shouted from below. We grabbed our coats, ready to make a run for the bunker. By the time all of us were assembled downstairs, the shooting had stopped.

"Guess we are not the target tonight," the young soldier said gratefully. Usually, it was Karlemann who shepherded us, but he had become almost invisible. We waited for a while, but the guns remained silent. We went to bed.

Erika ignored orders to switch rooms and move in with Ulla. We figured that if we had not caught their germs yet, a few more days together would not make any difference. Molkow was too drunk again to care.

Morning dawned on a more cheerful note. We awakened to Hannimusch's soprano voice, "Mail! Mail is here! Get your mail." She opened the door to our room only wide enough to stick her head in and hand us a fist full of letters. We bounded out of bed and snatched them from her hand. "Hope it's all good news," she said and went on to deliver the rest. "Mail...anybody interested in mail?" We could hear her sing up and down the hallway. This was only the second time that we had received mail.

We shuffled hastily through the letters--many were just fan mail--and opened them in order of importance. I found several from my mother. The most recent one was a month old. My stomach started to knot up. Heart pounding, I opened it, and as expected, it contained the blustery reaction to the news that I had been sent to the Russian front. "Papa exploded," my mother wrote. "He is trying, with the help of friends within the Nazi system, to bring you home."

I could picture the scene. My poor mother was caught in the middle, not only worrying about me here, but about my father, also, who might vent his anger at the wrong time and wrong place. He was in more danger, perhaps, than I was. We had a neighbor who had threatened my parents to turn them in for making derogatory remarks about the Hitler regime. He was a Nazi, and feared by everyone on the block. It did not have to be a Nazi, however, just someone who held a grudge, to turn somebody in and cause a catastrophe. Even a letter, if censored, as so many of them were, could prove devastating.

My anxiety over my parents suddenly intensified with feelings of guilt. Even if my father could effect my return home, I now wanted to stay. The soldiers for whom we performed every evening had become family. They were our brothers.

I quickly skimmed through the rest of my mother's letters in which she wrote about her everyday routine-- standing hours in line for a measly pint of milk, or an eighth-of-a-pound of butter, one person's ration for a month. Papa was trying to grow his own tobacco in flower boxes inside the kitchen window. They planned a trip to the country to barter with farmers for a little bacon and flour. Would it be all right, Mama asked, if she could trade my doll buggy for food? Saturdays and Sundays, if it did not rain or snow, they went to the woods to gather twigs and pine cones for fuel for cooking. It was still winter. They had run out of coal and had no heat.

In another letter, Mama explained how she was able to get a sack of coal for a rag rug she braided. She also braided straw into slippers for the market women who always complained that their feet were freezing. There, too, she was able to get a little extra; a few vegetables here, an egg there. My uncle Birke, she wrote--that big, jolly old soul, who was a family friend--had lost eighty pounds since I saw him. She did not think I would recognize him anymore. People who had no connections to farmers were literally starving to death. I also had a short letter from my brother Willi. "I am all right. Don't forget to write to me."

All letters from home sounded alike, no matter where they came from. Berlin, we found out, had nightly air raids. Hilde's aunt was bombed out and had to move in with her brother, sharing his two-room flat. Field Marshall Goering once bragged in a speech that he would change his name to Meier if one solitary enemy aircraft penetrated German air space. Well, that was what people called him now, among other names. Rumors circulated that Max Schmeling, ex-world boxing champion, had punched out Propaganda Minister Josef Goebbels, nicknamed "Stud of Babelsberg," for propositioning his movie-star-wife, Anni Ondra. Schmeling was arrested but released shortly afterwards because of public outrage.

In some of the letters, sentences or entire paragraphs had been inked out. People had to be careful what they said or wrote.

During lunch, Dr. Kurt came to discuss Ulla's and Erika's departure. As soon as suitable transportation became available, probably on a Red Cross train, they would leave to enter a sanitarium somewhere in the Thueringer mountains, away from the war and air raids. He promised to personally oversee and follow up on their transfer and to report back to us. We felt reassured.

After he left, a courier from headquarters arrived with a message that our show had to be cancelled that day because of troop relocations. Unofficially we learned that the Russians had amassed along the front lines, readying for an offensive. Only 50 kilometers south and east of Smolensk heavy fighting had already erupted and headquarters was preparing to evacuate.

Regardless of the cause, this was a much-needed break and we welcomed it. It was our first day off since we had arrived in Smolensk. Headquarters' message also included a dinner invitation for that evening from the General. For several days, high officials had been seen coming and going and we wondered if the dinner had anything to do with them.

Some of us did not want to go because Erika and Ulla could not come, but Molkow would not hear of it. We dressed in our best. Karlemann drove us there. Since the bombing of Hamburg he remained distant and preoccupied. I tried to show that I shared his concern, that I was there for him, but when he did not respond I withdrew, hurt and bewildered.

The room in which we had spent so many after-show hours was again transformed into a banquet hall. Long tables sheeted with white bed linen, decorated with colorful floral bouquets indicated that this was a special occasion. Officers in dress uniform with medals and sabers stood in clusters about the room and took little notice of our arrival until the General entered and introduced us. I saw only a few familiar faces among them. As usual, I was the General's table partner again.

"How are you, little Miss?" he greeted me and kissed my hand. "I am so sorry to hear what happened at the hospital. These are not the best of times right now," he said, patting my hand. His adjutant rushed in the room, whispered in his ear, whereupon the General excused himself and hurried out. While everybody stood around talking, waiting, aides passed around trays with drinks.

Forever fascinated by people's creativity and ingenuity to turn nothing into something, I was curious about the flower arrangements on the table. From afar, they appeared real. Flowers in March? In winter? Here? That just couldn't be, I thought. A closer look revealed that the flowers had been carved out of turnips and beets. Inge and I marveled at the delicate petals of replica roses when we heard, "Achtung! Herr General von..., Herr Oberst..." The announcer rattled off their names.

The big wigs, I thought, unimpressed. Model, Jodl, Rundstedt, Keitel, Mannstein: and so on and so on. In the course of our tour we would meet them all. However, I could not keep them straight and remember who was who. They were old men with whom I had nothing in common.

The officers clicked their heels and saluted, then ushered the honored guests to their places at the table and waited until they and we were seated before they sat down. Throughout the meal, the adjutant and messengers popped in and out of the room, delivering notes to the General beside me. "Damn...damn it all..." he cursed under his breath, "They are trying to pin this on us."

"Not the best of times, is it, Herr General?" I reiterated his earlier words. He took my hand, squeezed it, but looked past me as he said, "War is a terrible thing...worse if it's fought without chivalry and honor..."

The adjutant returned again. "The British refuse to come, so do the Swiss and..." He kept his voice low. I could barely hear what he was saying.

"Figures. Damn...! Well, keep Berlin on the line."

Through the course of the evening, from bits and pieces of the conversation between the adjutant and the General, I gathered that an extraordinary discovery had been made, and that representatives from various nations were asked to be witnesses, but they refused. I knew better than to ask questions, but I did not have to. The General told us later that just a few miles outside Smolensk, in the Katyn Forest, a mass grave had been discovered of what appeared to be Polish soldiers. They had been bound and shot execution style. There was no doubt that the Russians had done this but, of course, they would never admit to it, and neither could their Western allies.

The dignitaries and the General left shortly after dinner, and so did we girls. In case of an air raid, we wanted to be with Erika and Ulla. Molkow and Hilde stayed on. I hoped to catch a moment alone with Karlemann. Pretending I had lost something on the bus, I waited till everybody was out and inside the house.

"What are you looking for?" Karlemann asked.

"Actually...nothing," I answered, a little embarrassed. "I wanted a chance to talk with you."

"What about? I have to be back at headquarters to pick up the Molkows."

We were alone. He was only a foot away from me, but it could have been miles. "Are you mad at me because I pushed you away that night?" I stammered. My voice sounded hoarse. Tears welled up inside of me.

"I don't have time to talk to you now. Maybe later." He sounded cool and distant.

I stood there feeling like a fool. He did not even look at me. I turned and dashed past him out of the bus. Upstairs in my room I crashed on my bed and sobbed. Erika wanted to know what was wrong. She finally pried it out of me. "Forget him. He is not right for you anyway," she said, stroking my shoulder.

"But I love him. I thought it was mutual."

We were already in bed when I heard a faint knock at the door. "Elfi...Elfi..." It was Karlemann's voice.

"Don't answer...don't go." Erika practically begged me. But I already had my coat thrown over my pajamas and out the door I went. Downstairs in the hallway, Karlemann pulled me into his arms and kissed me, first my mouth, my face and down my neck. He had been drinking. He was drunk enough that I had to steady him. Temporary ecstasy turned to anger. I struggled free.

"What's the matter with you?" He staggered backward, a befuddled look on his face. "You wanted to talk to me. Well, then...?"

"Yes. When you are sober," I told him.

Then he insisted that that I go with him to his place, and when I said "No!" he became angry. We had words.

"I need a woman, not a child," he finally said, turned and staggered out of the building.

More miserable than ever I returned to my room, blaming myself for messing things up. He was probably right. I did act childish. But Erika breathed a sigh of relief when I told her what happened.

Two days later Erika and Ulla left on a Red Cross train. During a long, tearful good-bye, we promised to write each other often. I felt lost.

*****

Warm March winds licked at the snow and softened the ground. Travel on Russia's unpaved roads became difficult.

A new show with a famous movie star, Lil Dagova, arrived in Smolensk, replacing ours at the theater. We now visited units on the front. The pain in my leg had worsened. During the last performance at the theater I knelt down and could not get up anymore. Luckily, it happened at the end of a number. Molkow took me out of certain dances, but Dr. Kurt finally insisted that I stay off my feet altogether for at least a couple of weeks. The pain was excruciating. He wrapped my legs into long wire frames, making it impossible for me to go anywhere. Confined to my bed, I passed the time answering letters.

Another bundle of mail arrived.

"Dear Elfriede,"
my mother's letter began. "Oh, no, I thought, what is she mad about now?" She had a half dozen nicknames for me and never used my given name unless she was very upset with me. Reluctantly I read on.

"Your father and I debated whether or not
to tell you now or wait until you got home.
We have terrible news. Yesterday we
received a telegram informing us that your
brother was killed in action on New Year's
Eve, in Stalingrad..."

My mind locked on to that one sentence, reading it over and over and comprehending it less and less. My hands started shaking. "No! No!" I cried out. It scared Inge. "What's wrong? What's wrong?" she asked. The letter slipped out of my fingers and onto to the floor. Tears spilled down over my face.

"Willi...! It's Willi!"

Ilse, who roomed with us now in place of Erika, picked the letter up and read the first two sentences. "Good God!" she exclaimed and showed it to Inge. They grabbed my hands. The girls all knew my brother who had visited me every time we had a layover in Berlin. They thought he was great. He was a lanky six-foot-two with an infectious grin and a great sense of humor, a long distance runner who took fourth place in the 1936 Olympics. That earned him a cushy post in the army, out of war's danger. The Third Reich wanted to keep its top athletes. But because all his buddies had been sent to the front, he insisted on going as well. The last time I had seen him was five months ago. He had given me a recent picture of himself, joking, "I don't want you to forget what I look like." I needed no picture. I only had to close my eyes to see him in front of me with his head slightly cocked, smiling down at his little sister. His image was

126

etched in my mind and my heart forever.

"Willi...Willi...," I sobbed.

Inge sobbed along with me, as much for Willi and me, as out of anxiety about her own family's fate. Ilse left the room.

So much pain. How can anyone survive so much pain? Now I knew what my dark foreboding was about.

Hannimusch, Hilde and the other girls came rushing in with words of sympathy. Hannimusch sat down beside me. "I know how it hurts," she said, "but as days and weeks go by, you will start feeling better. Believe me."

At that moment, I really did not want to feel better. I considered it an act of betrayal if I ever again felt good about anything. "How can I go on living, dancing, smiling, pretending, when he is gone forever?" I cried.

"Give some thought to what you would want Willi to do had it been the other way around. Imagine what he would say to you if he could. The last thing he'd want is to cause you heartbreak and unhappiness. He is at peace now." Hannimusch's quiet voice fell soothingly upon my aching heart. I sensed that she had known and survived pain like mine.

Hilde offered me a sleeping pill and a glass of water. "Take it, it'll help you through the night."

Hannimusch, Inge, and Ilse stayed with me until the pill took effect. I did not even remember them leaving.

The first thought that came to my mind the next morning was my mother's letter, which I had not yet finished reading. It took several attempts before I could read beyond the second sentence. The letter continued:

> "...Actually, the telegram arrived just as I left the house to meet Papa at the train station. When I told him, it hit him hard. He went to pieces and screamed, "Murderers! Nazi murderers!" inside the crowded station. I was sure he would be hauled away and that we would never see him again. God help us if something should happen to you. It would be our death also. So, be careful, please. Don't let us wait so long in between letters. We worry so. Love and kisses,
> Your grieving parents."

God! Why do you give me a brother only to take him from me again?

Willi was my stepbrother. I did not grow up with him. Until I was thirteen, I did not know he existed. When I met him for the first time, I thought God had finally heard my prayers. When I was little and people asked me what I wanted for Christmas, my answer always was, "A brother or a sister." In the few short years we knew each other, we had grown very close. He was my joy. I was so proud of him. Now he was gone.

I let my arms sink down on the bed and stared at the ceiling. In my mind I revisited the many happy hours Willi and I spent together.

Inge and Ilse had gone downstairs for breakfast. I was alone when Karlemann knocked and entered. "I brought you coffee," he said, setting a tray on my bed. "You don't have to say anything. I heard about your brother and wanted to tell you how sad I am for you." He took my hand, kissed me on the forehead, then fluffed and stuffed pillows behind me so I could lean against them. He noticed the wire frames leaning against my bed. "How are your legs? Better?" I shrugged my shoulders. That pain was nothing compared to the pain I felt in my heart.

Karlemann insisted I eat a piece of jellied bread. "About us..." He hesitated. "You know what I mean. I wanted to talk to you but never found the right time or place, or the right words. I know this isn't the right time either, but..." He nervously picked on a blister on his hand, glancing at me once or twice. "I wanted to explain..."

"It's all right," I said resignedly. "It makes no difference anymore."

"I want you to know that I really care for you," he began, "but this damn war...sometimes I think I am going crazy. Not knowing if there is a tomorrow...I...I take what I can from today, like I want to drown myself." He paused, staring into the palm of his hand. If he waited for a reaction, I had none to give. I was overwhelmed by the loss of my brother and numb to any other feelings. If I could have, at that moment I would have traded his life for Willi's in a heartbeat.

"Elfi, say something," Karlemann pleaded.

I gazed at him with wondrous detachment. He was so handsome, so warm and friendly in a manly sort of way, but he was just a stranger now sitting at the foot of my bed. "I thought I was in love with you," I said quietly.

"Are you?" He leaned forward, looking at me as if trying to read my face.

For a fleeting moment I remembered the thrill, the electricity of his touch, his kiss, how I melted in his arms. Jubilant moments. Sacred moments.

"Are you...are you in love with me?" he repeated.

"I...I don't know," I answered.

Karlemann lit two cigarettes and handed one to me. Staring down at his hands again he said quietly. "I meant to tell you this earlier. I am married."

Funny, I thought. Erika had warned me. I did not want to believe it. She was right.

I caught myself vaguely smiling and nodding.

"Can we remain friends?" I heard Karlemann say.

At the moment I felt empty, just empty and betrayed. Betrayed by him. Betrayed by fate.

"I hope we can stay friends," Karlemann repeated.

I shrugged my shoulders. For the first time I looked at Karlemann as just a person, not as the prince of my imagination. He was in pain, too. Life was not a fairy tale with princes and happily-ever-after endings.

That evening I decided to rejoin the show in spite of doctor's orders. My legs still hurt, but a couple of days of rest and moist compresses eased the pain to where it was bearable. Molkow had no objections.

The next few days were hell for me. I tried to drink my troubles away. But after two drinks my chin turned numb, and not another drop could pass my lips. My body rejected it. Also, since we no longer danced on the stage at the Front Theater, my pains gradually and mysteriously subsided. It was Moedl, Inge's friend, who clued me in that my problems may have stemmed from dancing on a cement stage.

Day by day, the region became more unstable. German troops fought bitterly to hold their positions, but the Russians kept on coming and pushing them into retreat. The hospital was overwhelmed with casualties. Headquarters prepared to evacuate and debated whether to send us home. We still performed every night at different units, under conditions that truly stretched the imagination. One such performance took place in a dugout, a cave with dripping walls, a dirt floor, a few candles and no heat. But it did not really matter what we did or did not do. Just to sit with the men, to talk with them about home seemed to be enough. They had been in the trenches month after month, through the fighting, through the winter, through the mud. We brought them diversion, a few hours of relief and relaxation. Hannimusch, with her accordion and inexhaustible repertoire of songs was the star. The sing-alongs lasted into all hours of the night or until the Russian artillery zeroed in on us.

I now saw a very personal mission in what we did. Every time I made a soldier smile, or made him forget the war for a few hours, it was as if I lit a candle for Willi, or placed a flower on his grave. And each time my pain became a little more tolerable.

Finally, we received orders to leave the area. A few days before we left, we stopped at headquarters to say good-bye. Everybody was there who knew us, even the General. We shook hands, hugged, kissed, cried and wished each other luck. Dr. Kurt and Betty held hands as they talked quietly in a corner of the room. Inge had said good-bye to Moedl sometime ago, before he was shipped out. Molkow, losing his best supplier of booze and cigarettes, toasted the Quartermaster General literally under the table.

I asked the General if he had succeeded in getting his international committee together. "The Turks are coming," he replied sarcastically. Molkow got permission from him to view the site of the mass graves before we left, providing our bus could maneuver through the mud. Early morning would be the best time, we figured, when the ground was still frozen. "I do not recommend it for the ladies," the General warned, "it's a grisly sight."

Because the discovery was of such enormous international importance, we wanted to bear witness. Karlemann drove us there the following morning. It took him about an hour through mud and sleet to reach the area--a clearing in the woods, fenced off with barbed wire.

Guards allowed us entrance and Karlemann drove as far as he dared toward a group of German soldiers who were digging in the mud. He and Molkow got out; we had to stay behind. What we saw from the windows of the bus was gruesome enough. A row of badly decomposed corpses lay beside a ditch, bones protruding from bits of rotted clothing. Karlemann and Molkow stayed no more than a few seconds before they came back. Molkow was white as chalk.

"There may be hundreds, maybe thousands buried there. They have only dug up part of it." Molkow told us. "Russian savages!" He exclaimed. "Who else could do such a thing?"

We rode back to the Artist Home in silence.

Our last show in the area took place at a unit that had requested it ever since our first performance in Smolensk. They went all out, converting a rectangular wooden structure into a theater with a stage. It had a curtain made of blankets strung onto ropes fastened to pulleys, to open and close. Blankets also served as a backdrop and partitioned off a dressing area. Flags and sprays of wheat decorated the walls of the building.

As we prepared for the show, the unit's musicians volunteered to accompany us. However, they sounded so awful that Hannimusch declined. "It would take ten weeks and a prayer to get them to play right," she said under her breath to Egon. She opted to accompany us herself on an out-of-tune piano, but did select a drummer and a base player to fill in. They rehearsed while we unpacked.

It was time to get ready. Back stage, Hannimusch warned us, "Kids, you better be very quiet back here. I can hear every little sound out there, even a sniffle."

The curtain opened. Molkow finished the introduction and we were on. The piano sounded so awful that we could hear snickers coming from the audience. We did not dare look at one another for fear we would burst out laughing, too. But the audience did not care. The fellows clapped, cheered and stomped that the building shook.

In places such as this, without toilet and washroom facilities, we usually had two buckets back stage, one with water to wash our hands, the other for emergencies.

About halfway through the program Hilde had such an emergency. Molkow was announcing the next number when we heard chuckles from the audience, turning into roaring laughter. At first we thought they were laughing at Molkow's old jokes. We looked at one another. He had never gotten that big of a response before. Suddenly it dawned on us. Hilde sat still crouched over the bucket. Tinkle-tinkle-tinkle.

"Oh, my God! They heard everything! That's what they were laughing about."

No matter how tragically sad times were, moments like this opened a dam of pent-up emotions. We laughed tears and could not stop. Hilde made us swear a holy oath not to divulge her identity.

After the show, the men surprised us by unveiling a South Sea bar, complete with an imitation native in a grass skirt as bartender. Again, I was amazed at how anyone could achieve such impressive effects with bits and pieces of scrap lumber, branches, twigs and straw. The same musicians who had had such a hard time reading our music, struck up a Hawaiian melody, followed by nicely played dance and hit tunes.

Meanwhile, soldiers had put up tables, covered them with sheets, and set them with an assortment of nice china, gleaming dinnerware and candles.

"Where, in the name of Peter, do you boys get all this stuff? Here, where there is hardly one brick left atop another?" Hannimusch asked.

The fellows just grinned. "That's called procurement," one of them explained.

Glasses filled with red wine sparkled like rubies in the candlelight. We lifted them to toast one more day, one more happy hour, and wished each other well. After dinner of Goulash and potatoes, the fellows asked us to dance with them. Hitler had long banned such frivolities for the duration of the war. Should someone report us, Molkow would lose his license or worse. However, the unit's captain was willing to take the chance and the responsibility, and after a few cognacs, Molkow gave his consent, too.

It was this overwhelming affection we felt from the troops that kept us going. They went out of their way and spent their last rations to show us how much they appreciated us. It was a kinship beyond blood. They were our brothers.

I was lost in thought when Karlemann asked me to dance with him.

"It's our last evening together. Tomorrow it's goodbye. We may never see each other again." He held me close. A war of emotions tore at my heart. Tears welled up, but I did not want to cry. I was glad when a soldier cut in.

Suddenly, an explosion. Then another, and another. Knocked to the floor, I felt things falling on and all around me. A gust of wind blew out most of the candles. I heard the roar of engines and felt rain hitting my skin. Men shouted orders. More explosions, though farther in the distance. Flashlights flicked on. I raised my head and stood up. A section of wall was knocked out.

Immediately, men went to work to seal up the wall with boards and blankets, swept the floor and mopped up broken dishes and spilled wine, straightened tables, and relit the candles. In less than half an hour, the band resumed playing and the party and dancing continued as if nothing had happened. Most did not know that one man was dead. A splintered board had pierced his back. I saw two men carry him out. One put his finger to his mouth. "He's gone. Don't let the others know. Nothing can bring him back. Why spoil a good party. It may be our last. Who knows? Tomorrow it may be us."

I thought back to the night in Warsaw and the toast Dieter made. "Yesterday is gone, we don't know what tomorrow brings, therefore, let us live and enjoy this moment."

Molkow needed assistance again that night to get on the bus. Karlemann was also reeling but insisted that he was fit to drive. When we made it back without incident, Hannimusch bent down to kiss the ground. She, too, was not sober anymore.

Our suitcases were packed. We had no cause to get up early the next day, but for some reason, I woke up as dawn was breaking. I sat up and looked out of the window to check on the weather. I could not believe what I saw. Emmy and Karlemann, walking arm in arm from his barracks toward our building, stopping and kissing a couple of times. I turned away and buried my face in my pillow. I wanted to scream.

Around noon, we boarded a train to Roslavl. I was ready for a change. A large group of friends, including Katja, saw us off. We shook hands, hugged, and promised to stay in touch with each other. The only one I did not say good-bye to was Karlemann. I never wanted to see him again, ever.

At the very last moment a courier from headquarters arrived with a small package for me. It was a box, ornately decorated with flakes of colored straw on black lacquered wood. Inside was a note. "Good luck. Your General."

X

Russian Ways

The charred chimneys of Smolensk faded into the distance. From the windows of the train, we looked out over an endless expanse of flat, thawing land. Water from melting snow accumulated into countless puddles and pools. It had nowhere to run. We passed a mud-caked peasant leading his scrubby horse along a deeply furrowed road and watched him labor through the spongy, sticky soil. Russia had no network of paved roads, not even to connect its cities. Until the sun dried out the gray-brown clay, the land was virtually impassable.

March had faded away without leaving a hint of green on the barren, water-soaked land. By night, the soil froze hard again. Winter hung around like a tired old man, but with enough energy to whip up a freak storm.

The monotony of the landscape invited the mind to wander. At home, gardens and meadows would be in full bloom by now with crocuses, snowbells, primroses and daffodils, against a background of tender greens. Every time I thought of it a lump formed in my throat. I pictured the neat alpine villages against my beloved mountains. Willi and I had wanted to hike up mountain trails someday. I remember the time Erika and I took off on a hike up a mountain, got lost, and had to find our way back in the dark. We had missed our performance that night and Molkow docked us one month's salary.

135 .

The train was almost empty. We had a coach to ourselves. Hannimusch and the girls compared autographed pictures of Lil Dagova, the movie star, who had replaced our show at the theater in Smolensk.

"Where is yours?" they asked me.

"I didn't get one," I answered, wondering when, where and how I missed out. After the loss of my brother, little else mattered.

"Oh, well," I shrugged my shoulders, "no big loss. Never was one to collect such things anyway."

Ilse gasped. "But she is so famous, so beautiful. Did you know that she is sixty-two and has not a wrinkle on her face? Isn't that amazing?" she rattled on. "She doesn't smoke, doesn't drink anything other than water or milk, eats very little meat, and sleeps at least eight to ten hours every day, always on her back, never on her side so she wont crumple her face."

"She told you all that?" I questioned.

"Her maid told us, didn't she?" Ilse looked around for others to back her up. They nodded.

"How awful," was all I could say.

"What do you mean?" The girls looked at me as if I had lost my mind.

"That seems like too big a sacrifice for fame and beauty. Bet, she never feels the wind, the sun, the rain and the snow on her face either. That wouldn't do for me." I shook my head. "But, to each her own."

"All I can say is that I wish I'd look that good when I am sixty," Hannimusch said.

I studied the pictures for a while then handed them back. "At sixty-two, who wants to look like an uncharted map? I prefer a weathered face, a face that tells where it's been."

Ilse waved her hand at me. "You belong on a farm," she said. Her values and mine were poles apart. I knew that Erika would have agreed with me. How I missed her.

Uschi seemed bored by our babble. She suggested we play a game.

"Ohhh..." Ilse groaned, "not one of your brain exercises again!"

"Typical," Uschi sneered at her. "Those that need it the most want it the least." She handed each of us a sheet of paper torn from a notebook. "Pick your subjects," she said. "What'll it be--history, geography, literature, or the theater?"

We chose geography. The rules of the game, which we had played many times, were simple enough. We had to name a country, one of its cities, rivers, mountains and famous people, all starting with the letter 'A'. The first one to finish raised her hand and we moved on to the next letter of the alphabet. The one with the highest number of correct answers won. Sometimes, bluff was trump. But Uschi kept good records to settle disputes and challenges at some later date, when we had access to a library. In Russia, however, there were no libraries we could access. We were lucky to get hold of a book that someone left behind. Books were a rarity and precious, both for reading and for use as toilet paper.

The train moved along at a fair pace and stopped only once by a water tower. We reached Roslavl before sunset. Men from an engineering outfit picked us up and drove us in a truck to the headquarters of the *Organization Todt*.

Roslavl was badly damaged but, unlike Smolensk, still resembled a city. Its narrow cobblestone streets and gutted, soot-darkened stone and mortar buildings reminded me of cities in Poland.

A group of Todt engineers welcomed us at the steps to their headquarters and led us upstairs to a dormitory-style room. On the way, they explained that arrangements had been made for Molkow and his wife to stay in another building not far away. We could not believe our luck in escaping his scrutiny for awhile. Molkow, however, was upset for exactly the same reason.

"Keeping track of a bunch of girls is like running a flea circus," he complained to the captain in charge. Before he and Hilde left, he instructed Hannimusch to keep a tight rein on us. That was a joke.

Our dorm was straight across from the captain's office. It offered no frills, but the beds were clean and it was warm. The heat came from two radiators under long, bare windows from which we overlooked a cobbled courtyard, walled in by other buildings.

"Heavens!" Hannimusch exclaimed. "This is like a

fishbowl. We have to find something to hang over those windows." She started to make a mental list. "We need sheets or blankets, wash bowls, and buckets with water unless there is a toilet and a washroom somewhere."

"I'll have a look," I volunteered. Inge came with me.

A worn linoleum-covered corridor ran the length of the building with doors on either side and a window at one end looking down on a city intersection. The paint on the walls was a dull, dirty yellow and peeling.

"This reminds me of some old government offices back home. Depressing," I mentioned.

"I was thinking the same thing," Inge agreed.

"Did you ever notice how some people, who work a long time in places like this, seem to look just like them? They have no personality."

"Never thought of it. But now that you mention it... you're right."

When we could not find the facilities we were looking for on the second floor, we went downstairs. "There it is," I said, pointing to a door marked with two big zeros. We knocked first, then cautiously opened it and walked in.

"What is this...?" I exclaimed. I looked at a row of stalls without doors and without stools. Each stall had a hole in the cement floor with a footpad on each side, and high up on the wall of each hung a tank with a long pull chain.

Inge and I looked at one another, then burst out laughing.

"The stools are missing."

"What do you do here? Squat over that hole?" Inge giggled.

"I guess so," I said and pointed at the footpads. "You put your feet here so they don't get wet, then aim."

"Mensch! You better have a good aim." I pulled on a chain and water started swirling around the hole. Though the stalls were clean, the room reeked of urine. I wanted to get out of there. "Let's tell the others," I said and challenged Inge to a race up the stairs and back to the room.

"Come and see the Russian toilets," we announced.

"Why? Why? What's wrong now?" the girls asked. Giggling, Inge and I described our findings.

"I've seen those toilets." Hannimusch grinned. "They've got them in Poland, too."

"Let's go see. Yeah...let's go see!" The girls were curious.

The building echoed with laughter and chatter as all seven of us scurried downstairs. Doors along the corridor opened and men in long johns and various stages of undress stepped out and hastily retreated again when they saw us rushing by. Our noisy stampede also caught the attention of our hosts, who asked us what was going on. When we told them about our peculiar find, they roared with laughter. "Don't worry, we've installed some regular plumbing upstairs," they said and then led us to an unmarked door on the second floor.

"That's more like it," Hannimusch sighed with relief, after inspecting it. "Here we can even wash up and brush our teeth."

"You can also take a sauna if you like," our hosts informed us.

"A sauna...? That sounds...interesting," some of us agreed reluctantly.

Though we knew what a sauna was, none of us had seen, much less been in one.

The captain in charge looked at his watch. "By the way, I was just coming to tell you, we have a little cold supper prepared for you," he said. "Come on over when you are ready. We are just across from you. See you in about half an hour?"

"You mean at your office?" Hannimusch asked.

"Ja, just across the hall."

"I guess that would be all right," she agreed hesitantly. "I don't think Molkow would object."

The office, as it turned out, also happened to be our hosts' dining room, living room, bedroom and party room. Hannimusch's brows drew together with concern when she saw the cozy layout, and her eyes darted back and forth between the furnishings, our hosts and us. I knew exactly what she was thinking.

"Hmmm...quite comfortable. Has our director seen your...uh...your office?" she asked.

"No. Why?"

"Didn't think so. Never mind."

After the formal introductions, the seven of us and four officers crunched around a large round table in one corner, set up with candles, trays of sandwiches and bottles of wine. The rest of the room contained a long table strewn with maps, drawings and large sheets of paper, plus an assortment of angled measuring devices. Between two tall windows rose shelves filled with books and files, and at the far end stood several bunks. An archway beside us led to an adjacent room.

Conversation shifted from small talk to Roslavl, which had been the scene of earlier, heavy fighting. It had been declared a Red Cross town now. But because it was also a strategic stronghold, connecting rail traffic between east and west, and north and south, the Russians ignored the rules of the Geneva Convention and bombed it nightly.

The *Organization Todt* had been called in to restore bridges, build roads, repair power and telephone lines and the rail system--an impossible task because of chronic shortages of steel and other building materials. Moreover, what they restored one day, the Russians destroyed the next. "We have to rob Peter to pay Paul," the engineers told us, "We have orders; 'produce, or else.' They expect us to be magicians." The men were clearly frustrated.

The atmosphere was relaxed and genuine. Before the evening was over we drank brotherhood with them, which meant that we called one another by first names, dropping formalities of rank and status. Later, back in our room, we discussed how different these men seemed, compared to the formal, almost stiff posture of the officers at headquarters in Smolensk.

Next morning, we heard a sharp knock on the door. Hannimusch opened it and in stepped a Russian woman, short and stocky, wearing a traditional white kerchief over her graying hair. She informed us in broken German that the sauna was ready. We had no idea what to take along and showed her a bathing suit and cap. "No, no... no clothes," she gestured. We showed her towels and soap. She pointed to the towels and nodded, but waved her hand "No...no," at the soap. She walked to the window and pointed down to a low structure in the courtyard. "Sauna," she said.

"Thank you. We'll be down shortly," Hannimusch told her, holding the door open and invited her to leave. But the woman did not seem to understand.

"You may leave. We'll be down in ten minutes." Hannimusch pointed to her wristwatch, then held up ten fingers. The woman shook her head. "You come...now." Her tone of voice approached that of an order.

We debated whether we should leave a message for Molkow in case he should drop by, but decided not to, since we would not be gone that long.

"You come...now," the woman repeated, unsmiling and brusque. She remained standing broad-legged in the middle of the room and watched us get ready.

"Like a Russian tank," I whispered to Inge. "I don't like her...I don't like her at all."

Reluctantly, we followed her downstairs, out a back door and into a building reminiscent of a 19-century laundry house. Inside, two young Russian women abruptly stopped chatting as we entered. The 'Tank,' as we called this older woman, gave them orders and, evidently, told them to get busy.

Three immense vats filled with water took up most of the space in this stark, whitewashed room. Opposite the entrance, a few yards away from another door, the wall bulged out strangely, like the belly of a pregnant woman. The protrusion had a small iron door. One of the girls opened it and hurled chunks of wood inside. It was some kind of oven, nothing we had seen before.

Then the 'Tank' indicated that we should disrobe. Since we saw neither a bench, chair, nor hook, I draped my clothes over a broom handle. The others piled their coats and robes on a dry spot on the cement floor. Stripped to our panties and wrapped in towels, we stood on a wooden grid and waited. The floor was cold, but the air was warm and moist.

The 'Tank' shook her head. Pointing to her hip, making motions as if to pull down her skirt, she said, "off... off."

"Can you believe that? She wants us to take off our panties, too?" Hannimusch looked at us, unsure of what to do. I was ready to put my clothes back on and to get

141

the heck out of there. I did not trust that woman from the start. However, when some of the others started to comply, like a fool, I followed suit. The young Russian girls giggled their heads off when that older woman opened the door to the steam room and herded us in. A wave of heat engulfed us.

"Sit," she ordered, pointing to wooden risers filling one side of the room. Obediently, we sat down on the lowest rung, opposite a pile of rocks. In front of the rocks stood several buckets of water. As soon as we were seated, the woman picked up a bucket and splashed the contents against the rocks. The water sizzled and bubbled, and formed a cloud of hot, dense steam. It enveloped us so that we could barely see each other anymore. At first, the damp heat felt wonderful and relaxing. We even climbed higher up the risers where it was more intense. Then the woman, who had left the room, returned and threw another bucket of water on the stones. Heat and steam increased to a point where we had trouble breathing.

"Go, open the door, somebody," Hannimusch gasped, "I think I'm going to pass out."

I groped my way over to the door, but was unable to open it. "It's locked," I told the others and started pounding on it. "Open up...open up," I shouted, pounding on it even harder. No one answered.

"I feel like Gretl in the witch's house," I said, returning to my seat.

"I'm getting scared," Betty admitted.

"Maybe they are partisans and are going to kill us in here," Ilse added.

Comments like this flew back and forth. This was not funny anymore, especially as Hannimusch was having serious problems breathing.

"Come on down, it's a little cooler here," I told her. My heart thumped in my throat. Once more I felt my way to the door and pounded on it, screaming, "Open up, somebody. Open up...now!" Still no answer. My suspicions ballooned into panic. I was convinced that these Russians planned to do us in.

Suddenly, the door opened and in came the girls with bundles of twigs and sticks in each hand. Their entrance allowed enough steam to escape for shapes and faces to become recognizable again.

Hannimusch was lying on her stomach, too weak to budge. One of the girls started beating her back with the twigs. "What the hell...? What are they going to do to us now? Beat us to death?" she whimpered. The other girl approached me, smiling. "No hurt...feel good," she said, hitting herself with the branches to demonstrate that it would cause me no pain. She started swatting me up and down my legs. "Feel more good on back," she said, encouraging me to turn over. I looked into her blue eyes. There was not a mean streak in it. I started to relax. My skin began to tingle.

"You know...that really does feel good. Maybe they're not going to kill us after all," I said to the others. Pleasurable grunts eventually even escaped from Hannimusch. After everybody had a good massage the girls left and the Tank reappeared. "Finish...come out now."

"Thanks a lot, Warden," Betty growled back at her.

Crowding around the door, we waited for her to step aside. When she did, we surged out and...swoosh! The girls doused us with buckets full of ice-cold water. By the time we caught our breath, they had disappeared, giggling and laughing.

"I think, we just paid a few war reparations," Hannimusch quipped, still recovering. "What an experience!"

"Never again for me," Betty vowed.

But back in our room we had to admit that we felt totally revitalized.

Meanwhile, Molkow had been looking for us. Red with anger, he stormed in "Where the devil have you been?"

"At the sauna."

"What do you mean, taking off without letting me know. Damn it!"

"Now...now, Egon," Hannimusch tried to calm him. "We were just next door."

"You do that again and I'll fine all of you a month's pay."

"Big deal," I muttered under my breath. "Why bother to pay us at all? Take that, too. You take everything else."

"What? What did you say?" He lunged toward me, grabbed my arm and jerked me around. Before I could blink, the back of his hand struck my face. Hannimusch, the girls, everyone stood there, stunned, though this was not the first time he had slapped one of us.

"I'll remember that…" I said, looking at him defiantly, "that and a few other things you are doing."

He turned purple. He raised his arm, about to strike me again, when the captain walked in, grabbed him by his coat collar and yanked him backwards. "Hey…hey! Don't you dare lay a hand on these girls," he threatened him with his fist.

Caught by surprise, Molkow backed off, straightened his coat and scoffed, "This is none of your business. These girls are my responsibility," then he steamed out of the room.

"I'll make it my business," the captain thundered after him. Pausing for a moment to cool down, he turned to us. "What I really came over for is to tell you that breakfast is ready."

We finished what we were doing before Molkow's rampage. Hannimusch put her arm around my shoulders and said, "Come on, let's get some breakfast."

Molkow and Hilde sat at the far end of the long table, cleared now of papers, maps and blueprints. Hilde probably knew nothing of what just happened and we did not tell her. My face still smarted where Molkow struck me, but inside I brimmed with satisfaction. Someone had finally put him in his place.

That mean Russian woman served coffee and buttered bread.

"So, how was the sauna?" our hosts asked.

"Torture chamber is a better word for it," Hannimusch joked. "The warden that runs the place seems to get a perverse pleasure out of scaring people. I honestly thought we might not come out of there alive." When we told them what happened, the men shook their heads and laughed.

"We really ought to get rid of that dragon," the captain, whose name was Hugo, said.

Finished with breakfast, I got up and walked over to a window, looking down on a long, narrow city street. Blocks away, I saw a mob of people milling around, slowly approaching. Leading the crowd were two black-veiled figures, performing a grotesque dance, bending, swaying and flailing their arms. Right behind them followed a bearded man wearing a long black robe and a flat-topped, rimless hat, carrying a pole with a wrought iron icon. Behind him, people carried an open coffin with a corpse.

"What is going on down there? What are they doing?" I asked Hugo as he walked by. He took a quick look. "Oh," he said, "that's a Russian funeral."

As the crowd came closer, I heard the two black-veiled women hysterically screaming and wailing, accompanying their frenzied dance.

"Professional wailing women," Hugo explained. "The more important and revered the dead person was, the louder they cry. And the louder they cry, the more they get paid." He chuckled. "Behind them, carrying the cross, that's the priest."

So far, we had had little contact with the Russians, their lives and their customs. Fascinated, I watched the procession pass beneath the window. In the coffin lay a dead man, dressed in black, hands crossed over his chest, decked with a few flowers.

As I continued watching this strange procession, Molkow impatiently paced the floor. "Where is our transport to the theater? Should have been here a half hour ago," he growled.

A little while later, a covered truck arrived to take us and our equipment to our place of work--a musty old movie house somewhere in the heart of the city. Everything inside was filthy, from the small stage floor to the tables and chairs in a dinky dressing room. Before we could unpack, we spent an hour cleaning and dusting.

Hilde had one of her weird spells. Restless and irritable, she screamed orders at us, making very little sense. *"Der Geist ist wieder mal aus der Flasche."* I heard Hannimusch say to Uschi. "The ghost is out of the bottle again." I thought it meant that she was out of medicine. It had happened before. Hilde always carried a bottle with medicine in her purse to control what she called her "chronic intestinal problems." She sipped from it frequently, especially when under tension. It made her glassy-eyed, but seemed to calm her. When she ran out, she got the shakes and became irrational. At this moment, she could not hold a glass without spilling its contents.

Not knowing what to do for her, we began to unpack and hang up our costumes. Hannimusch had started to rehearse with a few Russian musicians. She came back a half hour later, raving about what a pleasure it is to work with such excellent musicians. "Especially the violinist. That man is a virtuoso," she marveled. "What an honor to work with him."

After a little snack and an hour's rest we put our makeup on and readied for the show. The theater filled up fast. People even packed into the aisles. In the front row sat the engineers.

The stage floor was worn, uneven, and awful to dance on. After the first few numbers we pulled splinters out of our feet, knees and behinds. Our costumes, shoes, hands, everything turned a grimy black. We gave a shamefully uninspired performance that night.

The first half of our program ended with Liszt's Hungarian Rhapsody--my favorite number and a hit with every audience. The curtain closed; we took our bow. The audience began to hiss and whistle, and threw coins on the stage. "Were we that bad?" I wondered.

Uschi picked up some of the coins. "Look," she said, fingering a good sized silver coin. "Isn't that a ruble?" We looked at it, then at each other, not knowing what to make of it.

Hannimusch met us back stage, very excited. "Guess, they really liked you kids. Half of the audience are Russians."

We heard a soft knock on the dressing room door, followed by a small voice requesting, "May we come in, please?"

"Come in," we answered.

The dressing room filled with people, Russians, shaking our hands and kissing the hem of our robes. "Bravo! Bravo!" they repeated and asked for autographs.

"I'll be the Tsar's uncle," Hannimusch postured, hands on hips, smiling at the confusion. It finally dawned on us that all the hissing, whistling and throwing of coins was the Russian's way to express approval.

That made us feel even twice as bad for giving such a lousy performance. We tried to do better during the second half of the show.

Hilde, of course, had to sit it out. She sat rigidly in a chair, shaking uncontrollably. After the show, Molkow wanted to get her to bed as soon as possible and kept at us to hurry up. When we dropped him and Hilde off, he gave Hannimusch strict orders not to let Inge, Ilse and me out of her sight or out of our room. But when we arrived at our quarters, the engineers had a little snack prepared for us. Since we had not eaten very much, it sounded tempting. Hannimusch told the fellows about Molkow's instructions to chaperon us and because of it had to decline their invitation.

"Oh, the hell with that old buzzard," Captain Hugo said. "He better not raise any fuss."

"Well, I suppose we could at least come over for a bite to eat," Hannimusch relented. "But only for a little while."

"Good enough," Hugo accepted.

"They sure are nice fellows," Hannimusch said. It had not escaped my notice that Gert, also a captain and engineer, paid her a lot of special attention and that she primped more than usual that evening. Gert was about her age, though short and stocky, but he was quite a character and lots of fun.

The fellows had set a table with a variety of open-faced sandwiches and a choice of drinks, from beer to soda lemonade. While we ate, Gert entertained us with one funny story after another.

"Tell them how you escaped through a sewer," his comrades prompted him.

"Culverts," he corrected them, and began to relate his adventure. "In Kiev, not so long ago, my outfit worked on the water mains when the Russians broke through and cut us off. Anyone of us would rather be dead than taken prisoner. So, we hid in one of the big culverts, debating what to do. Acquainted with the layout of the underground drainage system, we figured we could crawl through to the German side. These culverts were ancient and infested with rats. We didn't know how far they reached, or what shape they were in. But it was our only chance. Crawling on our bellies, we were quite a ways in already when we suddenly heard voices. Russians! They seemed to be coming from the other side! There was no turning back. We had to shoot it out. Hoping they had not heard us, we turned off the flashlight and remained still, counting on the advantage of surprise. Revolvers ready, we waited. We saw their lights coming closer. Suddenly, we were face to face, staring at each other. Neither side knew what to do. They did not even have their weapons drawn. I was in front. I saluted, and motioned them to pass. Hell, I didn't want to shoot them. Their front guy also saluted, smiled, shouted an order to the others, and they squeezed by us. What the heck! They only did what we did, trying to get back to their side. Can't blame them for that. We crawled on, in opposite directions and came out just behind our lines." Gert paused. For a moment he was lost in thoughts. With a quiet chuckle he reached for his glass.

"Well, here's to you, Fritzi."

"Who is Fritzi?" Hannimusch wanted to know.

"He didn't make it. He never made it into the culvert."

Time was racing by. Hannimusch felt a twinge of duty. "Kids, we better call it a day. You know what Molkow said."

"Ah...come on." We balked. "Molkow doesn't have to know about this."

The wail of an air raid siren interrupted our arguing.

"We better head for the shelter," Hugo warned. "This is supposed to be a Red Cross zone, but those Russkies don't pay much attention to that."

The shelter was a dark, dank hole in the basement of the building, lined from floor to ceiling with bunks, and already crowded by the time we got there. Men crammed like sardines on the double-decker bunks and smelled just about as bad.

"Find yourself a space," we were told.

The fellows crowded together even more, making room for one here, another there.

"Never thought it would come to this, finding myself in bed with five men," Hannimusch cracked up. "Somebody ought to take a picture of this."

"I think somebody just did," I said. A flash momentarily blinded my eyes.

"Something to put in your album," Hugo laughed, promising to send us a copy.

We had to stay in the cellar for almost an hour before the 'all clear' sounded.

When the Molkows did not show up for breakfast the next morning, we decided to check on them. It was a gorgeous, mild day. A walk would do us good. We passed rows of burned-out buildings, their outer walls still standing. Russian civilians and German soldiers cleared the streets of the bomb damage from that night and helped evacuate people from the ruins.

Following a hand-drawn map and verbal directions, we reached Molkows' place. They were housed in a low, modern complex, one of the nicest we had seen in Russia so far, surrounded by a garden and enclosed by a wrought-iron picket fence. We wondered what privileged individuals had lived there before the Germans took it over.

Taking a chance, we knocked on one of several doors and by luck it was the right one. "One moment," Molkow answered.

Hilde sat propped up in bed when we entered. Molkow was spooning her balsam tea to calm her nerves.

"Here," he handed us cup and spoon, "you stay with her. I have to find a doctor."

Some time ago, we had dubbed Hilde 'Fieseler Storch,' after a reconnaissance plane because, like her, the plane seemed to be made of nothing more than sticks and skin. It was Betty who drew the comparison the first time she saw one of these old planes, when it buzzed us while riding from Smolensk to a unit up front. It seemed to fit, more now than ever. Hilde looked pale and spent.

"Do you hurt? Can we do anything for you?" Hannimusch asked, stroking her shaking hand.

"I need my medicine," she answered impatiently.

Hannimusch picked up a bottle of pills from Molkow's nightstand. "Would these pills help?"

Hilde tossed from side to side, knocking them out of Hannimusch's hand. "No. I want MY medicine."

Molkow was gone for a long time. When he returned he brought a medic with him. He gave Hilde a shot. Seconds later she relaxed, thanking the medic with a grateful glance.

"You can go now," Molkow said to us. "She'll go to sleep."

"She can't do without that morphine anymore," Hannimusch mentioned, on the way back. "It'll kill her some day."

Morphine! I remembered having been warned by my parents. That came about after my dance teacher, Lisa Kresse, a world famous dancer, had told my parents of her addiction to morphine, and the painful withdrawal and rehabilitation she had to undergo. This nearly destroyed her career and her life. "Never, ever touch that stuff," my parents etched into my mind. To hear that Hilde had this problem not only shocked me, it floored everybody, but it explained Hilde's sometimes very odd behavior.

During our short stay in Roslavl, we became good friends with the engineers. On the evening before our departure they planned a farewell party for us. Molkow was still tied down with Hilde, so we did not have to worry about him.

As we returned from our last performance in Roslavl, the fellows surprised us with a room decorated with paper chains and candlelight. Gert stood bent over a large bowl in the center of the round table, pouring into it whipped eggs, finely ground coffee, a bottle of brandy and stirred and tasted it between each addition. He called his concoction "Russian Blood." It was fun just to watch him. By the time he ladled it into mugs, he was in high gear. I took one sip and lost my breath. It burned all the way down to my toes, but it tasted quite good. Hannimusch unpacked her accordion. We sang songs, linked arms, rocked to the rhythm of the music and toasted our friendship. Gert was in great form, keeping us laughing until we hurt. Yet, ever so gradually, our songs and stories became more melancholy and sad as the night wore on. What surfaced was our pain, our losses, the endless good-byes, the hopelessness of our common situation, homesickness, and the horrors of war we had to witness every day. Laughter dissolved to tears.

"What we need is some strong coffee," Hugo decided,

rising to his unsteady legs. He asked me along to help.

On a table in the adjoining room sat a camping stove with a teakettle. "You grind the coffee and I'll fill up the kettle and light the stove," Hugo said to me, steadying himself on the table. I was tired but felt fine. I had a built-in shutoff in my system. Once my chin turned numb, not another drop of liquor could pass my lips, and I never got drunk.

The coffee was ground. Hugo had filled the kettle and the tank of the burner, then lit it. "It'll take awhile before the water boils," he said. We might as well get comfortable." He stretched out on a corner bench and suggested I should do the same. I'll take this side, you can have the other." Our heads met in the corner. For a while we talked.

"You know, when this mess is over and I make it back home in one piece, I sure would like to see you again," he said.

"That would be nice," I admitted.

"I have a sister about your age. She and you would have a great time together. Do you have any brothers or sisters?

Oh, I wished he hadn't asked that, I thought. How can I tell him about my brother without breaking down. This was still a deep, open wound within my heart.

I did not have to answer. Hugo was snoring.

That is the last I remember until somebody shook me awake.

"Sooo...! That's how you make coffee in here. Nice going!" Hannimusch looked down on me.

"Come here, look at this," Gert roared, pointing to the kettle and the burner. "Can you believe it? They put the water in the tank and filled the kettle with the fuel." Turning to Hugo he heckled, "Nice trick. Did you think you could make water burn?"

"Man, you are crazy. I lit the thing. I saw the flame," Hugo defended himself, but upon closer inspection he just grinned. "Can't believe I did this. There must have still been fuel in the line, or I could not have lit the thing." Everybody laughed.

"I'll keep you in mind when it is time to send for the bony reaper," Gert teased. "I don't have to worry that he may get me too soon."

Though the incident revived everybody for the moment, we decided to skip the coffee.

The gray of dawn already hazed the sky.

XI

Spring comes to Russia.

It was no longer the stability of a region, but its accessibility that determined our itinerary. The thaw brought almost all transportation other than rail to a standstill. As we headed by train from Roslavl in a southerly direction toward Briansk, we saw numerous vehicles along the way mired in mud and abandoned. A dispatch from an armored division was supposed to flag down the train, pick us up, and take us to their unit. We could only wonder how.

A single line of railroad tracks ran straight as a ruler as far as the eye could see, dividing the landscape into two identical, boring halves. Earth met sky to the right: earth met sky to the left. We were on the train for about three-quarters of an hour when it suddenly braked. About twenty yards from the tracks stood a mud-caked truck and beside it an equally muddy motorcycle with sidecar. Molkow stepped out on the coach's open platform to meet with two men in uniform and leather jackets. They, too, were splashed with mud from their knee-high boots to the collar of their jackets. Assuming they had come for us, we wondered how in heck we would get from the train to the truck. Molkow, the train's engineer and the two men, presumably officers from a panzer division, pondered the same question. Two more men, the driver of the truck and another soldier, waited by their vehicle for a directive. What they faced was no easy task.

They would have to wade back and forth through this muck, carrying twelve large suitcases, four large trunks, Hannimusch's accordion and odds and ends, over to the truck, piece by piece.

We watched this transfer with apprehension. The men were careful. Their slipping and sliding, sinking ankle deep into the goo with every step made us nervous. We fully expected to see one or the other item they carried land in the mud. Hannimusch was especially concerned about her accordion. Then it was our turn to cross over. Thankful for our army boots, we proceeded carefully with skirts and coats drawn up, placing one foot in front of the other like high wire artists. By the time we reached and climbed onto the truck, we had mud on our clothes, our purses, even on our faces. "How far do you have to take us?" Molkow asked the truck driver before getting on.

The two men sized each other up. The driver lit his pipe, leisurely puffing on it before he answered. "About forty kilometers."

"What if we get stuck?"

The corner of the driver's mouth drew up in a crooked grin. He scanned Molkow up and down, from his hat, sunglasses, white scarf, black leather gloves to his now clay-coated boots. "We made it here. We'll make it back. Got two men to push. With you that makes three."

Molkow was not amused. "What's your name, soldier?"

Instead of an answer, the driver slammed the cab door shut, started and gunned the engine. Molkow scrambled to get on the back, and did just in time. The wheels of the truck spun and spattering mud in all directions like a fountain. The vehicle lunged forward, fishtailed, spun out, but gradually advanced, yards at a time. The motorcycle took off ahead of us, making a lot of noise and going nowhere fast. Meanwhile, the train had left and we sat in the middle of this no-mans-land. Suddenly, the tires of the truck grabbed on to something solid and the truck took off as if to make up for lost time. It was a washboard ride. For miles and miles, we rode on a one-lane road made of side-by-side logs, so many, it must have taken a forest to build it. We crossed the flat, treeless plain shimmering under the sun from its millions of puddles and pools. It had its beauty but offered the eye no point of reference.

Eventually we came to a cluster of small, thatched-roof houses built on stilts. Narrow boardwalks led from one house to the other. The officers on the motorcycle had gotten there ahead of us and stopped the truck. After a brief discussion with Molkow, they assigned us two cottages on opposite sides of the road. One could only house four, the other had beds for eight. Hannimusch moved in with the Molkows, and we girls moved into the other, temporarily displacing a major and his aid. These rustic, cabin-like homes made of rough, weathered lumber, wrapped around one central hearth. Ours had two rooms with two small windows, furnished with cots, a table and chairs. A few personal belongings such us photos, a saber and a Russian helmet left behind by the officer, decorated the walls. Floor, ceiling, walls, all were made of pine boards. Above an arched opening of the white-stuccoed hearth hung kettles and cookware. The entrance led through an enclosed porch on the west side of the house and served as a drop-off for boots and coats, and storage for buckets, shovels and tools. It also offered an unobstructed view across the endless plain toward the curving horizon. It was one of the better houses we had been in.

We had gone through the usual arguments over who sleeps where, when Emmy called us out there to witness a spectacular sunset. "Hey, everybody! You've got to see this!"

A sun bigger than anything I had ever seen touched the earth's edge and transformed the water-soaked land into a sea of shimmering gold. In awe and reverent silence, we watched this gigantic sphere melt down into the horizon, fusing land and sky with blazing light. It was a sight so grand, so wondrous that I half expected angels or God himself to appear.

As the sky darkened we lit candles, rekindled the fire in the hearth, unpacked, cleaned up, wrote letters, talked and just relaxed. Such rare, quiet moments allowed us to think and reflect. Shelved worries and heartaches resurfaced. Inge still had not heard from her folks since the massive bombing of Hamburg. Meantime, Berlin and Munich had come under heavy attack. We knew only what we occasionally heard on a radio. Deaths reportedly numbered in the hundreds, the homeless in the thousands. It would take weeks before we knew if our families were among them. As long as we were busy, we could push such fears out of our mind. On stage we smiled and went through our antics; off stage we babbled a little too much, laughed a little too loud, and drank sometimes more than we should have, then felt guilty afterwards.

After I scribbled a few letters, one to my folks and another to Erika, I went to bed early. Sleep was another way to escape. When I did not think of my brother, I worried about my folks, or thought of Karlemann. I still could not look at Emmy without resentment and a gnawing pain. And I missed my friend, Erika. She was the only one I could really talk to. I wondered where she was and how she was doing.

On the verge of drifting off, I felt something bite me on the legs and snapped wide-awake again. "Bugs," I shouted, jumped out of bed and checked my sheets. Little black, round dots, the size of pencil erasers, scurried into the folds and out of sight. "Bedbugs!"

Panic struck us. We tore our beds apart, stripped them, shook out blankets, sheets, pillows, moved the beds away from the walls and dripped hot wax into the wooden joints of the bunks. Only after we could think of nothing else to do, we went reluctantly back to bed. The bites itched mercilessly and I scratched myself raw. It was close to daybreak by the time I fell asleep.

Shrill rings from a telephone woke me up. It came from a field telephone left by the officers. Betty answered it. I would not have known how. It was Molkow informing us of the day's agenda, beginning at noon with the routine of unpacking, ironing and mending of costumes.

Before I got out of bed, I counted the red, pea-sized bumps all over my legs, arms, and body up to my ears, but there were just too many of them. "Great heaven! Look at me. How can I go on stage like this!"

"You won't have to wear a costume tonight," Inge joked about my polka-dotted skin. Everybody had bites, but nobody had as many as I did, nor the huge welts they caused.

I dressed and headed over to Hilde for sympathy and hopefully a remedy. The itching almost drove me insane. "Oh, dear," she exclaimed when I showed her my arms, legs and rump. She dabbed the welts with pure alcohol, which burned like fire where I had scratched. Even that was more tolerable than the itching. "You'll have to cover them with makeup and powder before you go on stage tonight," she said. "And don't scratch anymore."

"Sure. That's easy for you to say," I grumbled.

Overnight the ground had frozen hard again but began to soften where the sun hit. By noon it was mud. A staff car took us to the theater--a recently constructed barn-like shed with a stage and rows of bench seats. Its walls still gave off the scent of fresh cut pine.

We checked out the stage. The floor bounced like a trampoline when we jumped and we sounded like a herd of elephants crossing. It also had ridges and was full of knotholes and gaps.

"We can't dance on that, at least not on toe," we concluded. We could easily trip or twist an ankle or knee. When we expressed our concerns to Molkow, he dismissed them with a wave of his hand.

"Must be expecting some big shot tonight," I speculated, "or he wouldn't risk that any more of us became disabled."

Hannimusch looked for the piano. "Egon! Weren't they supposed to furnish a piano? Where is it? No piano!"

"Damn it," he cursed. "No piano. No heat. No lights. Damn!"

It was cold inside the building. With our coats still on, we unpacked our costumes while Hilde went over each one to see what needed mending. "Can't we do this some other time?" we pleaded with her.

"It's got to be done," she insisted. She was again in one of her weird moods.

Barely able to hold a needle between our cold, stiff fingers, we grumbled and made faces behind her back, while she checked and rechecked each costume, finding ever more things for us to fix.

Finally, Molkow decided that there was no point in hanging around as long as we had no lights, no heat and

157

no piano.

My bites itched viciously. I could not wait to strip and dab them with alcohol again, and put hot compresses on. My scratching drew blood and caused the bumps to swell into big, ugly welts.

For the night's performance, soldiers rigged up generators to run lights, put a kerosene heater in the dressing area, and even procured a piano. Hannimusch was relieved when she saw it, otherwise she would have had to accompany us on the accordion. She did not like that, and neither did we. But when she played the first chord, she burst into shrieking laughter, which turned into a wail. "Listen to this...just listen! You could never tell that I just played a major scale."

"That's what that was?" We grimaced.

While putting our makeup on, Hilde rechecked the costumes, nit-picked and criticized everything we did: the ironing, the mending, even the way we hung our costumes up. The more she looked, the more she found wrong, and the crabbier she got. Behind her back, Betty did her famous impression of a Fieseler Storch--the skinny plane that we nicknamed Hilde after. It never failed to break us up laughing.

"What's so funny?" Hilde asked, looking over her shoulder at us. Betty switched quickly to her most angelic expression, only to resume her antics as Hilde turned away again.

"What are you giggling about," she finally demanded to know, suspecting that she was the source of our amusement. Her eyes darkened with anger. Somehow, that made it even harder for us to restrain our laughter. Uschi was the first to explode and that started a chain reaction. We burst out, one after the other, laughing out of control till tears rolled down our cheeks and we gasped for air.

Hilde was livid. She called her husband.

"Silence!" Molkow demanded. Even he could stifle our laughter only for as long as it took to swallow, then we burst out anew. Uschi stood closest to him and caught the back of his hand across her face while he threatened us with everything he could think of, including getting us kicked out of the theater guild. I turned away and bunched a towel over my mouth. My sides hurt. But this was not the sort of laughter that bubbled from the heart, more like heaves from our souls.

The show was about to begin. We tried to pull ourselves together but with the first awful sounds from the piano we broke out all over again, and again as we stepped onto the bouncing, thumping stage. The audience laughed right along with us, or at us, we were not sure.

During intermission, Hannimusch rushed into the dressing area, "What in heaven's name is going on?"

"They have gone berserk," Molkow fumed. "But they'll pay for this, that's a promise."

Now Hannimusch began to snicker and quickly covered her mouth and dashed out.

"Not you too," Hilde cried after her, wringing her hands.

In spite of Molkow's threats and purple fury, we could not stop. Uschi was the worst. Her whole body convulsed and she constantly reinfected us. Toward the end of the show she staggered about like a drunk and was unable to go on stage anymore. Intermittently, she switched from laughter to sobs and back to laughter again. Molkow finally realized that this was more than just an act of insubordination and called for a medic, who took one look at us and prepared to give Uschi a shot. "Russian Koller," he called our condition (a kind of hysteria peculiar to men at the front lines). "Have seen it often enough in the trenches up front. We all have limits as to how much we can take." He left us some pills. "Take them and go to bed," he advised.

By the time we reached our quarters, we were totally exhausted. We took the pills, and slept like the dead, bedbugs and all.

First thing the following morning, feeling embarrassed and very foolish, we apologized to Hilde.

"You belong in a nut house," she said, grudgingly accepting our apology.

In the afternoon we visited a division very close to the front, not to perform there, just to spend a few hours with the troops. Under beautiful sunshine we rode in open commando cars and watched the land change from

159

soggy brown clay to greening fields with shrubs and trees. Leaving the log road, we followed a deeply furrowed dirt road for awhile. Drainage ditches bordering the road had made it passable. It led to a village where houses had shingled roofs, sun bleached stick fences, and many greening plants and trees. A few chickens scurried out of our car's path, squawking.

Our vehicles had not yet come to a stop when soldiers swarmed around, shouting to one another "They are here...they are here!"

"Any of you from Berlin? From Schweinfurt...Essen... Bremen...?" They bombarded us with questions, wanting to connect with someone from home. Then they asked about conditions at home, about air raid damage, availability of food, questions we could not answer since we had not been home ourselves for almost four months. However, many of these men had not been home for over two years and were eager to hear anything we had to tell them. I wished I could have spent more time with them and resented being whisked away again by officers as if they had a monopoly on us.

At the commando center, a former schoolhouse, we joined our hosts and a few Russian civilians for drinks. One of the Russians, a well-groomed woman in her late thirties, a teacher, spoke fluent German. I practically held her hostage with questions. How did she come to speak such perfect German? What was life like under the communist regime? Was it better than under the Tsars? How did people feel about Germany's invasion? She was gracious enough to answer most of my questions.

"The village we are in," she told me, "is an old German settlement." That accounted for her competency in the German language. "I taught the children of the village. This building here was our schoolhouse."

"What was life like under the Bolsheviks?" I repeated my earlier question.

She took a deep breath. "It was difficult. We lived in constant fear. They came and took everything away that they deemed unnecessary for our survival. They took our land, and when the war broke out, they took our men and our children."

Our conversation attracted more and more listeners,

including Molkow and his wife.

"German settlements had fared better under the Tsar. As per agreement, the Germans owned their land. The Russian peasants owned nothing. They worked as serfs for the aristocratic landowners who cared little about them. Often, they died like flies during long and harsh winters, running out of food and fuel. The communists provided them at least the barest necessities." The teacher gazed wistfully into the distance. She continued. "Once a year, a government truck came to the villages and distributed goods such as boots, a pair of trousers, a shirt for the men, a dress and apron for the women-- never mind the color, style or fit, it was more than they had ever had. The government also established schools for them. A poor but bright, talented child could hope to become a doctor, a teacher, a scientist, an artist as long as it conformed to the party line."

"Just like in Germany...tow the party line or else." I thought of my application to the university. The moment my cynical comment slipped out, I knew I should not have said it in the presence of people I did not know. I tried to bridge the sudden silence with more questions, but Hilde cut in.

"How come they build houses on stilts?"

"They store straw and hay under them in the winter. It keeps the floor insulated against the cold, and later becomes food for the animals.

"Are you from here? Where did you study?" Hilde asked.

"I am not from this village, but one like it not far from here. I went to school in Moscow."

"That explains why you stand apart from average peasants around here. You could pass as one of us," Hilde said, referring to her more cosmopolitan appearance and demeanor.

"You must have been glad when our troops marched in," Molkow assumed arrogantly.

"Many never lived to see it," the teacher answered dryly. With that she excused herself and left the room.

Our hosts, meanwhile, prepared to take us to a shooting range to show and teach us how to shoot guns. They also promised to take us to a lookout and to the trenches from where we could see over to the Russian side with a pair of binoculars.

To think we were that close to the front caused some anxiety. Hilde was particularly nervous. "What if they start shooting?" she asked.

"Don't worry. Until the ground dries we won't see much action," officers assured her. Nature seemed to do her best to stop the war, first with a hard, hard winter, then turning the ground into a bottomless morass. But mankind remained determined to fight on.

At the firing range we viewed an assortment of weapons, from revolvers to machine guns, and our hosts encouraged us to try them out. "Try this," one fellow said and handed me a stubby rifle, something between a machine gun and a revolver. He showed me how to hold and brace it against my shoulder. Though I feared and despised guns, I did not want to appear a sissy. "Now aim and pull back slowly on the trigger," the fellow instructed me and helped me point the barrel toward a mound of bailed straw. I did as he said, and slowly pulled the trigger. The butt of the gun recoiled, knocking me backwards, while it fired in rapid succession. I screamed and dropped it on the ground. The fellow laughed. "Thank you, but that's not for me," I told him, shaken and bruised. After that, Hannimusch, Inge and I watched from afar. My blood ran cold when I thought that I could have easily killed someone.

Next, the officers took us to the lookout. It was nothing more than a mound of dirt on elevated ground. Standing in a hollow, we looked across a field at a long ridge of piled dirt where the Russians had dug in. Though this was all we could see, being so close to the enemy was a weird feeling, like walking along the edge of a cliff.

Our hosts then took us even closer, to the front-most trenches, guaranteeing that it was perfectly safe as long as we did not pop our heads above ground. We followed reluctantly.

Soldiers held watch in trenches that snaked around a hill. Our appearance rendered them speechless. The last thing they expected was female company from home to drop in. Once over the initial shock, their first concern

162

was for our safety.

"Whatever you do, for God's sake, keep your heads down," they warned us right away. "Those Russkies itch to find a target, any target at all, to shoot at." To prove their point they demonstrated. One of the men lifted a steel helmet on a stick inches above the ground. Bang! A bullet hit it just like that.

Beneath the hill, the men had dug out a large cavern they called home. Reinforced and lined with log beams, it was furnished with bunks, table, a plank for a bench, a few crates in which they stored their few belongings, and a spirit burner with a pot sitting on it. Everything pointed to the fact that they had been there for a while.

"Sit down." The men directed us to the bunks. We did, avoiding the places where water dripped from the ceiling.

"By God, this calls for a drink," a sergeant said, still not quite sure whether we were real or a strange apparition. Looking around for his buddies, he yelled, "Any of you jokers have a bottle stashed away?" The men shook their heads regretfully.

"Oh, well, we'll fix that." He reached into his pocket, pulled out a box with cigarettes and counted them. "You guys, come on, kick in a few sticks," he urged his comrades and went around collecting from them.

"You watch!" He grinned, grabbed a small megaphone, aimed it over to the Russian side and shouted into it. "Hey, Russkies! Got any vodka? Have cigarettes."

A short while later we heard from the other side. "Skohlka cigarette, skohlka vodka."

The sergeant counted the bunch in his hand. "Twenty," he yelled back.

"Nyet. Fifty."

"Twenty-five."

"Nyet. Fifty."

"Fifty? Kiss my ass...forget it. No deal."

We could not believe what we saw and heard. This was war. They were ready to blow one another's head off. And here they were swapping goods.

"What kind of war is this?" I asked a fellow standing next to me. "I don't understand how one minute you trade with them, then can turn around and kill each

163

other. This is crazy."

"Hey, that's nothing," the soldier bragged. "Hell, sometimes we play cards together. They are just guys like us, bored and tired of just sitting in foxholes. They don't want a war any more than we do." He chuckled, "But don't stick your head above ground. When it comes down to it, we are still enemies."

"Eh...Germansky? Forty..." The bargaining began anew. Finally, they settled on thirty cigarettes for one bottle of vodka. The sergeant lifted and waved a white rag on a stick, waiting for the other side to do the same. Then, they exchanged whistles and he walked, holding the white flag, to meet a Russian half way. They made their trade and he returned with a bottle.

Hannimusch was beside herself. "This is the craziest thing I've ever seen. This whole damned bloody war is a bloody farce. But people die."

"All wars are crazy. We don't hate those guys over there, they don't hate us, but...we have to fight each other. If I don't shoot them, they shoot me. That's how it is."

"I'll never understand," Hannimusch said, shaking her head.

"Don't forget," one of the men added, "we got guns in front AND in back of us. What choice do any of us have? We wouldn't be here otherwise." He sounded cynical, even bitter.

I thought about my brother. He did have a choice. Why did he have to volunteer?

If nobody wanted to go to war, how then could one man mobilize millions to march, to kill, and to be killed? I recalled the cheering young replacements in the Poznan station, how eager they had been to come out here to fight. And with a stab of guilt, I remembered how excited I was when the principal of my school announced that the war had started. For us kids it was like a holiday. I did not think of people dying. I had not lost anyone yet. I had not heard the wounded moan and scream. And I could have never imagined the destruction war could bring. War was glorified by colorful parades, with flags and medals, and speeches about honor and duty. What does youth know about war if it had never been in one?

These short few months had given me much to think about.

The minute we got back to our quarters the telephone rang. Betty answered again. "Scala Berlin here," she joked. The Scala was the last legitimate theater our company had performed in before that, too, was bombed out. Betty listened, smirked, then relayed this message: "Somebody wants to talk to the 'blond doll'!"

The only blond in our group was Ilse. Betty handed her the receiver. Ilse hung on that phone for more than a half-hour as a group of tank commanders evidently tried to persuade her and us to come to their place to party with them.

"If we don't go over there," Ilse related and squirmed, "they'll come over here. What should I tell them?"

"Just hang up. If they don't understand 'no' maybe they will understand that," Uschi suggested. Ilse finally did. Immediately the phone rang again and kept on ringing. It was always the same bunch of guys. We took turns giving them a piece of our mind. Then we packed the bell with cotton to muffle its ringing and simply did not answer anymore. We also bolted our doors.

It was past nine o'clock, pitch dark outside. Already in pajamas and nightgowns, hair in curlers, we sat around playing cards when we heard strange noises outside. "The tank commanders," we suspected. We blew out all the candles and stayed quiet, hoping they would soon give up and go away. We waited, still hearing noises around and even under the house.

"Strange, that they don't knock on the door or say something?" I whispered.

"They're trying to scare us," Betty whispered back.

"What if it's not them but Russian partisans?"

That was always a possibility. The thought sent shivers down my back. We ducked into the most sheltered corners around the room. For awhile, all I heard was my heartbeat.

"Someone is trying the door handle," Betty murmured low. I had heard it too. Then everything remained quiet for a long time.

"I have a good notion to tell those guys off," Betty

fumed. "I just know it's them."

"The phone..." Ilse remembered. "It isn't ringing anymore? Maybe we should call somebody?"

Betty was already on it. She cranked it "Hello... hello...?" Nothing happened. "It's dead," she said, toneless.

"Hush...I hear something again," Ilse cautioned. I scooted over to the window and peeked out into the darkness, just barely making out the shape of the next house and nothing else.

"We can't just sit here on the floor all night long. We have to do something," Uschi grumbled.

"Quiet!" Betty hushed us. "I think I hear a car."

Suddenly we saw flashlights and heard men's voices outside. Then a knock at the door. "Are you all right in there?"

Betty lit some candles. "That's darn dirty of them to scare us like this," she said and went to the door. "Are you the jerks that kept calling us?"

"Yes...until the phone went dead. That's why we came to check if you're all right. Some Russkies are prowling around again. Can we come in and talk to you?"

Betty reluctantly opened the door. "Sure it wasn't you doing the prowling around?"

Three men from the tank squadron pushed their way in, two officers and a corporal. I could smell their liquored breath from ten feet away.

We looked awful--hair in rag curlers, no makeup except smeared mascara, in long flannel nightgowns, long johns underneath because of the bugs, wrapped in robes, and faces greased to blind a bat--but suddenly nobody cared.

The fellows told us a tale about partisans sabotaging telephone lines and equipment in this area, and offered to post a guard at our door for the night. We almost believed them until one pulled a bottle from his coat pocket, helped himself to glasses and set up drinks for everyone.

Emmy and Ilse took admiring notice of the three as they stood in front of us, tall, trim and handsome. They also were the first to accept a drink. Betty, on the other hand, squinted at them with contempt and asked them to leave, convinced that they had staged this scare.

Right then Molkow burst in. "What's going on here?" He saw the bottle on the table, the drinks poured, the fellows, and exploded. "You men get the hell out of here, this instant," he ordered. He was about to sweep the drinks off the table with his hand when one of the officers shoved him back. The situation ignited into a brawl. Molkow threatened to call their commander. That's when two of the men picked him up, carried him outside, and dumped him in the frozen mud. The fellows finished their drinks, said they would send someone to fix the phone line and to stand guard, then left. We locked the door and went to bed laughing, losing no sleep over who would win this fight. Only Emmy expressed some regrets. "I think that's the last we will see of them," she sighed.

In spite of all my precautions, next morning I woke up with fresh bites. I cursed this place and was glad that we had spent our last night in it.

Betty had problems of another kind. "Women just aren't meant to go on expeditions," she groaned, bending over with cramps. Her nightgown and bed were soaked with blood. "Now I have to do laundry before we leave." Every drop of water had to be hauled in from an outside well and heated in a kettle over an open fire. We shared one wash bowl between us, drawing numbers to see who got it first. Since Smolensk we had not taken a bath, unless we counted the dousing we got in the sauna in Roslavl.

The next stop was a small township. Troops as well as civilians turned out to welcome us. We stayed with Russian families who opened their homes and hearts to us, mostly older people with a few very young children, the first children we had encountered. Their small log homes, furnished with only the barest necessities, were meticulously clean. A special place in every home was set aside for a small altar with a picture of the black Madonna, surrounded by photographs of the extended family.

Because the people were so kind and friendly, we wanted to show our appreciation and do a show especially for them. Hilde and Hannimusch together approached Molkow with this idea and, surprise of surprises, he agreed.

We held a matinee. Molkow stood at the door to the theater greeting the people as they entered. One of them handed him a couple of eggs. Somebody else handed him a couple more. He filled his coat and suit pockets until he ran out of room. Still the eggs kept coming and people insisted that he take them. His pockets bulging, his hands full, he did not know where to put them anymore. Somebody finally brought him a basket. By the time the theater was full, so was the basket--a small laundry basket full of eggs.

"What a treat," we thought. "Fresh, soft boiled eggs every morning! Great!" We ate them morning, noon and night; scrambled, boiled, poached, until the mere sight and smell of them made us sick. We passed the last batch on to soldiers.

The fields greened, the air warmed, and on mild evenings around sunset, people gathered on their cottage steps, singing melancholy songs accompanied by someone strumming a balalaika. Once in a while we gave a matinee instead of an evening performance. Then in the evenings, we sat and listened to the Russians sing. They had the most beautiful voices, so rich and deep. We waited until the sky darkened and all the stars came out, millions of them, more than we had ever seen. They seemed close enough to touch. My heart opened wide, taking in the peace and glory of the evening.

Daily sunshine gradually solidified the ground, making it passable. We traveled again by truck from place to place, outfit to outfit, along rutted dirt roads, edged with grasses and weeds. Sometimes a Fieseler Storch spotted and buzzed us, tipping its wings in greeting. On these one-night stops, all we seemed to do was pack, unpack and pack again. We performed in halls, in tents, in the round, and even outside on quickly constructed platforms. Most nights we slept on straw beds in bug-infested huts. I could not find an inch on my skin without bites. Heaven was a bucket full of hot water for a sponge bath. Incredibly, we held together, inspired by the smiling faces of the soldiers at these isolated outposts.

Fighting had resumed all along the front. Several times, we came under heavy artillery fire and had to sit it out in one of the thatched-roof cottages. Not much protection. Terrifying as that was, when the canons stopped firing, we relaxed again. It was over, until the next attack. The gnawing concern for our families back home never ceased. It haunted us day and night. Reports of continuing air raids, extensive damage and steadily rising death tolls, not knowing if our loved ones were among the dead, the homeless, or those that had survived, kept us in an emotional turmoil--an agony we shared with every soldier on the front. We looked forward to Briansk, the next large city on our schedule, where we would get mail again.

XII

Friend or Foe?

Our first stop in Briansk was at headquarters to pick up a stack of mail. Most of it was at least a month old. We were eager, yet apprehensive to open the letters from home, expecting that the news in general would not be good. For Inge the news proved devastating. It was the first word from home since the brutal air attack on Hamburg in early March. Now it was the end of April. She read parts of her mother's letters aloud, with frequent interruptions to wipe away her tears and to blow her nose.

"Everybody is alive and well," her mother wrote, "but there is nothing left of our home and belongings." Inge's mother described how her family cowered in the cellar during the bombing. "Explosions pulverized mortar, stone and cement. The air was so thick with dust that it was impossible to breathe. We had to get out or choke to death, but found ourselves entombed under tons of rubble. With a cloth tied over nose and mouth, we dug through the debris only to surface into a hellish inferno. Raging fires lit up the night like a midday sun. Bombs exploded right and left as we ran through the burning city looking for shelter. Between explosions we heard people scream. Some staggered aimlessly through the burning streets, calling out names. Some just stood and wept in front of what was their home. Little children, injured, lost and alone, cried for their mothers. Buildings collapsed around us. Heavy winds whipped up the flames and hurled debris around." Inge's mother went on to describe how she, her husband and Inge's younger siblings walked for hours that night through the treacherous, blazing rubble to a relative's house. Once familiar neighborhoods were no longer recognizable. They got lost.

"Oh, my God!" I mumbled and buried my face in my hands. I had not yet opened my letters from home and now was petrified. Sniffles filled the pauses between Inge's reading. Hastily she opened the next letter. In it, her mother wrote that the government had resettled her family in the country, forcing a farmer to take them in. They shared one room between the four of them. Her father, who worked in the city, had to stay there with friends and saw them only on weekends. Thousands of bombing victims from Hamburg alone faced the same fate.

I listened, and tried to imagine what it was like not to have a home anymore. My mind visited familiar scenes... my mother in the kitchen, bent over the kitchen sink washing dishes; my father watering the potted plants that crowded the window sill; our cat Pussy curled up atop the kitchen buffet. Home consisted of a thousand such familiar images. Just to know that it was there, waiting, gave me a sense of security. Inge had lost that. It must be, I thought, like grieving over the death of a kin. I felt terribly sorry for her. Inge looked up from her letters, took a deep breath and said with a hollow, toneless voice, "Thank God they are alive."

Emmy received news that her parent's home near Berlin had caught on fire during a napalm attack, gutting the roof and the upper floor. Hannimusch's friend wrote that the raids over Cologne continued though there was little left to destroy. He managed to save her possessions by moving and storing them in the country. My parents, who still struggled to accept the death of my brother, had survived a March air raid on Munich without major damage to their apartment unit. In one of Mama's letters she described how my father and a neighbor had saved our apartment unit. During an air raid, as the two men patrolled the building, two stick bombs pierced the roof and landed in the stairwell. Quickly, they picked them up and tossed them out the window before they could explode. It could have cost both men their lives. Just a spark from the phosphorous contents of these bombs could burn through flesh and bone.

My mother also wrote about a friend who was arrested for complaining about the awful shortages and deteriorating condition back home. She had been standing in line an hour to buy a few sheets of writing paper. When her turn finally came there was no more paper. One fanatical person in the line overheard her angry comments and turned her in. She spent three terrifying days in Gestapo custody.

All letters were subject to random censorship, therefore carefully worded. However, we could glean from them a growing, widespread discontent at home. People were fed up with the war, the bombings, the scarcity of food and other necessities. Even party loyalists had become disenchanted with the lies and propaganda of the Nazi government.

On the brighter side, we also received many letters from friends. Erika and Ulla wrote that they were doing well and hoped to rejoin us soon. Inge received several letters from Moedl, which softened the terrible news from home. Betty heard from Kurt. I got a note from Karlemann in which he mentioned that Smolensk was under siege. He and his bus had been reassigned to another troupe, and he hoped to run into us again somewhere. The mere thought of him still stabbed at my heart and my conscience. Mad at myself, I ripped the letter into little pieces, wishing I could do the same with the memory of him. I glanced at Emmy. Had Karlemann written her, too? She did not mention it, and I was not about to ask. From all indications, she still knew nothing about Karlemann and me, and I thought it best to leave it that way.

Briansk was a city as big or bigger than Roslavl, not quite as gray and drab, but just as badly damaged. I saw no great loss in the destruction of some of the old, outdated buildings, but felt a sad kinship with the people who had once called them home and now had nowhere to go. Newer buildings on the outskirts of the city--long boxes with rows of small windows--had even less eye appeal.

Headquarters assigned us a bus and driver to take us

to the theater, located on a main street. We passed the twisted frames of burned out streetcars, still on track, and through streets choked with people on foot and on bicycles, or crowded atop horse-drawn carts.

When we reached our destination, before unloading anything, we checked out the theater. One look at the stage and we panicked. The stage was tilted. It sloped toward the audience, something we had never encountered before. "We can't dance on that. We'd have to dance up-and-down-hill. This is ridiculous!" Our reaction was instant and unanimous. We took our concerns to Molkow.

"That's the way it is. If you can't handle it, you might as well forget about ever dancing at the Paris Opera, because it and many other major stages are built that way," Molkow replied. "Better get used to it. Greater dancers than you had to adapt." However, he did at least, schedule a rehearsal before the show.

"Good luck!" Ilse said and rolled her eyes. "I can already see myself landing in the orchestra pit."

As soon as we had unpacked our costumes, we ran through some of our numbers, especially those with many turns. Up hill was a struggle; down hill a catastrophe. We staggered and stumbled through our routines as if stone drunk. Molkow yelled at us, calling us a bunch of clumsy cows. While we rehearsed, he paced back and forth on the stage's apron, having stagehands raise and lower available backdrops. He backed up against the footlights to gain a proper perspective, and went just a little too far. Not used to the incline either, he lost his balance and fell with a thundering crash backwards into the orchestra pit. For a second, everyone froze, then rushed to the scene, only to crack up laughing. He had fallen onto a big kettledrum and had broken through. Only his legs, arms and head were sticking out. Cursing and kicking and flailing, he struggled to get out. I felt like applauding.

"This is divine justice," Uschi mumbled between bursts of laughter. She still held a grudge against him for slapping her. So did I. We could not hide our gratification, but felt bad about the damage to the kettledrum.

Molkow was lucky. He escaped with bruises. But he fumed and glared at us as if we were to blame. While we were laughing, it crossed my mind that the same could still happen to us.

That night's performance was our worst. Fighting against gravity, trying hard not to crash into one another, was all we could concentrate on. Besides, after so much bad news from home, our heart was not in it.

Our stay in Briansk was short. We resumed visiting the units up front. During the warm, dry weather, we danced outdoors on quickly built stages, right behind the front lines. Loudspeakers aimed at the Russians encouraged them to surrender by broadcasting music, propaganda messages and advertisements for our show. They usually answered with a thunder of guns that we could barely hear our music. Nearby explosions flashed across the sky like lightening during a storm. Our instinct told us to run for cover, yet we kept on dancing. Most of the time there was no cover anyway. As long as the soldiers remained in their seats, we kept on dancing. Medics carried casualties past our stage to waiting aid cars. We kept on dancing. Less then a mile away, men killed one another. We kept on dancing.

I had reached a point--perhaps, we all had--where I was mostly numb. Like in an emotional coma, I felt nothing anymore. Occasionally, one or the other of us flew into a rage, or exploded in uncontrollable sobs or laughter. However, in the journal I kept, and in long letters to my parents, I reported happenings and events, but no longer expressed what I thought or felt about them. It felt like I was dead inside.

At another small outpost, the Russians suddenly broke through the German lines and cut us off. We were trapped with about a hundred landsers who had come to see our show, and got caught in heavy crossfire. All communication with other German units was lost. A cluster of wooden buildings, a former collective farm, provided a crowded, primitive shelter. Close by was a small pond--or large mud puddle, depending on one's point of view--and beyond that and all around us was an area of thick brush with small, deciduous trees that had not fully leafed out.

Among the soldiers was a lieutenant we had met earlier, wearing the *Ritterkreuz*--a medal of the highest honor awarded by the *Fuehrer* himself. He took charge. After assessing the situation, he called us together for a briefing. It looked grim. If our forces could not repel the Russian advance, we faced certain capture. The men, armed only with rifles and little ammunition, could not defend us for long. Someone suggested that they should save one bullet for each of us. It was better to die quickly than at the hands of the Russians. We agreed, remembering what had happened to a troupe like ours that the Russians had captured and tortured to death.

Strange as it may seem, we remained calm and oddly detached as if this was not real at all, as if we were discussing or rehearsing a play. The prospects facing us were so horrendous, so numbing, we simply could not accept or believe that this could be happening to us. My mind played with questions 'What if...?' I listened for that inner voice again, but since that night in Smolensk during that terrible air raid, I felt disconnected from myself. My body went mechanically through the motions, performing routine tasks like a machine. I heard myself talk, saw myself walk, and thought "how weird," like there were two of me, side by side. I wondered if this was some defense mechanism against the ultimate fear of dying as fainting was against pain. And I wondered if soldiers experienced a similar shutdown when they faced battle and certain death.

The buildings temporarily housed a small infantry unit, and consisted of two long wooden structures divided into small sections, each with a door and window. One contained a hearth, a long table with benches and served as a cookhouse. We spent the first night in a room next to it, on crude bunks collected from all the other rooms. Keeping our darkest fears to ourselves, we boosted each other's morale by anticipating a quick resolve of this crisis. By nightfall the guns quieted. All we could hear was the frog song from the pond. It lulled us to sleep creating an illusion of rural serenity. The lieutenant sent out scouts and posted guards for the night. But with the first light of morning, gun and artillery fire resumed. We did not seem to be a target, but heard the shots whistling past our ears.

I wandered with Inge and Ilse over to the pond and

watched the frogs and little salamanders in the weeds along the edge. The ground felt spongy and smelled of decaying plants. The sun rose higher and hotter, sucking the moisture out of the swampy ground. With nothing to do we stretched out on a large pile of hay and sunned ourselves.

That evening, the unit's cook announced that he was low on food and water. We still had a few private rations left and told ourselves that we would be rescued before they were gone. I had gained a few pounds and did not mind losing them again.

During the second night, scouts sighted a column of Russian tanks rolling westward no more than three kilometers from us. Came morning, the shelling intensified. On the third day, all the cook had left was a sack of barley. He boiled it in the brackish water from the pond and served it for breakfast, for lunch and for dinner.

After the fourth day, nerves began to unravel. Scouts proposed we make a break for the German lines by night. It was risky, but the noose had tightened, the pocket was shrinking, and we really had no choice. Anything was better than sitting and waiting for the end.

Again, I listened inside for that trusted little voice to tell me "You'll be all right," but I heard only the pounding of my heart. I offered to lay cards, hoping to reawaken that sixth sense of mine. But nobody had a stomach for it. The situation was just too tense and too grave.

Evening came. We gathered around the table in the cookhouse for another bowl of barley. Molkow ordered us to eat, to retain our strength. He plunged the ladle into the steaming mush and dished it out. We watched him put the first spoon full in his mouth and chew on it like a rabbit. "Eat!" he ordered. Spoon in hand we stared into our bowls. "Eat!" he repeated in a threatening tone of voice. Ilse, who sat between him and me closed her eyes, put the spoon to her mouth and retched. So did I and the others. The air was charged. It felt like something was about to happen when Betty piped up, "The cook said it should taste better today because he snared a crow and put it in the soup." Face down over her bowl, her dark, beady eyes scanned our faces for a reaction. Suddenly, this whole freakish scene--Molkow bent over the steaming cauldron like a conjurer of evil, dishing out a mystic potion to his repulsed subjects; grotesquely contorted faces; Hilde's glazed stare; the smell of sweat mixed with perfume--everything seemed so bizarre and suddenly terribly funny. Before I could swallow the barley in my mouth, I exploded with laughter. Barley spattered everywhere. It sprayed Molkow's glasses, the girl's hair and faces and clothes. That was all it took. The room rocked with laughter. Pent-up tensions erupted like a volcano. Molkow turned purple, threw down his spoon and left the building. Hilde joined in the hysteria. We got up from the table, cleaned ourselves off and staggered outside into the waning sunshine, taking a deep breath for life.

The Lieutenant, together with the scouts, mapped out an escape route. We packed and stored our belongings under the buildings, out of sight, keeping out only the barest necessities, and went to bed. I fell into a fitful sleep on a bunk nearest the door. The door had no lock. Since guards patrolled back and forth in front of our hut, we felt protected. My body and mind had adapted to the constantly varying conditions that I could sleep on and through just about everything. Lately, however, I had horrible dreams. Current and past events played themselves out in bizarre nightmares. Sometimes I woke up bathed in sweat, kicking and screaming. That night I dreamed fighting off an intruder, who had thrown himself on top of me, fondling me indecently. I could smell his foul breath and felt his weight on me. I heard myself scream. The dream was so real--too real. Next I heard "Elfi, wake up, you are having a nightmare again." But this time I was not dreaming. The weight slid off me while a hand covered my mouth. Next I heard the door squeak open and close. "I am awake. I was not dreaming...I was not dreaming," I screamed, overcome with sudden panic.

"What's going on?" Molkow growled from his bunk and flicked his flashlight on.

"There was a man on my bed," I cried out.

A quick, frantic search of the room turned up nothing. "She was dreaming." Molkow concluded. "Go back to bed."

"No. I don't think she was dreaming. Somebody was in here," Emmy, who slept in the bunk next to mine, confirmed. "I heard and saw a shadow groping around, but couldn't tell who it was."

The search extended briefly to the outside where Molkow alerted the patrol. They claimed they never saw or heard anything unusual, only their comrades walking to the latrine.

"It had to be one of them," we reasoned. "One of our own!" It was a betrayal of the worst kind for one of our own to exploit our mutually desperate situation. The enemy seemed to lurk everywhere, not just on 'the other side'. I lay in my bunk with my eyes wide open, afraid to go back to sleep.

Morning dawned. The air was hot and humid. The lieutenant cautioned us to stay inside the buildings, move around as little as possible and not make any noise. But the heat and humidity inside became unbearable. Some of us sat on the wooden steps outside to catch a breeze. We spoke in whispers.

Near noon, we heard the faint sound of an engine. It grew louder, closer. We ducked inside and listened with hearts drumming. Soldiers took up their defense positions. Everything fell quiet as if the place were deserted. The engine noise grew louder. "It's one of us," a soldier yelled and came running from his post. I often marveled how they could tell. Their ears could identify by the sound what gun, what tank, what car it was they heard, and whether it was German or Russian.

In a spray of gravel and dust an armored car careened into our camp and skidded to a stop. Someone yelled for us 'show people' to jump in. We did not question it and piled into the vehicle. Seconds later it raced away with us through brush, through mud, over stumps and bumps. One man drove, a second man manned a machine gun at the back of the vehicle. Both wore large sun visors but looked vaguely familiar. I do not know how long it took or how far we went. Ducked down, on top of one another, we did not lift our heads until the car slowed and we were told to relax. Only then did we recognize our rescuers. It was Captain Ernst and his corporal, longtime acquaintances of ours whom we had met on an earlier tour. They happened to be in the region, heard of our predicament and took action, risking their own lives. We could not thank them enough. Their heroic act redeemed and restored my faith in men. In tears, near collapse, we were sent immediately to a field hospital for a week of rest.

Miles from the front, spread out over a dusty prairie, rose a city of barracks and tents, filled with the wounded, the sick and the shell-shocked. The staff put us in one of the barracks, which was divided into two sections. Day and night we listened to the moans and screams coming through the thin walls from deliriously ill patients.

"If that isn't a joke to send us here for our health, I don't know what is," Hannimusch scoffed. "If we are not sick or crazy now, we will be before the week is up."

Molkow echoed her sentiments, complaining that he could not survive one more week cooped up with us cackling hens. He paced the floor and fumed, demanding private quarters but to no avail.

After the first few meals--no barley, thank God, and no eggs--we regained our strength and wanted to get out of there. Our costumes, Hannimusch's accordion, our makeup, sheet music, everything had been left behind when we were rescued. What now? We could not do much of anything. Inge hoped we would be sent home. Molkow thought it was the end of him and his company. Some of us feared that this might be the end of our careers as well. My main concern was, that if we stayed much longer in Russia it would be the end of us. How much longer could our luck hold? We had already outlived more than nine lives.

Before the week at the field hospital was up, we received news that our troops had recaptured the area. Our baggage were safe and on its way to Briansk. We cried and cheered. That ended our stay at the hospital, which had become the ultimate test of our sanity, as well as our mostly amiable relationships within the group.

Good news in Briansk helped heal our battle scars. Molkow had a message from his secretary that he was on his way to us with a fresh set of costumes, our summer clothes and, circumstances permitting, planned to bring Erika and Ulla with him. They would arrive in Orel around the middle or latter part of May.

Erika is coming back! That was what I needed to hear. It changed my whole attitude. I had something pleasant to look forward to.

The latest map at headquarters showed Orel with the region's largest airfield kneeing deep into Russian territory, making it vulnerable to attacks on all sides. Soldiers we spoke to considered it a powder keg, ready to blow up.

In the meantime, we resumed performing on outdoor stages close behind the front. In spite of the physical hardships, it actually drew us there. We realized how much our visits meant to the men who had not had a furlough for months, sometimes years. And on the front it was always twelve o'clock midnight when masks came off and each person was what he was. Without facades, friendships progressed and solidified quickly, severed only and too frequently by death. Though we were dancers, not soldiers, we felt a kinship between them and us. Here we met the real heroes. Sometimes, too, their ugly counterparts. Time spent on the front was the most meaningful, often paid for with most bitter tears.

At one of these outposts, we befriended a young captain and some of his men. He was the German equivalent of a Greek God--tall, straight, strong, blond and blue-eyed. He was devoted to the men under his command. In turn, they had only the highest admiration for him. He came to our attention when he thanked us after a performance. We asked if we would see him later at a party given by officers in the region. He responded, "I only go where my men are allowed to go."

He touched on a subject that had bothered me for some time. Though we served our fighting men by performing, much of our free time was spent with officers of higher rank who had the facilities, the extra rations, and the clout. Molkow was not about to dally with troops when he could tank up on brandy and make deals with the brass. He had accumulated two big wooden crates full of booty, from cigarettes, booze, blankets, to rare canned goods, and planned to ship them back to Berlin with his secretary.

This young captain's remark ignited what had been smoldering inside me for a long time. Looking into the faces of the young and not so young soldiers, who waited so patiently after our performances just to shake our hands, to exchange a few words about home and family, it had bothered me that we had so little time for them. "Hurry up! Hurry up!" Molkow always nagged.

Molkow had walked on ahead to the building where the party was. As usual, trained to obey, we hurriedly followed. On a sudden impulse I stopped. "Wait a minute," I turned and said to those following behind me. "Let's just stay here for a while and spend a little time with the boys. Isn't that the reason we are here?"

"Are you crazy? You want to start another big row with Molkow? No thanks! Count me out," the girls objected.

"Ah, come on. You know it's the right thing to do," I challenged them. "After all, these are the guys who have to take the heat, who are stuck in the trenches, who get shot at first. I thought, that's why we were sent here, for them, not just the fat-cats and officers."

"Yeah...! Yeah...! That's right! We risk our necks, we do without, while they skim the cream off the top."

I perched myself atop a fence railing to the cheers from the troops.

"What about Molkow? He'll have a fit," Hannimusch hesitated and shook her finger at me. But the enthusiasm of the men persuaded her to stay, along with Inge and Emmy. All four of us sat perched like sparrows on the fence, surrounded by the men, having the best time, laughing, joking, talking, and more laughing. When Molkow found us missing he checked on us, not appreciating one bit what he saw, but just as I figured, there was nothing he could do short of starting a riot.

That is how we came to know the captain and his men a little better, and in the days that followed we saw quite a bit of them. They thought we were special. And we had great respect for them, especially the captain, for his deep concern and devotion to his comrades in arms. On the day before we had to move on, they went on a special detail, but promised to be back to see us off. "See you tomorrow," they said.

For the captain and six of his men tomorrow never came. They had been killed and were buried already by the time we found out. Stick crosses, like the ones we saw from the train on the way to Smolensk, marked their graves. Inge and I picked wildflowers along fences and fields and placed them atop the earthen mounds. We said good-bye, our tears falling on the broken earth, and we wondered if their spirit was still around to see and hear us.

The weather turned cold and rainy. Roads quickly slicked with mud. We came to a village with an old glass factory in a territory occupied by the SS. Upon arrival, the commander asked if we were interested in touring a Russian factory. Of course we were. He assigned a young lieutenant, a good looking, cocky young fellow, barely twenty, to take us there and show us around.

As we entered the factory, a large, barn-like wooden building with a dirt floor, I would have given anything to be a painter. An enormous bell-shaped furnace with large arched openings occupied the center. Heat from its core as intense and blinding as the sun's, lit up the immediate surroundings and reflected in shades of red off bare-chested, sweat-glossed workers, accentuating every muscle in their lean bodies. Using long poles they extracted globs of molten glass from the white-hot center of the oven, blew into them, rolled them into shapes on some sort of bench, returned them to the furnace and rolled them some more. Intermittently, steam hissed and puffed from water troughs into which they snipped red-hot ends. Other workers, among them women, moved phantom-like in and out of the shadows, stacking the finished, gleaming product--mugs, steins and bowls--on wooden planks. This all took place in relative silence without the hum and roar of machines. I stood transfixed. Time seemed to have stood still here and it felt as if I had stepped back into the Middle Ages. Someday, somehow, I promising myself, I would try to recapture this scene on canvas.

Spellbound, I watched the play of light and shadow, wanting to etch every nuance of color, every shading into my memory. While standing there in awe of this visual drama, an old woman rushed up and fell to her knees in front of me, kissing the hem of my coat. She clasped her gnarled hands, looking up at me with tearing, pleading eyes and said something in Russian which, of course, I did not understand. Her abject posture embarrassed me, but the desperate expression in her aged, wrinkled face was a cry for help. I bent down, wanting to raise her up, at the same time I looked around for some one to interpret. The young SS officer stepped up, kicked her to the ground with the heel of his boot, and then lashed at her with his swagger stick as if swatting at a fly. "Get...get... get! Away with you, old hag," he shouted.

Without giving it a thought, I shot up, lunged at him and pushed him away.

"What...what the hell are you doing?" I was dumbfounded. "Why did you do that?"

"She is just a dirty old Russian," he said with a sneer.

You...you...you ought to be a shamed of yourself." I could not even find words right away to express my outrage. "Only a coward would kick an old woman to the ground. You are not fit to be an officer."

Molkow grabbed hold of my arm, trying to pull me aside. "Shut up...shut up," he hissed. "This is not your business."

The shove I gave the lieutenant had knocked him slightly off balance. His look of surprise gave way to a cynical grin. Molkow pulled my arm. I shook him off and knelt down by the old woman. She was too shaken and afraid to get up. She grabbed my hand, held and kissed it. Tears streamed down her face. She tried to tell me something. Helpless, not able to understand, I looked at the other workers. "Is there anybody here who can interpret?" I asked. They went about their business as if nothing had happened. I could not understand why nobody came to my aid. Molkow pulled on me again and cursed, "Damn you! Get up, I say. Get out of here."

"Leave me alone!" I yelled at him and jerked out of his grip. "Why don't you go after that brute over there. He is the one that ought to have his face slapped."

I felt like I was taking on a whole army. Nobody wanted to take my side. My colleagues stood frozen; fear written on their faces. Finally, one of the workers, an older man, came up to us, cautiously, keeping an eye on the SS man and on Molkow. In broken German he explained that the woman had wanted to know what happened to her daughter. Germans had loaded her on a truck one day with dozens of other females from the village, and carted them off. She had not seen nor heard from her since.

"What do you know about that," I turned to the SS lieutenant.

"They were put to work in Germany," he answered with cold indifference.

I helped the woman to her feet and told the interpreter, "Tell her that her daughter will be all right. Most Germans don't act like this jackass in an officer's uniform," I assured him.

Molkow was pulling on me, fuming. Before he managed to drag me outside, I kissed the woman on the cheek and thanked the interpreter.

Outside, Molkow lit in to me. "You apologize to the lieutenant," he demanded. "I have not come this far in my life to risk it all over a snot-nose like you. He is an SS officer! You've insulted and ridiculed an SS officer."

"Apologize? Me apologize to him? It is he that owes me and that woman an apology." I answered.

The SS lieutenant took us back to our quarters. On the way, my anger turned on my colleagues. "What's the matter with all of you lame-brains? You just stood there and did nothing."

Hannimusch bit her lip and dropped her head. "You could be seen as a sympathizer, a collaborator with the enemy," she said in a low, quiet voice. Molkow had to try to stop you, or your actions would incriminate him, too, if not more so."

"What did I do wrong? What did she do wrong? Do you think it's right for this guy to kick an old woman to the ground?" Not one of the girls would look me in the eye.

"By interfering, you could have actually made things worse for that woman, and the man that interpreted for her," Hannimusch added.

They had not heard the last of it from me. I hoped the commander of this SS outfit would invite us that night, so I could get this matter off my chest, and tell him of his officer's brutish behavior. Unfortunately, he did not. I stewed over this incident until the following night when I did get a chance to talk to the commander. He was a balding man in his late forties, gentlemanly but aloof, short on words, and always surrounded by other officers.

It took a while before I found the courage to approach him. "*Herr Oberst*?" I addressed him. Internal tensions raised the pitch of my voice, making me sound like a little child. "May I speak to you...?" I glanced at the other officers and added "...in private?" He looked slightly puzzled. One corner of his mouth turned up into half a smile. He nodded and said, "Of course, of course." With one hand on my shoulder, he steered me out of the room onto a porch. "Now then, what can I do for you?" he asked. Leaning against the railing of the porch he pulled an etui from his chest pocket and offered me a cigarette. I was nervous and accepted gratefully. First, I asked if the code of conduct for an SS officer differed from that of other officers. The *Oberst* (German for Colonel) glanced at me with raised eyebrows. "Are you trying to tell me that one of my officers misbehaved?" he asked. "Yes," I said, then I went on to tell him in the fewest words possible what had happened at the factory. "That poor old woman--a mother, worried about her daughter, her child--I can not get her out of my mind," I said in closing. "He kicked her so hard that she fell over." By now, tears streamed down my face. A flicker of compassion warmed the *Oberst*'s stony face. Again, he placed his hand upon my shoulder and assured me he would reprimand the lieutenant and to put the woman at ease, maybe even try to find out about the whereabouts of her daughter. We walked back into the room. My face must have reflected my doubts, because he added, "I give you my word of honor as an officer and a gentleman," and he saluted, not with the Nazi salute, but with a soldier's. It was this gesture, this distinction that made me believe that I could trust him to keep his word.

When I told the girls later what I did, they gasped. "You didn't. You are crazy. Molkow is going to have your hide for this." But Molkow never mentioned this incident again, and I felt a foot taller.

Not far from where we stayed was a stable where some of the officers kept riding horses. The following day an aide asked me if I would like to ride the major's horse. As long as I could remember I had wanted to learn how to ride a horse, but in every dancer's contract was a clause forbidding certain activities. Horseback riding was one; so were skating and skiing. The reason given was the risk of injury. It made me laugh. Nobody cared about the risk of injury when they sent us to the Russian front. Therefore I said, "Yes. I would love to go riding, only I don't know how."

"Nothing to it. I'll teach you," the aide said. We set a time and a place to meet.

Before I sneaked off, I stopped by the Molkows to make sure they would not come looking for me. If they found out what I was up to, I would be in even deeper trouble than I was already.

The meeting place was a grassy field by an orchard hidden from the village's view, where the aide walked a horse, all saddled up. I knew little about horses, but this one seemed monstrous, like the kind I saw pulling beer wagons back home.

"This stud hasn't been ridden for months. He might be a little frisky," the aide warned as he helped me up on the saddle. "But don't worry, I'm holding the reins. You hold on to the saddle."

The horse's back was so broad that my legs reached nowhere near the stirrups. The aide knotted the straps so I could put my feet in there.

"We'll take it easy," he said, leading the horse around in a circle, nice and slow. "But if you want him to go faster just kick him in the flanks."

I had to laugh. "I can't even reach the flanks, much less kick them."

He had the horse trot slowly round and round so I could get the rhythm. Then one of his comrades showed up.

"What's the matter with this lazy beast? Can't he go any faster?" he said and swatted the stallion on the behind. The horse reared and whinnied, then bolted off straight toward the orchard. I held on desperately to that saddle while branches flung and ripped at me. The only reason I did not fall off was because my feet were caught in the straps. When I finally got one foot out I tried to slide off, but the other was still caught. The horse dragged me on the ground over prickly weeds, rocks and protruding roots. I covered my head and face with my arms. Finally I freed my other foot also and fell to the ground and just lay there, afraid to move, afraid to find out how many bones of mine were broken. The horse took off. The aide and his buddy came running, huffing and puffing.

"God damn," they swore, "that stud is heading straight for the Russian side. He is gone. We'll never see him again."

Then they looked at me. "Are you all right?"

I was not sure. I hurt all over. Blood was running down one side of my face. When I tried to stand up, I could not bear to put my weight on my left foot.

"You damn moron," the aide turned on his buddy. "It's all your fault."

"Gee...I'm sorry...I'm sorry. I just wanted to help," he said.

The fellows had to carry me back to my quarters. Inge was the first to see me. "Holy Bimbam!" she exclaimed. "What happened to you?"

"I fell."

"Off what?"

"A horse."

"Man! Will you ever be in trouble when Molkow finds out!"

"If you don't blabber he doesn't have to know. I'm going to tell him that I fell. That's all."

By now my eye and my ankle had swollen and turned color. I had scratches and bruises all over my arms and legs.

"How in heck can you dance tonight? You can't even walk," Inge worried.

"I'm going to try."

I cleaned the blood away and put cold compresses on the swollen areas, and later applied makeup over the most obvious spots.

"Why do you always do things you are not supposed to do? That's why you're constantly in trouble. You know the rules about horse back riding." Inge scolded me, sounding like Erika.

"Rules..." I mocked. "Is that why all of you just stood there and did nothing when that SS lout kicked that woman? It's forbidden to ride a horse but it's all right to kick an old woman, and all right to send us to the front lines? Did it ever occur to you that if people didn't follow so many rules and did their own thinking, maybe there might not be a war?"

"All I know is, that if you had followed the rules, you wouldn't be hurt now."

"Yeah...maybe. On the other hand, if everybody thought like me, the generals would not get an army together to fight a war."

Inge threw her hands up in the air. "You are incorrigible."

I was able to conceal my injuries until we got ready for the show. "My God, girl, who ran into you?" Hannimusch noticed my injuries first, alerting Hilde, and Hilde told Molkow. They wanted to know what happened. I made up a story. When they did not believe the first one, I made up another one, more ridiculous than the first, until they gave up interrogating me.

I paid for my transgression with excruciating pain during the show. When I tried to go on toe, my ankle simply gave out. But I did not asked to stay out of the show, and nobody offered it to me. It was my decision to ride that horse, I figured, and I had to pay the consequences.

Afterwards, the major's aide came backstage, telling me so everybody could hear, "That stud never did come back. He went over to the Russians." I signaled him to shut up, putting a finger over my mouth, though Molkow and Hilde must have figured out by now what really happened. I never did learn what story the aide gave the major. The following day, however, the horse came trotting back to the stable, spry and unhurt.

Russia's weather heated up. We rode toward Orel in our bus, bumping along rough, unpaved roads and stirring up clouds of fine, powdery dust that penetrated everything. Grit got between our teeth and into our eyes. We had just enough water with us to take a sip now and then, not enough to rinse our dry mouths, or quench our thirst. Farmers out in the fields sprayed the land with honey-wagon-scent. The landscape looked peaceful and soothed our frayed nerves. But the war was never far away.

We came to a roadblock within view of a village.

"What's going on?" our driver asked the patrol.

"They are smoking out partisans."

Minutes later the air vibrated with explosions and a black cloud of smoke rose into the sky. The whole village suddenly stood ablaze and we heard machine gun fire.

I did not have to ask about the people in that village. There would be nothing left of them.

"Rules!" I reminded Inge. "That's the result of people following rules." Her face expressed horror, as did the faces of all the others.

"This is barbaric," Hannimusch said to the patrol.

"It's barbaric when they poison our water supply, not only killing our guys, but their own as well." He went on to tell us that his units had lost more men at the hands of the partisans than in the fighting.

"It's their lives or ours," the soldiers said.

Them or us. That was the bottom line.

Capt. Hugo - Roslavl

Hannimusch

Orel

From top to bottom — Theater, Dr. von Rauffer, Hospital

In Orel

Picnic with Russian Peasants Looking On

Hours before we were cut off by advancing Russians

Hilde Molkow kissing a *'Ritterkreuz'* recipient

Ilse, Inge and Elfi sunning on themselves

XIII

Orel

Traffic increased the closer we came to Orel. Military vehicles, hand carts, donkey-drawn carts, Russians on bicycles and on foot jammed a cobbled road dotted with potholes. A streetcar bulging with people clattered toward the heart of the city, stopping frequently to let people on or off. Our driver, a middle-aged infantry corporal, leaned on his horn when stops dragged out too long; otherwise he was resigned to wait for an opportunity to pass. That did not come until the street widened, leading to a bridge over the Oka river. In the afternoon sun the river glistened like a frayed ribbon of gold. Twisted metal and concrete boulders jutted out of its waters and cluttered its shores. Just beyond the bridge we turned right and stopped in front of one of several identical three-storied buildings.

"The artists' hotel," the driver announced. From the outside it looked like a newer apartment house. On the first floor it had a community kitchen, a dining hall, and toilets. The upper floors had large rooms, each with four to six beds and a wash basin with running cold water. Hannimusch immediately tried one of the faucets. It worked. "What do you know! Back to civilization," she cheered.

A Russian maid and the driver helped us carry our suitcases to the second floor where Molkow was engaged in the ritual of assigning rooms. I shared one with Inge and Ilse, reserving a bed next to mine for Erika, who would be arriving sometime soon.

Before doing anything else, I looked out of one of two large windows with a view of the river, the bridge, and a main street with little shops and a lot of traffic. Bathed in sunlight, Orel had none of the gloom of other Russian cities. It bustled with activity, simulating a sense of normalcy in spite of its ruins and battle scars. I felt I was back in the twentieth century and was a human being again.

As I stood there gazing out, hands reached up from behind and covered my eyes. I could not believe it, but it had to be. "Erika!" I squealed, turned and embraced my friend. She, Ulla, and Molkow's secretary had arrived ahead of schedule and had been waiting for us at the hotel.

"Let me look at you." I held Erika at arm's length. "You've never looked better."

"And you've put on a few pounds," she teased me. I was sorely aware of that, but not exactly pleased to hear her point it out.

"It must have been the barley soup," I joked. "But I'll tell you about that later. We have so much to catch up on, it'll take weeks." The few pounds I had lost over the barley diet, I had put back on again.

After unpacking, we met in the dining room downstairs. Neither of us noticed what we ate that evening. We were much too excited to be back together again, and too interested in what Molkow's secretary had to report from the home front. He was actually an Italian Count with a long, unpronounceable name that started with the letter M. Thus we addressed him either as *Herr von M.*, or *Herr Baron*. He confirmed what we had read in letters. Berlin and other German cities were under siege. Thousands had died under the hail of bombs. Thousands more had lost their homes and everything they owned. Having no place to go, people took up residence in subways or cavities beneath the rubble of former dwellings. Some starved or froze to death. Some wandered the streets in madness, searching for family members they would never again find. Hand-scribbled messages posted on ruins everywhere asked for or gave information about the where-abouts of those who had lived there. One of the saddest scenes to witness, the Count said, was when wounded veterans returned home, looking for their families, only to learn they had lost both.

In Berlin services such as water, electricity, gas, tele-phone, trains and transportation were often disrupted for days, weeks and months. Prisoners--criminal, political and POWs--cleared the streets, disarmed bombs which had not exploded, and took care of the most necessary and urgent repairs to keep life going. Food rations were further reduced from month to month. Without some connection to a farmer and with nothing to trade, people hungered down to skeletons. The black market flourished in spite of the death penalty for anyone caught dealing in it. Farmers cashed in on their good fortune. The poorest among them suddenly had expensive carpets covering dirt floors, and mink coats hanging in their closets. They squirreled away chests full of silver and gold, including wedding rings, collected in trade for a few eggs, a little butter, a chicken or a ham. Long the underdog, looked down upon by city folk, the butt of jokes, the farmer was now king. Not all, but quite a few took vengeful advan-tage of the situation, reveling in the sudden humility of the high and mighty, who formerly would not allow them to cross their front door, much less invite them into their parlor. These snobs now bowed at their feet. "Everyone for himself. That seems to be the motto of the day," Herr von M. concluded.

We hung on to every word he said, way into the night, and forgot for the moment all about the suitcase full of mail he had brought from the home office and the boxes with our summer clothes. That had to wait till morning. As we trailed off to bed, I passed Hannimusch, Ulla and Hilde standing in a huddle in the hallway, whispering. I overheard Hannimusch gasp and say, "I didn't know he is Jewish."

Wonder what that's about, I thought, but shrugged it off as something that did not concern me.

Later, after Inge and Ilse were already asleep, Erika and I were still talking. She told me that the Baron came close to being arrested when the border control at Brest checked his pass and ID. She had been surprised to learn that he was of Jewish descent.

"I thought he is an Italian Count," I said.

"He is, but his mother was Jewish." According to Erika, the military patrols interrogated him, but finally let him go. "He was extremely nervous from then on and started to shake every time a patrol came around to check our papers."

I had always been curious why he worked for Molkow. He seemed too elegant, too suave, too manicured to be working as a mere secretary. His title fit him perfectly. He also could have passed as a movie star. I could picture him in the role of a high-class spy.

"He mentioned being indebted and very grateful to Molkow for giving him this job," Erika reported.

"Molkow...?" I shook my head, "It's not like Molkow to stick his neck out to do somebody a favor. There's got to be something in it for him."

"I don't know." Erika yawned. "Maybe Molkow is not as bad as you think."

Erika and I talked until sleep finally overpowered us. Morning and the wake-up call came much too soon. It took some effort to drag ourselves out of bed.

"Come on you two, today is payday," Inge urged us along.

Payday in Russia did not excite me because there was nothing to buy and what small salary I got went straight away into a savings account. The only money I spent was on tips here and there.

At breakfast, Herr von M. had all the payroll receipts and deposits ready for us to sign. My check was for 180 marks for four months.

"How come only 180 marks?" I questioned. "That should be 240 marks plus our combat zone bonus?"

"Herr Molkow deducted 60 marks, one month's salary for an evening in Warsaw."

"Oh? I thought Dieter and Herr Molkow were treating us?"

"I wouldn't know anything about that."

"And what about the combat bonus?"

"Herr Molkow does not have you on the list to receive a combat zone bonus," the Baron answered in a cool, business-like manner.

"What list? It's not he that's paying it; it's the military. We are all in the same zone, so we should all get the same bonus."

"I am sorry. You have to take that up with Herr Molkow." With that, he turned to the next one in line, intimating that his business with me was finished. His aloof, capsuled manner left no room for questions or debate and was intimidating. He was a master at keeping people at a distance, using a minimum of words.

Left standing there I did not know how to respond. Boiling inside, I threw my head back and stomped out of the room. In the hallway I stopped Ilse, "Did you get your bonus?" She only shrugged her shoulder, not wanting to be drawn into a dispute. Back in the room I asked Inge. "No. I didn't get a bonus. And that cheapskate even deducted 60 marks for Warsaw," she griped.

Only Uschi admitted, "Of course. We are all supposed to get combat pay."

"Well, I didn't. Inge didn't either," I complained.

A little later at lunch I was still brooding over what to do when Erika nudged me. "What's the matter with you?" she asked. "You have hardly said a word all morning. Are you mad at me for something?"

"Why no, silly." I smiled and gave her a little shove. "I am mad all right, but not at you." Molkow was sitting at the other end of the table with Hilde and his secretary. I do not know what gave me the courage, but I suddenly got up and walked over to them. "Herr Molkow," I said, "I would like to talk to you about the combat pay."

Conversation around the table suddenly hushed.

"What about it?" he answered with his mouth full of food.

"Do you want me to discuss that here, or later in your room?" All eyes focused on us. Hilde elbowed her husband while pretending to search through her purse. Molkow looked around and saw all eyes staring at him. "After lunch then," he grumbled.

My heart pounded with stage fright as I later knocked on Molkow's door. "Come in," Hilde answered. Molkow was playing solitaire, not even looking up as I entered.

"Herr Molkow," I approached him. "About the combat

zone bonus...as I understand it, the military pays that to anyone, soldier or civilian, who works and serves within a combat zone. So why do you withhold that from some of us? We are exposed to the same dangers, suffer the same hardships. We are entitled to it."

Molkow continued with his solitaire game and said nothing. Feeling awkward just standing there, with anger building inside me, I brought up another sore subject. My voice sounded hoarse, my heart pounded wildly, but I was determined not to let him scare me off, or freeze me out, or sweep my complaints under the table. I tried to remain businesslike and polite.

"I also would like you to explain how you justify paying me only 60 marks per month, yet you feature me as first soloist. My contract with you describes me as an apprentice, meaning that I am in training under you in preparation for the State exam. But for the year-and-a-half that I have been with you, the only thing I've learned are the numbers in the repertoire. Technically I have been sliding backwards. I know I won't pass my exam as a dancer six months from now. Something is not fair or right here."

Molkow's face turned red. I expected him to rear up from his chair at any second and spew fire. Hilde sat at the edge of her bed manicuring her nails, looking up every so often in nervous tension. But Molkow finished his game, folded his cards, got up from his chair and walked toward the door. "Your contract mentions no bonuses of any kind," he said before he walked out.

"Nor did it mention that I would be spending six months on the Russian front. I'll have to check into that a little deeper," I said. Anxiety and anger consumed my voice. He probably did not hear me anymore, but Hilde did.

"He'll do what is right. You'll get what you are entitled to," she tried to assure me, feeling obligated to smooth things over. But she could not look me in the eye.

Suddenly, like in a jigsaw puzzle, all the pieces fit into place. Herr von M. had reason to be grateful to Molkow for giving him a job and, perhaps, protection. None of us would have ever guessed that Herr von M. was half Jewish, had it not been for the German military border patrol who checked his papers. He did not have to wear an arm-band with the yellow star and the word '*Jude*' on it. This obligated him to Molkow who, on the other hand, needed the Baron to keep quiet about the books and the money he was siphoning off from us. He could count on Herr von M. to reveal or say nothing against him. That all made sense to me now.

Getting back to my room, the girls wanted to know how I had fared. "He didn't kill you? What did he say?"

"Not much," I answered.

I gnashed my teeth and looked at Erika. "Maybe he's not as bad as I think, you say? Hah! He is more crooked than a vine on a grape stake," I told her. "But I won't let him off the hook. You can bet on that."

Meanwhile the girls had claimed their packages and were unpacking their summer clothes plus some treats from home. Ilse received perfume and a lipstick from Paris where a relative of hers was stationed. Erika's mother had sent her dried fruit from her own orchard. Inge received pictures of her family and dog, taken before they were bombed out. Most of these packages had been sent at least eight weeks ago to Molkow's home office. I inquired about mine.

"You were with Molkow when Herr von M. brought them into the dining room. Hannimusch helped him. Ask her," the girls answered.

"Then mine must still be down there." I flew down the hall and down the stairs, taking two...three steps at a time only to find the dining room empty. Back up the stairs I ran, knocking on Hannimusch's door. "Have you got my package in there?" Hannimusch let me in. "No," she said, "we handed out all the packages that were there."

"But I didn't get mine yet."

"I don't remember seeing one for you. Better ask Herr von M.. He has the list." Panic settled like lead in my legs. My knees threatened to buckle under me. Nothing was going right that day. I dashed out of the room, al-most knocking Uschi, who was coming in, to the ground. Out of the corner of my eye I saw the Baron in the hall just as he entered Molkow's room.

"Wait...wait..." I yelled. Herr von M. leaned back out

of the doorway. "Can you tell me where my package is?" The Baron opened the briefcase he had clutched under his arm and took out a sheet of paper. "It looks like all the packages have been distributed. I brought with me everything that arrived in Berlin before my departure." He studied the list and shook his head. "I don't see your name on the list. Maybe your parents didn't send your things in time, or they got held up somewhere. I am sorry."

I was in shock. All strength drained from my body. "Not one summer dress, no shoes...what am I going to do for the next three months in this heat?" With tears streaming down my face I returned to my room. The lightest clothes in my wardrobe were a wool skirt with two short-sleeved, frayed and worn out blouses.

"Maybe, we can lend you something," Inge and Erika tried to console me. They themselves did not have much to wear, and whatever they had did not fit me.

I was devastated. I saw myself as the Cinderella in the group, minus a fairy godmother. "My folks couldn't have forgotten to send my things, knowing how badly I needed them."

"The package may have gotten lost, or delayed," Erika consoled.

Whatever the reason, I threw myself on the bed and sobbed.

Ilse, who had the largest wardrobe of any of us, felt sorry for me and offered me one of her summer dresses. "I never liked it on me anyway," she said. Luckily, it did fit me. One silk summer dress with klutzy and worn out brown saddle shoes. It did nothing for my ego. Only minutes before I had felt really proud of myself, quite smug, actually, for having found the courage to confront Molkow. That did not even seem important now.

To cheer me up, the girls and Hannimusch coaxed me into walking with them to the theater. It was not far and we could explore some of the shops along the way, especially a little ice cream parlor we spotted coming into Orel. This was the first time in Russia that we saw shops open for business. Armed with a few Russian words-- please, thank you, hello, good bye, how much, yes and no--we were eager to investigate what they had to offer.

202

The ice cream parlor was nothing but a hole in the wall, cluttered with buckets, sacks, bags, and rusty tin cans filled with colored, crushed ice. It looked more like a paint shop than anything else. Against one wall stood two small round tables with chairs, already occupied by dozens of flies. After a quick survey of the place we retreated, waving to the young girl who came to serve us, "Nyet... don't bother."

"No thanks," Hannimusch said and grimaced as we walked away. "I wouldn't put anything into my mouth coming from this place." A bit further down the street we came upon a hair salon. In it sat women looking like Medusas with black snakes growing out of their scalps. A strong smell of ammonia made our eyes water.

"They are doing permanents here," Inge exclaimed. "Maybe we can get our hair fixed." Our hair had become unmanageable, oily, with split-end frizz, because we had to put it up in rollers every night. Desperate enough, we went inside and asked with a lot of hand motions if we could get our hair cut and permed. An attendant, who spoke a little German, answered our questions, and gave us a hand-on-heart assurance they would do a good job. We agreed to come back the next day.

Just a few blocks from there was the theater. Another slanted stage. A group of Russian singers had just finished rehearsing. We had a friendly exchange with them, and they stayed to watch our rehearsal. They seemed as curious about us as we were about them.

I could tell that we would give a good performance that night. Ulla and Erika were back in the show, we had fresh, clean costumes and had a clean, decent place to stay--all reasons to lift our spirits. Even I looked forward to the show and I danced my heart out. I had to. It was one way to rid myself of all my pent-up anger and frustrations. Since Smolensk, I had no more problems with my legs. It was all caused by dancing on that cement stage. I could leap again higher than anybody in our company and could do Russian wheels and understeps without even having to breathe hard.

That night, our performance ended in triumph. After the Hungarian Rhapsody the audience went wild. People threw money on the stage, clapped and stomped and would not let us get off the stage. And every time I took my solo bow, the applause rose even higher. I Knew I had done my job, and done it well. Most of the audience, we were told, came from a nearby hospital, including the staff, the recovering wounded, plus many Russians who worked there. After the show, the hospital staff invited us to a reception.

When we arrived there, I found myself instantly surrounded by a group of officers who showered me with compliments about my performance, and insisted I join them at their table. Flattered, still glowing and happy over our success, I just smiled and let them usher me to their table. One of the men introduced himself as Chaplain Albert Schmidt. Tall, trim, with dark, hypnotic eyes and a cynical smile, he looked every bit the villain in a seductive sort of way. His black hair came to a sinister point in the middle of his forehead. I pictured him in the role of the evil *Iago* in *Othello* or the *Mephisto* in *Faust*, yet he was a pastor. This intrigued me. Next to him stood his total opposite, a short, stocky, round-faced major whom the chaplain introduced as his friend Dr. von Rauffer.

During the course of the evening I learned quite a lot about each, partly from what they told me about themselves, and partly from the quick-witted repartee between them. Dr. von Rauffer was a highly respected, well known surgeon from Poznan and also an accomplished baritone. He was asked to sing a couple of arias later on and I was amazed at the volume, warmth and beauty of his voice. He was also nice to talk to, open, kind, with a wonderful sense of humor. I felt truly honored to have the attention of these two most interesting men.

What the chaplain lacked on vocal talent, he made up for in the way he could make his words sing. In a low, soft tone he uttered flattering comments, one after another, making each word feel like a kiss. He made my heart pound and my reason fog over. Sirens should have gone off in my head.

At one point Dr. von Rauffer warned, "Don't trust his collar. He really is a wolf in sheep's clothing."

"I believe you," I admitted laughingly. But that was what fascinated me about him. Never before had I met a pastor, a chaplain who whispered such outrageously seductive things in my ear. He compared me to a goddess, made references to the curves of my body and my 'alabaster' skin, saying he felt the urge to kiss every inch of it. Not in my wildest dreams would I have expected such beguilement from a man that preached the gospel. Not once did he refer to my soul, or even mentioned God.

"What made you decide to become a pastor?" I could not refrain from asking.

"Because the propaganda minister's job was already filled," Dr. von Rauffer intercepted with a wink. He referred to Josef Goebbels, Hitler's smooth-tongued mouthpiece, also known to be a womanizer and an eloquent liar. The Chaplain just laughed it off.

Taking my hand, Dr. von Rauffer asked me, "Do you like horses?"

"I love them. I love all animals."

"Can you ride?"

I told him what had happened to me not too long ago on the back of that big stallion that charged through an orchard and almost delivered me to the Russians.

"I would never put you on a horse like that. And you don't have to ride if you don't want to. But a friend of mine, a cavalry captain, oversees a former hunting lodge with large stables not very far from Orel. It is a beautiful place, very peaceful, where one can forget the war for awhile. Would you like me to take you there?"

"That sounds wonderful. Only I would need my boss' permission."

"I'll talk to him. If it's all right with him, is it a date?"

"Oh, yes," I said eagerly.

"You waste no time," the pastor jested, "taking her to the woods with you."

"You would, undoubtedly, invite her to church to pray with you?" Dr. von Rauffer bandied, laughing a hearty laugh.

"Unfortunately, I must bow out of the competition for a couple of days, but when I come back, watch out!" Pastor Schmidt warned. He continued all evening whispering seductive intimacies into my ear. Once, when Dr. von Rauffer briefly left the table, he leaned forward, gazed into my eyes and said, "Do you believe in destiny? Do you believe in love at first sight? I have a feeling we were meant to meet," he hummed. His eyes burned deep into mine. He was overpowering. I felt physically weak, ready to melt into his arms. Never in my life had I met anyone like him and thought such men existed only in romance novels. Face to face with one, I was overwhelmed. I was glad when Dr. von Rauffer's returned.

My feet, I could have sworn, did not touch the ground as I floated back to the hotel that night. Erika chatted all the way but I hardly heard a word she said. I went to bed in a daze.

The next voice I heard was Erika's. "Elfi, Elfi," she shook me and waved her hand in front of my face, "Wake up, we have to go to the hair dresser."

It was another gorgeous warm day. Inge, Erika and I strolled across the bridge, past the hospital, the theater, and the ice cream shop, catching the eye of German soldiers walking or driving by. Some yelled at us in Russian, others made remarks in German, none of them quite sure to which side we belonged.

"We must be looking pretty ragged if they can't tell us apart from the Russians anymore," I concluded. Russian women, even the young, wore drab, colorless clothes. I had not seen one who looked particularly well groomed. Young girls sometimes wore flowers in their hair, or a bright scarf. From what we had observed so far, women were the work horses in Russia. In the fields, we had seen many times men leading the horses and women doing the planting, the bending, the lifting, the hauling.

By the time we arrived at the hair dresser's Erika had changed her mind and backed out of having her hair done. "I want to see how yours turns out first," she said.

I was ushered to a chair in front of a counter and immediately asked to hold my head over a large, chipped enameled bowl in front of me. Without towel, frock or anything else to protect my face and clothes, a woman attendant poured a pitcher full of cold water over my head. Then she wrung out my hair like a rag and when it quit dripping she used a dingy, frayed cloth to squeeze it out even more. A man from the shop lit a spirit burner and set on it a ball shaped, copper vessel. At the same time the girl dowsed my hair with ammonia solution and rolled it onto short, thumb-sized tubing. My eyes teared. I coughed and gasped for breath. "My Lord, how can they stand this stink all day long?" I shouted over to Inge, who underwent the same treatment. She could not reply because of a choking spell.

When steam flowed out of the holes in the copper ball, the man attached a half dozen rubber hoses on to them and connected the other ends to the tubes in my hair. After about fifteen minutes--I thought my scalp was on fire--he detached the long tubes and inserted them into the next section of rollers. After my hair was cooked and the last rollers had cooled, the girl removed them and again doused my head with cold water. As before, she wrung my hair out and said I was finished.

"Finished?" I questioned.

"Da," she answered with a nod and pointed to a broken mirror on one wall. I took one look and flinched. Inge and I paid and fled without even attempting to comb through our wet, kinky manes. Once out of earshot Erika let loose with laughter and opinions about Russia's antiquated hair salon. "They don't bother with shampoo, they just incinerate the dirt," she chortled and backed away, holding her nose, every time we came too close to her.

"Bet you, I'm going to have burn blisters all over my head. Didn't your rollers get hot?" I asked Inge.

"Hot?" she repeated, "I was afraid they'd cook my brain."

"That's also a good place to pick up lice," Erika warned.

"No way," I assured her, "lice don't hang around a place like that. Only we are that stupid."

The first person to see us when we got back to the hotel was Hilde. "Holy Mother, what did you do to your hair?" she screeched. "It looks like the inside of a horse hair mattress." She was not exaggerating. Inge and I immediately asked for hot water so we could, first of all, shampoo the smell away, and secondly, relax the tight curls. Touching our hair after it dried was like touching steel wool.

"By the way," Ilse remembered, "that short, chubby major you sat with last night came by. He left you a note." She pointed to my pillow. I picked it up.

207

"Liebes Fraulein Elfi," it read,
"Everything is set for tomorrow noon. Am on duty until then and may be delayed. Therefore, please meet me at the hospital. Ask any aide. They know where to find me. I'll try to catch the show again tonight; otherwise I'll see you tomorrow.
    Yours, von Rauffer."

I was pleased to hear from him.

Whenever we performed at a place longer than a day or two, we attracted our individual cheering sections, who came night after night. We loved to flirt and interact with our audiences, which made the show more fun for us and more spirited, too. Again, like in Smolensk, invitations poured in from near and far to visit, party, or perform at the various units around the city. Competition for our company was keen, making us feel like celebrities.

Molkow accepted a late dinner invitation from headquarters in a place called 'Mäuseturm' (Mouse Tower). We were told that the aristocracy of the military would be there. Names being tossed around included Jodl, Model, von Manstein and Prince von Metternich. It sounded very impressive. Ilse was in her glory. The way I fell for dark eyes, she fell for titles. When we arrived there, Ilse immediately focused on a handsome young officer who, someone told her, was a prince. She pulled all her wily routines, even faking a faint, collapsing in front of him. As a gentleman would, he lifted and carried her to a chair. But as she seemed to recover he left her in the hands of an aide. She did not get to sit with him. Knowing each other so well, the rest of us knew what was going on and watched, totally amused.

The evening passed quickly and we returned to our hotel at a decent hour. Erika and I talked for awhile then went to bed. I looked forward to the next day and my date with Dr. von Rauffer and a horse.

I arrived at the hospital early. A medic gave me directions to Dr. von Rauffer's office. The hospital was huge. I walked up the broad stone steps divided by a polished brass railing, and along a wide corridor with many doors, most of them open, allowing a look inside large wards filled with men patients. In the air hung the familiar odor of ether, blood and iodine. At the end of the hall, where I was told I would find Dr. von Rauffer's office, the door stood open. I stepped in and stopped cold. Not ten feet away, two men in white aprons with a cloth over nose and mouth, were sawing off a man's leg. I froze. All the blood in my body seemed to drain into my feet and everything went black.

Returning to consciousness, I found myself propped in a wicker armchair by a window with a nurse in attendance. "Do you feel better?" she asked.

A little confused at first, I nodded, "I am fine." Then I remembered. "Guess I just blacked out. I've never seen an amputation before."

The nurse handed me a cup of tea. "The doctor will be with you shortly."

"Dear child," Dr. von Rauffer said, rushing through the door. "This must have been a terrible experience for you. I am so sorry you had to witness this. Never even thought that you would be walking in." He patted my hand. "If and when you feel up to it, let's get out of this place. What do you say?"

I was ready. We did not walk, we ran down the stairs and out of the building and to where his motorcycle was parked. As if we could not escape this place fast enough, he jumped onto the seat and I climbed into the sidecar and off we rode. We rode to the end of the city, into sun-baked country, leaving a cloud of dust behind us. By a grove of trees Dr. von Rauffer throttled the engine and stopped. He took a deep breath and said, "I do so love the country." Peasants worked in the fields, unloading and scattering manure from atop an oxcart. The air was potent with freshly plowed, dunged earth.

The doctor inhaled deeply. I made a face and pinched my nose. He looked at me and smiled. "You pinch your nose," he said, "but have you ever given it a thought when you eat a slice of freshly baked bread, that this is where it begins?" He pointed to the fields. "This dung-covered soil produces the grain from which bread is made."

"I had never thought of it that way," I answered.

"Think about it. You'll find that this is so with many things. Everything has its cycle."

"Everything?"

"Everything," he confirmed. "Think of the seasons, think of the water in the ocean, birth and death."

"What about death? When a person dies that's the end, isn't it?"

"We don't know that. I am certain that the law of nature applies to us and to our death as well."

I looked at this man beside me. His deep-set eyes wandered over the fields to the horizon. His round, clean shaven face mirrored a gentle, inner calm.

When we arrived at the lodge, his friend, the Rittmeister, came out to greet us. He was a somewhat older man with a moustache, nearing fifty maybe, slim and straight. "Come on in. Come on in. Lunch is waiting and I am hungry as a bear," he welcomed us. On a large, open porch stood a round table, already set with odds and ends of dinner ware, and around it stood four comfortable looking wicker chairs. "Sit wherever you like," he said, "this is quite informal."

While the two men exchanged bits of personal news, my eyes wandered around the house. It was built out of solid logs sealed with mud, atop a stone foundation. On the outside as well as on the inside hung hunting trophies; antlers, stuffed animal heads and birds. Large French doors opened to a huge room with a massive stone fireplace. A long, heavy table with legs carved into animal paws, and matching leather-upholstered, straight-back chairs occupied the center of the room. In one corner next to the fireplace, a leather couch and several round leather armchairs made a cozy seating arrangement. On the other side, a steep set of stairs seemed to lead to a loft. Everything about this place was massive and masculine.

"Well, what do you think?" Dr. von Rauffer asked me.

"This is quite a place," I answered. "To whom did it belong? Nobility?"

"At one time, yes, it did. But wait till you see the stables."

An orderly entered with a bottle of wine and filled our glasses. The Rittmeister proposed a short toast.

"By the way, my friends call me Rauff," the doctor said to me with a wink. "And him they call Ritt." So, Rauff and Ritt it was, and we drank to that.

The orderly placed a large bowl of stew on the table and started serving. It smelled wonderful.

"We had to kill a horse the other day," Ritt mentioned to Rauff, then promptly caught himself with a sheepish grin. Rauff glared at his friend.

I took one bite of the stew and knew what Ritt stopped short of telling. Horsemeat has a peculiar sweet taste. I remembered it from my childhood days. I used to like it. Now it made me gag. I ate very little. It was almost as bad as the barley soup.

Finished with lunch, we headed for the stables. Inside, pointing at long, double rows of stalls, Ritt explained, "This stable was full only six months ago. Today we have only five horses left and even they may be shipped back to Germany shortly."

"The way the war is going, so are we," Rauff added.

I did not understand much about horses, but the ones left were beautiful, sleek and graceful, not like that monstrous stallion I had ridden a while back.

"Oh, if only I could ride one of them," I sighed.

"Why not?" Rauff encouraged me.

"Why not," I echoed, once again breaking the rules.

Rauff rode out with me into the open country, patiently teaching me some of the fundamentals of riding until I got the hang of it.

"Do you have horses of your own?" I asked him.

"In Poznan, yes. My entire family loves and rides horses," he said with pride. He reached into his pocket and pulled out a leather wallet with pictures of them. "Just got them in the mail," he said and showed them to me. "My wife, my sons..." he explained who the people in the pictures were.

"How long since you've seen them?" I asked.

"It's been over a year," he sighed and looked at the pictures for a long second before putting them back into his wallet. "As long as the wounded keep pouring in I can't get away. There is a shortage of surgeons," he said. He told me about his family, his home, his estate in Poznan. His voice became hoarse with emotion. Suddenly, he spurred his horse and charged a short distance ahead.

I understood. Pain and sadness had become the warp in the tapestry of our lives.

My horse wanted to follow his. I could not control it. When it caught up with the Doctor, he smiled at me. "You have to learn to control this beast."

The hours flew by. I finally got the hang of a gallop and the two of us raced each other from one clump of trees to another. Then it was time to return. Rauff and I rode slowly toward the stables and talked. He asked me about my family. I told him about my brother. We talked about the war and that he feared having to move his family westward. "Before the year is up, the Russians will be in Poland," he guessed. "It's going to be a fight for survival from now on."

We said good-bye to Ritt, then drove back to Orel. In the hallway of the hotel Rauff kissed my hand. "You are a dear," he said. "May I call on you again? Tomorrow?"

"I would be delighted," I replied with sincerity.

XIV

Small Victories

A good part of our audience every night came from a large air base near Orel and it just so happened that a Stuka pilot, a childhood friend of mine, was stationed there. He saw our show, recognized me and came back stage.

I just stared at him, speechless.

"*Geh, schau net so dumm. I bin's, da Alex!*" he greeted me in true Bavarian fashion, grinning from ear to ear. "When I saw you up there I asked my buddy to pinch me to make sure I wasn't dreaming. That girl up there, I told him, looks like the girlfriend of my best friend's sister."

"Alex!" I squealed. "I can't believe it is you! Where did you come from?"

The last time I had seen him he had just turned nineteen. That was about a year ago. I punched him in the arm like I used to do when we were kids and he teased me.

"When did you get your wings? I must say, you look mighty sharp in that lieutenant's uniform."

"Hey! You don't look so bad yourself. A long shot from that scrawny kid we chased down the street with those big grasshoppers. Remember? Bet you still haven't forgiven me for that," he laughed.

Molkow prodded me to hurry and get dressed.

"Wish we had time to chat. Can you get away during the day some time?" I asked, feeling pushed.

"I'll do better than that. I'm going to get you kids out to the base. My old man is the commander there."

His buddies grew impatient, too, yelling for him to get on the bus.

"Got to go, or I'll have to walk back," he said, "but I'll be seeing you. You can count on it."

That is where we had to leave it for the moment. Molkow had accepted an invitation and was eager to get there. He acted antsy. It was to be another special affair for the high command with the generals.

The bus dropped us off in front of a large iron gate leading to a garden. We passed under a long canvas awning screened off with mosquito netting, where an earlier reception must have taken place. Nearly empty punch bowls, empty trays, glasses and plates cluttered a long, sheeted table. The party had moved to the inside of an adjoining hall--a former gymnasium--where officers from various branches of the military stood around in clusters, waiting for dinner to be served. When it came time to sit down, Molkow placed me across the table from him next to a bull-necked Colonel with a monocle. "Another dull evening," I said to myself, and immediately thought of ways to shorten it. During dinner, the colonel complimented me on my dancing and my figure. "It is nice to see a dancer with curves," he said. "Most are flat as a board." He expounded on what he thought to be the ideal size and shape of a woman's breast. Oh, God, give me a break, I thought.

Immediately after dinner I excused myself and left the room for a breath of fresh air. On the way out I met Erika who was equally bored and tired and we decided to sit this party out under the stars. Passing the banquet table under the canopy, I noticed that the punch bowls still had all kinds of fruit in them--canned peaches, pears, and fresh strawberries--delicacies we had not tasted for a long time.

"Hey, Erika," I nudged her. "How is this for dessert?" No one was around, so I quickly skimmed some fruit into a couple of glasses and then the two of us reclined in lawn chairs and munched on them, feeling quite smug. The fruit was delicious. I sneaked back several more times for refills. We had a great time talking and laughing, and filling each other in on our experiences during the time we had been apart.

That was the last thing I remembered.

My eyes opened to a bright midday sun. At first I did not know where I was, or how I got there. It took a while before I realized that I was in bed...in my bed, thank God...but for my life I could not recall anything that happened between the time I sat with Erika slurping fruit and the present. My head felt like a balloon about to pop. When I tried to sit up, the room spun around like a whirlpool. I felt sick to my stomach. "What happened?" I groaned. Inge and Ilse were all dressed and ready to go somewhere. "My God, what time is it?" I mumbled bewildered.

"It's noon," Inge said. "You better get up."

From the direction of Erika's bed came a long, drawn-out moan. I tried to turn my head to look but the slightest move activated hammers inside my head and made me even more dizzy and nauseous. Out of the corner of my eye I saw Erika sit on the edge of her bed holding her head between her hands. "Someone please tell me what happened?" she groaned.

"You got drunk. That's what happened," Ilse jeered. "You couldn't even walk, we had to carry you back."

Slowly, I propped myself up, feeling even woozier when I tried to stand. The floor seemed to slant uphill and my body tried to compensate by leaning into it. "How could I have gotten drunk? I did not have a single drink," I defended myself.

"That's a laugh! You are disgusting." Ilse reveled in righteousness.

A little later Hilde came in. "You made a proud spectacle of yourselves, getting that drunk. You ought to be ashamed," she scorned.

"But...but...we didn't even have one drink. Honest! We just had some fruit from those punch bowls outside. That's all," I insisted.

"Great God!" Hilde rolled her eyes upward and hit her forehead with the heel of her hand. "Well! That explains it! How stupid can you be? Don't you know that fruit soaks up the alcohol? Eating it is like drinking straight brandy."

215

Erika and I looked at each other, dumbfounded.

"Oh, yeah...? Well, we know now," I groaned.

Hilde gave us a couple of aspirins and sent Inge to the kitchen for coffee or tea.

I felt so sick that I could barely dress myself. Before I could put a comb to my wild, kinky hair, a maid brought a message that Dr. von Rauffer was downstairs wishing to see me.

"Oh, no! Not now!" I winced, wishing I could disappear into thin air. "What am I going to do?" Still unable to walk straight, sick to my stomach and looking every bit as bad as I felt, I did not know what to say. "Tell him I'm not here," I instructed the maid to say, but retracted it a second later. What if Hilde had already told him? "No...no...wait. Tell him I'll be down in a few minutes." If I did not go downstairs to meet Rauff, he would probably come up, especially if he thought I was sick. I really did not want him to see me this way. With makeup I tried to cover the deep circles under my eyes and the gray-green color of my face. I turned to Erika, "How do I look?"

She squinted at me for a second then said, "Like leftovers."

"Just don't breathe on anybody," Ilse volunteered, fanning her face as I passed by her.

Rauff took one glance at me and asked. "Are you sick?"

I nodded, then told him the whole horrid story. He started laughing till the tears rolled down his cheek. "I'll bet this will cure you forever to pick the fruit out of punch bowls."

"Forever," I assured him.

"Let's go for a walk," he suggested and offered me his arm.

"I don't know if I can," I told him honestly. "All I want to do is go back to bed."

"The best thing is to sweat it out," he insisted.

Since Molkow had already given his permission, I suffered along. It was a hot day. The bright sun hurt my eyes. Rauff walked me to the hospital, got me a tall glass of lemonade, then we strolled up and down along the river. Oh, I was sick. But he talked to me and coaxed me along. After an hour I returned to the hotel well enough to put cold towels on Erika's head. By show time we both felt better but had more trouble than ever navigating up and down that slanted stage in our still woozy condition.

That night the chaplain sat in the front row. That made my head spin even more. I felt a rush of nervous energy, and by the end of the show I was exhausted. Molkow, who had a hangover himself, decided to go straight to the hotel. I was glad.

Like headquarters in Smolensk, the hospital became our anchor point. Any night our group was not committed to some other place, we stopped there and always, there were Rauff and the chaplain. It was Rauff who had my unequaled respect and admiration; but it was Albert who activated my hormones and fanned my romantic fantasies. In Albert's presence I felt vulnerable and tempted. "Damn," one voice inside me scolded, "pull yourself together." Another voice argued "Why? You might be dead tomorrow." My fascination with the Pastor was tempered only by Rauff's wise and patient counsel. He allowed me to test on him my innermost thoughts and feelings about life and death, and love and war. Through a serious exchange of values and ideas, I gained confidence in my own judgments.

I learned that the chaplain was married. It did not hurt me this time like it did when Karlemann confessed that he was married. However, it still was a betrayal. Albert was a chaplain who daily preached the Ten Commandments and the word of God. I often wondered if preachers believed in what they were preaching. With Albert it was "Do as I say, not as I do." The next time he whispered seductive flattery in my ear, I confronted him-- I had the grit to do that now--and asked for an explanation. He laughed it off and continued right on with his ardent pursuit. What a cad, I thought. Still, every encounter caused my heart to flutter and my blood to pound in my ears with the roar of an ocean. Part of me rejected him, and another part attracted me to him beyond all common sense and reason. I could not understand myself. Was there something wrong with me? When I fell for Karlemann I thought it was love divine; love that could only happen once in a lifetime, and that it would last just as long, like the love between my parents. It was different

217

from the crushes I used to have, the kind Erika kidded me about. I felt the same excitement over Albert as I had felt over Karlemann, and that scared me.

Rauff was a good diversion, and I really liked being with him. I felt comfortable to talk to him.

Before our now, almost daily rides into the country, I accompanied Rauff on his hospital rounds. Many of his patients were amputees and often despondent, unable to face going home as cripples. Some were angry with the doctor, who, in order to save their lives, had to take off a leg or an arm. "You should have let me die," they complained bitterly. One now and then accused him of being a butcher.

"Indeed, I feel like one at times. Day after day I amputate, cutting young men's bodies to pieces, as well as their hopes and dreams. His hands tightened into fists. "So much young blood is being spilled...and for what?"

Separated from the large wards lay those already under the shadow of death, clinging to life with only a breath. Some had no arms, no legs, or even a face left. Horrified, I turned on Rauff. "Why do you try to save them? Why don't you end their pain?"

"Sometimes I would like to put a gun to my own head out of compassion for myself."

I wished I could retract what I had said. The only way I can describe his eyes and his face is by comparing it to a broken window on a burned-out house--desolated. I reached for his hand and squeezed it, hoping to convey just how sorry I was for saying what I did.

Later, on our way to the country, he pointed to a small church up on a hill. "Would you like to take a look inside?" he asked. "It's one of the oldest churches in the region, built in memory of crusaders who never returned."

I loved old places, and churches in particular. This one was a perfect example of early Gothic architecture. Except for the pointed arches of a massive portal and several side windows, no other adornments interrupted the straight, clean lines of the structure, including its spire. That was its charm. Rauff told me a little of the church's history. During the revolution, this monument to Christendom became a meeting place for the Russian underground. When the Bolsheviks discovered this, they raided it and slaughtered everyone inside. Later they turned the church into a shrine for fallen revolutionaries, replacing the cross with Lenin's picture. Now it was a church again.

Rauff opened the massive door. We walked into the cool, dim interior that echoed with our presence. On tip-toes we walked between the pews toward the simple al-tar--a table covered with a white, lace-trimmed cloth on a raised, stone platform. In the center of it sat an urn, em-bellished with an ornate cross, flanked by two candela-bras. Offerings of flowers haphazardly placed on the floor decorated the front of it.

An old Russian woman, shrouded in black, knelt on the stone steps to the altar, her eyes fixed on a picture of the black Madonna that hung above it. Her hands folded, absorbed in fervent prayer, she did not notice us.

"What God could refuse her prayer," I whispered. Rauff smiled and nodded. We did not want to disturb her and quietly exited.

Outside, Rauff confessed that he came here often. "In the cool, quiet solitude of this church I can get in touch with my soul, and with my agony," he said.

We rode off. When we came to a grassy knoll over-looking the river and parts of the city, Rauff stopped. He pulled a blanket from a knapsack, spread it over the grass, then unpacked some bread, salami, and a thermos with lemonade. We ate, soaked up the sunshine and let our eyes wander about the panoramic view, then stretched out and watched the clouds drift across the deep blue Russian sky. With every breath we drew in the soothing scent of this peaceful meadow. It was heaven. I thought of how lucky I was to be alive and to enjoy this serenity with Rauff, who had become my friend and men-tor. Simultaneously, I felt guilty to be so content, think-ing about the many who had died, and who were dying at this very instant while I enjoyed myself. I thought about the tragic casualties left behind at the hospital. I saw the faces of my brother, the young soldier in Smolensk, who died while I held his hand, and the captain and so many others.

"What do you think happens when we die?" I asked

Rauff.

My question did not seem to surprise him. "It is the end of pain," he said after a long silence. After another long pause he added, "And in one desperate moment not long ago, I forgot that it is also the end of joy." He reached for my hand. Staring at the sky, he added, "You see, about three weeks ago I tried to take my life."

I had heard a rumor, discarding it as impossible. From Rauff emanated such peace and inner strengh. But what I had seen in the hospital wards, what he had to do every day, I could not even blame him. Not knowing how to respond, I remained silent.

I thought of the Russian who jumped off the railcar, and the soldier who shot himself. I had moments myself when I did not care anymore if I lived or died.

"I think I understand," I said quietly.

Both of us lay quiet, staring at the clouds. Rauff still held my hand. "I don't know if you can understand," he broke the silence, "but these outings with you have meant so much to me. At first, you were just this vivacious dancer I admired and wanted to meet. I did not expect you to spend so much time with me, when you had so many admires to chose from. I am grateful. You allowed me to look at the world through fresh eyes.

"I have been enjoying every minute with you," I replied.

Back at the hotel, cheeks aglow from the sun, weeds still clinging to my hair, the girls razzed me. "Well, look at this wide eyed, blushing little Miss Innocence," Hannimusch joined in. Ilse was the worst. She referred to Rauff as the short, fat little doctor. "What's that cuddly, soft, stuffed teddy bear got that we have overlooked?"

"Oh...go slide off my back. It's none of your business anyway," I snapped at them.

"By the way, your flyer friend, Alex, dropped by. We are all going to the base tonight," Erika informed me. I was sorry that I had missed him.

It was still early in the afternoon. My mind lingered on the afternoon with Rauff. Suddenly, anti aircraft guns shattered the peace with deafening fury. I ran to the window and saw puffs of smoke explode against the blue sky. "An air raid? In the middle of the day?" Minutes later the big guns fell silent, replaced by a roar and the screaming of climbing and diving planes, and the ra-ta-ta-ta of machine guns. We could see them now.

"My heavens! There must be fifty planes up there and we are right underneath them. Let's get out of here," I yelled, running downstairs with Erika and Inge at my heels. There was no shelter in the building, or anywhere close by. We watched what we thought was the battle of all battles from under the doorway. The planes criss-crossed, dove, climbed and banked in wild pursuit of one another. It was hard to tell which were Russian and which German. We counted at least sixteen that went down. Some broke up in mid air; others spiraled down leaving a trail of black smoke. Some went into a dive from which they could not recover and crashed to the ground. Shrapnel and debris, small and large, hailed down around us. Windows shattered. The ground trembled. We ducked inside the building. The battle raged on and on. When it was over, we joined some civilians on the street collecting debris as souvenirs.

That evening, the air base was in the middle of a victory celebration when we arrived. Claim was that our side had shot down thirty-four Russian planes in the battle over Orel alone. Men toasted and dowsed each other with beer. Arms around each other's shoulders, they re-hashed the day's events, laughed and sang and got drunk. Our arrival remained unnoticed. We stood by the door of the officer's club like invisible intruders. My eyes searched in vain for Alex among the celebrants. Finally, an Air Force colonel approached and ushered us to a couple of tables away from the bar and all the activity. He apologized that the commandant would be unable to join us. I asked if he could let Alex know that we were here. "He is the commandant's son," I added. The colonel's face froze. He seemed at a loss for words. When he collected himself, he said that some flyers had not yet returned from their mission. That seemed strange. My sixth sense told me that something was wrong. The colonel left but returned shortly with a message from the commander that he wished to see me.

"Maybe he wants to prevent his son from getting mixed up with a dancer," Erika quipped. Dancers, enter-

221

tainers and artists were generally welcome at parties and banquets, but not in certain social and family circles.

Biting my lip, not knowing what to expect, I walked into the commandant's office. A tall, trim, gray-haired man approached me with outstretched hands and a pleasant smile. "So, you are the young lady my son told me about. Never met you before, have I?"

"I've never had the pleasure," I answered politely, all the while studying his face. Maybe everything was all right, and Alex really was just late.

"I am sorry to have to tell you. Alex is not coming back," the commandant said and drew up a chair. "Please sit down." He remained standing, leaning against and holding on to a desk.

"He is missing?" I asked.

"No. His plane exploded in midair. It was quick."

I swallowed hard but could not hold back my tears.

"I am so sorry. I am so very sorry," I stammered.

"Would you like a glass of water?"

I shook my head. What I needed was a handkerchief. I fumbled around in my purse and pockets without finding one. Alex's dad noticed and handed me his. He put his hands on my shoulders and said, "I am sure you understand why I won't join your group this evening. You are all very brave to come here to the front and deserve our overwhelming respect and gratitude. I apologize for my absence. Please pass that on to your colleagues."

I rose to leave and stretched out my hand. "Thank you for seeing me, and for telling me," I said quietly.

When I returned, our group was ready to leave. Most of the men from the fighter squadron were too drunk to care anyway, and Alex's friends had made only a polite appearance and left. Erika, Inge, Ilse and I spent part of the night remembering Alex, remarking on how odd it felt to be with a person one moment and find out the next that he is dead. With him died part of my childhood; memories of exuberant play and innocent delights.

Pain and sadness weighed down my spirit.

Our time in Orel came to an end. Molkow's secretary had already left for Berlin. At least for the moment, I forgot about my wage dispute with Molkow. It seemed so trivial in view of all that was happening. I had mentioned the matter to Rauff, who advised me to wait till we got back to Berlin, and to keep notes and records in the meantime. There was nothing I could do about it in Russia, except make myself totally miserable, having Molkow at my throat.

Rauff and I planned to drive one last time to Ritt's lodge. I was surprised that Molkow voiced no objections to me seeing so much of Rauff. As a matter of fact, he was almost civil to me lately. This made me nervous, like waiting for the ax to fall at any moment.

All the while, the chaplain continued his amorous overtures, again and again pressing me for a date. Every day it became a little easier for me to say no to him, but my insides still fluttered when he appeared on the scene.

It was around eleven o'clock in the morning, the time when I usually walked over to the hospital to join Rauff on his rounds. I was ready to leave when the pastor suddenly appeared at the door. "Thought you might like to join me for lunch," he said. He leaned against the door jam and casually lit a cigarette.

"Oh...! I didn't expect you," I muttered awkwardly. "Dr. von Rauffer is expecting me at the hospital in a little while."

"Well, he sent me to take his place while he is detained."

"He did?" I looked at him with suspicion. Something did not add up.

"Do you find that so strange? Aren't we always together?"

Erika and the other girls had gone with the Molkows to pick up our new rations. I was alone. The heat in the room suddenly became unbearable. I could hardly breathe.

"I'm just taking you to the hospital canteen. When Rauff is ready, he will join us," the chaplain assured me.

My intuition flashed an alarm, but it seemed reasonable enough to have lunch with the pastor at the hospital, especially since he indicated that Rauff might join us there. I went with him.

"Let me show you a short cut," the pastor said. He took me out the back door of the hotel across a grassy lot between other houses and to a rear door of the hospital.

We climbed a narrow flight of stairs to the second floor and wound up at his dark office. Instead of raising the window shade, he turned on a small lamp.

"Please, sit down," he said after first fluffing up a couple of pillows on a sagging armchair. "I have to quickly take care of a few things," he explained, "but I won't be long. Make yourself comfortable. Relax." He left.

The room looked cluttered. A large table took up half the space and was strewn and stacked with papers and books. Between it and the shaded window stood a high-backed chair with wooden arm rests. On the wall to the right rose shelves crammed full with books. Behind me stood an armoire with a padlock, and to the left of me a low, small table and another chair. A cot made to look like a divan filled the corner behind the door. Inconspicuously, next to the bookshelf hung a simple wooden cross. I was about to take a closer look at his books when I heard him return.

"Here we are," he announced, setting a tray full of sandwiches on the little table before me. "Thought it would be a lot cozier to have lunch here than in the canteen, don't you agree?" He unlocked the door to the armoire, pulled out two glasses and a bottle of red wine.

"What about Rauff?" I asked, beginning to sense a plot.

"Don't worry, he'll find us," he said and poured the wine.

I really did not care for any except that I needed something to wash down the dry sandwiches.

The pastor sat down in the chair next to me. "Now isn't this nice?" he commented. "All we need is a little soft music. And, if we close our eyes, we can pretend to be somewhere else, on the Riviera, or in Venice, perhaps. Have you ever been there?"

Disregarding his question I asked him, "Are you sure Rauff is going to find us here?"

Tight as a spring, I expected him to make a pass at me. Surprisingly, he behaved. He was actually very proper, making small talk, and only once in a while threw in a little compliment, or made a reference to how well the two of us got along. He was not overdoing it and I began to relax.

He poured me a second glass of wine though I really did not want any more. "We have to drink a toast to the future where we surely are meant to meet again," he said and reached for my hand. "You and I and the world."

He talked about places I had never been, sights I had never seen, and said he wished to take me to all of them. His words painted vivid pictures of all the places I dreamed to see. Still holding my hand, he leaned close to me. I shrank back. "Don't fight it," he whispered. Life is to be lived, to be enjoyed. Let's not waste precious moments on doubts and inhibitions." He stood up and pulled me close. The wine, his overwhelming presence, visions of life as it could be, tempted me briefly to sink into his embrace, to escape the brutal reality of the times and my heartaches. I wanted to forget and not to hurt anymore. My defenses weakened, but a small voice needled, "You fool...you wretched fool. He is married. He is just another Karlemann." His lips touched my forehead, my eyes, my cheeks, my mouth. At the brink of total surrender, I suddenly panicked and squirmed out of his embrace.

"Don't fight it," he said again, "I know you want me as much as I want you."

I grabbed my purse, dashed out of the room, down the hall to the stairs and out of the hospital without stopping to catch my breath. I ran most of the way back to the hotel before slowing down to an energetic walk. "Damn! What a fool I've been. I should have known," I scolded myself, but I also could pat myself on the back. I had passed the test.

"Would you please tell me where you've been?" Erika accosted me as I entered our room. "The doctor was here, waiting at least half an hour for you. Did you forget that you had a date with him? He looked very disappointed... actually quite worried, I'd say. Regardless what everybody says, I think he is a very nice guy. You shouldn't have done that," she scolded.

"What time is it?" I asked.

"Too late to run over to the hospital." Erika read my mind as usual.

I was so glad to hear Molkow announce later that we would stop at the hospital after the show to say good-bye. This would give me a chance to explain and apologize to Rauff. Thank God, he was there. Guilt must have been written all over my face because when I approached him he immediately put his arm around my shoulder and said, "I know. He told me. He tried and he lost. I am only sad that he stole the last hours we could have spent together. I can't get away tomorrow."

"And we have to pack." I added.

Around noon the next morning we left Orel to head south toward Kursk where the heaviest fighting took place. Our friends saw us off. Rauff came also; the pastor did not.

"I'll miss you, young lady," Rauff said. He gave me a hug and kissed me on the forehead. "If ever you get to Poznan, stop at my place even if I am not there. My family knows about you and you'll be welcome anytime. Keep in touch. I'll write to you. Maybe I'll even come to see you." We both wiped away tears when the bus started up. I missed him already and felt lost without his wise counsel and friendship.

XV

When is Enough Enough?

Enroute to our next destination we came upon a garden party of sorts, put on by the Red Cross. A large white tent with the Red Cross sign stood next to a grove of trees. Nurses in blue and white striped dresses and white aprons served coffee and streusel cake to soldiers sitting around picnic tables. A manually operated gramophone cranked out typical coffeehouse music, while an old biplane circled overhead and dipped its wings in salute. Neither the weather nor the setting could have been lovelier. Green, gently rolling hills dotted with clusters of trees created an illusion of pastoral serenity, yet only miles away our troops fought the hottest battle of the region. The music from the gramophone muffled out a faint but steady roll of thunder from the front.

A stocky, gravelly-voiced nurse with slicked-back gray hair twisted into a knot atop her head seemed to be in charge. Not wasting a smile, she invited us to stay. Actually, it sounded more like an order. She wanted us to mingle with the soldiers who got a short break from the fighting to rest and clean up. We stayed for less than half an hour, because we would have been late for our next show. Making small talk with the fellows, I wondered what was going through their minds. Within hours they would be back to what they described as hell. "If I'm lucky I'll get wounded," one young fellow said to me with a forced smile. I could see the terror in his eyes.

We were scheduled to give a matinee in a small town near by. Pressed for time, we did not even stop at our lodging first and went straight to the place where we had to perform. Our bus pulled up to the side door of a solid looking stone and wood structure, standing by itself on a large, graveled site. We followed Molkow to the door. When he opened it, a horrible stench forced us back. Holding a handkerchief to his nose, Molkow made a second attempt to enter and signaled us to follow. We found ourselves in the back of a theater. It was terribly hot inside and we immediately opened windows in the dressing rooms on either side of the stage to air the place out. Covering nose and mouth, we searched for the source of the odor, sure we would find a dead, decomposing animal some place. Nothing else could smell that bad. From beyond the closed curtain came sounds as if the audience was filing into the hall already. We peeked out and could not believe what we saw. Wall to wall, from front to back stood cots next to cots with wounded in various stages of suffering and dying. Now we knew what smelled so bad. It was the blood and rotting flesh from the wounded. Our first reaction was that somebody had mistakenly booked us in here. We ran to tell Molkow. He took one look and sent for the person in charge. No mistake, he was told. The units in the area expected a show in here. While Molkow negotiated with an officer, we sat on the steps outside the stage door fanning ourselves and fighting off nausea. We could hear Molkow protesting and the officer apologizing. Overwhelmed by casualties, the officer explained, his unit simply ran out of space and had to put them in here. He pleaded that we overlook the macabre circumstances and not disappoint the troops that were waiting and looking forward to our show. After he talked to Molkow he also talked to us. Resistance melted when he challenged our dedication to "our boys." Sick enough to vomit, with perfumed handkerchiefs tied over nose and mouth, we got ready for the show.

When is enough enough? Hannimusch finished playing the overture on a piano in the wings. The curtain opened. We pranced out on the stage and whirled through our first number. At our feet a chaplain gave last rites to the dying and the medics gave shots and bandaged wounds. This was Theater of the Absurd. It was surreal; it was madness. Everything inside me recoiled.

"Where, in God's name, do we draw the line? Next they'll ask us to dance on coffins and corpses. Of course, we'll do that, too," I raged, I cried, I retched. When I refused with some of the other girls to go back on stage, Molkow steamed. Fortified by swigs from a bottle he always carried around in his suit pocket, he accused us of mutiny and treason. Hilde, already glassy-eyed from sipping on her morphine medication, stared into space. Had it not been for Hannimusch who suddenly collapsed, Molkow would have torn into us as never before. Because Hannimusch fainted, everyone's concern shifted to her. Molkow had to call an intermission.

For some time, Hannimusch had been suffering from frequent gall stone attacks, some more severe than others. We called a medic who gave her a shot. She recovered enough to finish the show which Molkow cut to just a few more numbers.

I went through the motions like a zombie. Why am I doing this? I asked myself. How far do we go to follow orders? This is wrong! This is so wrong!

Between our numbers, we ran outside for a breath of air, or to throw up. When the curtain fell, troops that packed into the rear of the hall responded with subdued applause. I left the stage ashamed; ashamed that I could be made to bend so low; to go against everything I felt and believed.

Beaten and sick, emotionally too stirred up to go to sleep, we sat around Hannimusch's bed, talked, cried, and fed her chamomile tea, brewed in an empty tin can over Hilde's spirit burner. Hannimusch required another shot and finally fell asleep. At the early light of dawn, we went to bed ourselves.

Hilde had a terrible time waking us the next day. Neither her urging nor Molkow's threats could get us to accelerate beyond a crawl. Tired, depressed, cranky, we dragged ourselves into the bus. The driver started the engine and the bus heaved into motion. He had not even shifted gears when a huge explosion shook the vehicle. Out of the rear window we saw flames leaping through a cloud of dust. The house we had stayed in was gone. It blew up, as well as other houses. The area had come under sudden artillery fire. Our driver did not pause. He gunned the engine and headed out of that town as fast as he could. Erika clutched and kissed the medallion of a patron saint she wore around her neck. Hannimusch crossed herself. "I wonder how many more times we can cheat that old bone-merchant before he adds us to his collection," she mumbled. Hilde railed at us, "Because of your dawdling! We could all be dead now."

It was not the first time that a place blew up shortly before or after we occupied it. This time, it just happened in full view.

A mid-day sun broiled the earth. Our bus tracked slowly along a furrowed road, churning up clouds of pulverized clay. This fine dust stuck to our perspiring skin, caked the membranes of nose and throat, and crunched between our teeth.

A column of armored vehicles and trucks approached. Our driver tried to steer the bus to the side of the road to let them pass, but the bald tires could not bite through the powdery sediment and spun out as if driving on ice. Weary men, covered with sweat and baked-on dirt strained to push us out of the way. This delayed us for a good forty minutes. Next, we had a flat tire, then we ran out of fuel, having to beg passing troops for what they could spare. Fuel was as precious a commodity as water is in a desert. We collected it by cupfuls to keep on going.

Hours into the journey it became clear that we would not reach Gomel before nightfall. A roadblock caused further delays and forced us to detour many miles to the north. Meanwhile Hannimusch was in terrible pain again, moaning, crying, screaming. Bedded down in the rear of the bus, we took turns holding her hand, scared she might do something crazy. Once, when her pain had become unbearable, she had tried to jump out of a second story window. What we needed was a place to rest, and a place to stay for the night.

At the first opportunity, as we passed a unit hooked up to a field telephone, Molkow placed a call up the chain of command for someone authorized to modify our orders. Finally, we were redirected to a place southwest of Briansk.

Dirty, sweaty, tired, thirsty, hungry, we arrived at an isolated farm co-op. Expecting to find few comforts, we were happily surprised, overwhelmed in fact, to find clean, decent lodgings waiting for us. Another group of entertainers, who had also become stranded, welcomed us. Heavy fighting and Russian advances created total chaos with schedules. It came true just as we had feared when we received our orders in Poznan; we were caught in the middle of it.

This outpost was like an oasis, a resting place for travel-weary troops, equipped to feed and house a company or two. For the evening meal, we joined the other show people in a sort of commons. Except for one woman, all were men, too old or physically impaired to be drafted. We exchanged information about places we had been. Briansk was under siege now, they said. Smolensk was already in Russian hands, and so were many other places where we had been or traveled through. They feared, like we did, that they would not get out of Russia alive. Their tour was only for one month. When they learned that we had been sent here for six months, they gasped. "I wish somebody would kill that lunatic and his henchmen before they kill every last one of us," said a gray-haired performer, a magician, sitting at the other end of a long table. "They don't care, they have no conscience." Leaning forward, he said with a smirk, "Did you hear the joke about Hitler flying to Berchtesgaden?

The woman sitting next to him, his wife and assistant, jabbed him hard with her elbow. "You deserve what you get, if you can't keep your mouth shut." Not being encouraged to continue by anybody, he shut up. Most of us had heard that joke before. It was one of the cruder ones that made the rounds: Hitler had an intestinal emergency on the plane, used his cap, then tossed it out the window. A peasant later found it and thought he had found Hitler's cap with his brain in it.

I sat with Erika and Inge by a corner window overlooking a small square. The sun had already disappeared below the horizon but day lingered on. A sudden commotion outside made us look up. In the square, Emmy, Ilse and the Molkows stood around a tall, blond fellow in black uniform, shaking hands, laughing. "Karlemann!"

Erika and Inge ran out to greet him. I remained seated. I could not move. It seemed so long ago that I had met him, swooned over him, and we had kissed and embraced each other so passionately. I knew I had to go out to say hello. My absence would raise questions and suspicions. I joined the others, and Karlemann and I exchanged casual hellos and shook hands. He looked haggard, run down, and in need of a shave. His hands trembled as he lit a cigarette. I was surprised at how distant I felt, almost as if he were a stranger. With a gesture of intimacy he put his hand around my waist and drew me close. I pulled away. He turned and focused on Emmy.

The fire was out. In bed later, I let tears flush away the last ashes. Hard reality had replaced girlish fantasies, ideals and dreams. I felt old beyond my years.

Karlemann left the next morning. I did not speak to him again. A day later, Hannimusch recovered and we, too, moved on. We continued performing outdoors on makeshift stages along the ever-changing front lines. Sometimes we came under fire and had to evacuate in the middle of a show. Every night now, we slept in different, bug-infested Russian huts. Scabs and welts covered every inch of my body. I never felt clean anymore. We slept on floors, on tables, with rats and livestock sharing our space. One time I awoke to Ilse's screams and stared a cow in the face. The animal had simply walked in, followed by chickens and a hog, and licked my arm with its sandpaper tongue. Ilse in the bunk below cried out hysterically, "Help! Help! Get these animals out." Frankly, I preferred the animals to the bugs any day. In spite of all our precautions--moving bunks away from walls, setting the legs of the bunks in kerosene-filled cans--the bugs simply fell from the ceiling like a steady rain. Then there were the fleas. A couple of times I slept outside on the ground, partisans or no partisans. I just could not take it anymore.

I often wondered what kept the Molkows going. They seemed to be desensitized to it all. Of course, they took the better places to stay, got the better service, swam in booze, but here on the front, even the best was sheer misery. Molkow still barked and flared into drunken rages, but cared less and less about the performances,

sinking into a state of apathy. Back stage, between em-
ceeing, he played solitaire and did not wish to be dis-
turbed. I changed the choreography of my solos. He did
not notice. But one day when I decided not to go on toe
anymore, he exploded. I showed him my raw, bloody feet
and the broken down toe shoes held together with surgical tape. He insisted I wear them anyway. That was too
much. I ripped the slippers apart and threw the pieces at
his feet. Molkow stared at me, then at the shoes, then at
me again. Finally he said, "Well...try on Erika's...or
Ulla's. Take any pair that fits you. I want you on toe,"
and he walked away.

Two weeks out of Orel we revisited Roslavl, which had
changed hands twice. Our friends, the Todt engineers,
were long gone. We stayed at the outskirts. It was close
to noon, we had just received a bunch of mail and were
reading it when a courier arrived with a message for me
from Rauff. He handed me a sealed envelope. Since this
was a little unusual, everybody gathered around as I
opened it.

"Dear Elfi," it read.
"I am on my way home on a Red Cross train.
Would like to see you once more. Found   out
you will be in Roslavl about the time the train
stops there. My messenger will take you there
if you can get away.
Affectionately, your friend Rauff."

"Oh my!" I exclaimed excitedly, "That's this afternoon."

"Molkow won't let you go," Ilse speculated.

"It's quite important that you come," the courier
urged. "The doctor had an accident. He is in bad shape."

I had noticed that the handwriting was not his, but it
had not occurred to me that he could be hurt.

"Please, dear God," I closed my eyes, "please...I can't
stand losing anyone else I care about."

The courier went with me to see Molkow. He promised
to have me back in time for the show. I had already made
up my mind that if he said no, I would go anyway. But
Rauff's messenger was smooth. He knew exactly what to
say; and probably had been coached by Rauff or the hos-

pital staff. He began by relaying greetings from the general and the quartermaster, who wanted to know how we were doing, and if they could be of any assistance. I observed with pleasure how he manipulated Molkow, who finally consented with a sour smile.

Moments later I sat in the courier's small, open car and we raced off toward the train yard. When we got there, the Red Cross train was already in and loading. We ran up and down a long chain of cars in a frantic search for the coach Rauff was in. When we finally found him, I was devastated. He lay in a cast from his neck to his feet, totally immobilized. I bent over him. "Rauff." I touched and squeezed his limp hand. "What happened? How bad is it?" He smiled. Little lakes formed in the recesses of his eyes and spilled over onto his pillow.

"It's so good to see you," he whispered. "I was afraid you might not be able to come."

"Please, tell me, what's wrong with you."

"Remember old Ritt? We went riding, I got thrown and broke my neck."

"Will you be all right again?"

His thoughts seemed to travel far away, his eyes stared into space. "I'll be all right," he finally said. He looked at me again, radiating such affection as I have seen only on my father's face. "Remember the long talks we had about life and death, and the purpose of it all?"

I nodded, trying to swallow my tears.

"After every winter comes a spring. Don't forget that. We are part of this big, cyclic cosmos. Have faith, think big, and stay the way you are."

"Rauff, will I see you again?" I pleaded.

"If I survive. I will let you know. My chances are not good."

"I won't ever forget you. You'll be part of me as long as I live," I promised.

"We had been told to leave several times already. In parting I kissed his loving eyes, buried my face in his hand and whispered, "So long my dear, dear friend. Please, don't give up. I need you."

Whistles blew. Coach doors slammed shut. One last time I squeezed his hand and had to go. I knew I would never see him again.

On the way back the courier mentioned that Dr. von Rauffer had not been expected to last this long. "I think, he hung on just long enough to see you and to say goodbye. The doctor had doubts about making it home to see his family again."

When I got back, I threw myself on the bed and sobbed. At that moment I wished I were dead, anything to stop this terrible pain that gnawed on me inside.

I often saw myself in the role of Leoncavallo's Pagliacci--the clown that had to laugh while his heart was breaking. His famous aria became my theme song: "*Lache, Pajazzo!*"

But whenever I felt sorry for myself, someone always came along with troubles worse than mine. During the next few days in Roslavl I became acquainted with a young Russian girl about my age who did the cleaning and washing in the place we stayed. She spoke German quite well, seemed very pleasant, and worked hard to please us. One day, I caught her crying and asked what was wrong. After some prodding she confided that she was pregnant by a German soldier who had to leave the area. As a Russian she had no rights, did not know how to find or contact him, and was scared to death to be left behind when the Germans retreated. She feared what her own people would do to her for getting involved with a German soldier. I could see the terror in her eyes. "How can I help?" I asked, questioning myself if there was anything I could do. I asked where she was from and if she had family. She was from Orel, she said, and her parents were dead. The only relative she had left was an aunt who lived in Minsk, but she had no way of getting there and was unsure if she would be welcome. I had to leave her, but promised to give the matter some thought.

I told Erika and some of the other girls. They, too, were eager to help. Somehow we had to find a way to get her to Minsk. At least she would be safe from the Russians for awhile. The girls and I asked around for available transports to Minsk. There were trains, but not for Russians. We needed someone to smuggle her there. Then we found out about a mail truck that left the area once or twice a week. We sweet-talked the driver into hiding her aboard and giving her a ride to Minsk. When we told the Russian girl, she fell to her knees, kissed our hands, cried and thanked us again and again. I held my breath and hoped all would go according to plans. We got her on the truck and then just hoped for the best. Helping her was therapy for me.

Buried in my purse was a bundle of unopened fan mail. Many letters came from homesick and love starved soldiers. A few even contained proposals of marriage. As I read through them I came upon one with a picture of a young enlisted man who swore he would kill himself if I did not become his bride. He was not bad looking except for his unusual eyes. They were deep set and close together. I brushed it off. We tried to answer as many letters as we could. This one landed in the fire because of its aggressive tone.

I had long forgotten about it when one day he surfaced. I was just stretching and warming up in the wings of one of those township theaters when a fellow approached me. "Remember me?" he asked.

"No." I said. "Should I?"

"I sent you a letter with a picture of me."

It was pretty dark back stage and quite noisy. Hannimusch rehearsed with a few musicians in front of the curtain. Somebody hammered nails in the dressing room walls.

"We get so many letters...and pictures, I..." Before I could finish the sentence, he put his hand over my mouth and pushed me between two large stacks of folding chairs.

"I'm AWOL," he said. "If you scream and they find me, I'm as good as dead."

He scared me. I tried to free myself, making as much noise as possible, hoping to attract somebody's attention. He was strong. He pinned me against the wall. My grunts and struggle drowned in the already present din.

"You have to go with me. We'll hide. I know where to go," he whispered.

He is crazy, I thought. Molkow? Where in hell are you now when I need you? I tried in vain to twist out of the fellow's hold. I had to think of something. Maybe I could pretend to faint. Maybe I could knock the chairs over. Maybe I could play along, calm him until he let go, then break away. My mind raced through all these options. I stopped fighting and turned quiet.

"If you don't come with me, I don't care what happens to me. If I go, you go." he muttered.

In spite of his threat, I had a gut feeling he would not harm me. I stopped struggling and he loosened his hold. He still had his hand over my mouth and my head pressed against the wall, but I was able to turn my body and brace my foot against the stack of chairs. One hard push against the stack, I thought, might knock it over and draw attention. Instead, I knocked the soldier off balance and into the other stack, which then gave way. Chairs cascaded to the floor in a clatter. People came running--stage hands, the girls, Molkow. I got away. Somebody turned on the lights. Crouched, with his back against the wall, a bayonet in hand, the fellow cowered like a cornered animal, threatening to kill anyone, including himself if they tried to close in on him. A stagehand, a soldier, diverted his attention and others jumped in and subdued him. In the light I recognized his face, those deep set, narrowly spaced eyes of the soldier whose picture I had tossed in the fire, who had threatened to kill himself if he could not marry me. Completely limp and sobbing, he was led away. I was shaken, but felt no anger toward him, only deep pity. Another young life wasted.

The weather had changed. June brought one storm after another, drowning us in torrential rains. Dust turned into mud again. Each day, conditions turned more chaotic. Army columns, tanks, guns and fleeing civilians choked the roads. We no longer had an itinerary and often performed on the spot, improvising and adapting to spaces not much larger than two picnic tables. Molkow wanted nothing to do with the planning and staging of it. He left it to us while he played solitaire.

One day he called me to his room. What have I done now? I wondered. Hilde let me in. "Egon and I had a discussion about you," she said.

Oh...oh, I thought, here it comes. I'm going to get punished, fired or demoted.

"You are high-strung and rebellious, but you also show a talent for leadership. Perhaps, if you were given more responsibility, you might learn better self-control. Anyway, Egon wants to make you Captain of the ballet."

I stood there with my mouth open and dry as desert air. I did not know what to say.

"This means," Molkow took over now, "that you have certain duties--conduct classes whenever possible, hold rehearsals, and also adapt the show to the facilities. You complained that you don't learn enough, well here is your chance."

What in hell was he up to now? I wondered. Ever since I had confronted him in Orel, he had treated me differently. He let me go with Rauff just about any time and any place. He hardly yelled at me anymore. He also kept me in most of Ulla's solos, much to her chagrin.

"You will also get part of the cigarette rations from now on to send home to your father," Hilde added.

"Well?" Molkow expected an answer.

"I...I don't know what to say," I stammered, completely taken off guard.

"A simple 'thank you' would do," Hilde smiled.

"Thank you." I forced it out, wondering what I thanked him for.

"That's all. You can think it over." Molkow dismissed me.

I slouched back to my quarters, not sure if I was promoted or sentenced. Erika waited to hear what had happened. From my expression she guessed the worst. When I told her that Molkow wanted to appoint me Captain she was surprised and immediately urged me to accept.

"But I am the youngest. Do you know where that puts me? Whatever I suggest from now on will be taken as an order. The older girls, especially Ulla and Betty are not about to take orders from me."

"You don't have to do anything different from what you've been doing already. It'll be all right. They'll get used to it."

My hands turned sweaty just thinking about it. I knew my parents would be so proud of me.

"Is he giving you the combat pay, too?"

"He didn't say. I forgot to ask."

That same day Molkow put me in charge of the show. Right away problems surfaced. Everybody was on edge, including Hannimusch, who had to accompany the entire show on her accordion. The instrument was heavy. She could find no music stand and no place to sit where she could read the notes. The girls squawked about the cement floor, the long trip back and forth to the dressing area, and the way I rearranged the numbers. Inge and Erika supported me. "What do you expect from her? She has no magic wand to convert this stable into an opera house." Next, they accused me of playing favorites when I had to decide whom to cut out of a dance. Some did not like to be cut, others did not like to stay in, but the choice depended on how much time each had to change for the next number. Maybe I tried too hard. I wanted to do a good job.

"I should have never accepted this position," I told Erika later. "Molkow is probably laughing to himself."

"Oh, just give it a chance," she encouraged me. "You'll get used to it. And the kids will, too."

"I don't think this was a promotion. It is Molkow's strategy to divide and conquer. He can play solitaire, I work my fanny off and take all the heat. No! This was no promotion. It's punishment."

"Why are you always so suspicious of him?" Erika reacted, irritated.

Only two weeks into my new position and I had never felt more miserable and alone. In groups, the girls talked, laughed, then suddenly fell silent the moment I approached. If I had not written my parents already about my big promotion, I would have told Molkow to stick this job.

June rains, wind and cloudy weather ceased, the sun and heat returned and our show moved outdoors again, back to normal programming. Tensions eased.

"Guess who's going to be in the audience this afternoon," Hilde announced. "Count von Moltke and Prince von Metternich."

Both of these names were familiar to us from history as those of famous strategists during earlier wars. These men were their descendents. We peeked at them from the curtained off dressing area. The entire front row was filled with the luminaries from the military and nobility. A soldier rattled off their names and pointed them out.

After the show many came to shake our hands. They thanked us, and signed our journals.

At a reception later, Ilse was in her glory among the generals, counts, dukes, and barons. We grouped around a piano and joined in a sing-along of college songs and old battle hymns. Ilse sang the loudest. Somebody flattered her about her strong voice, which was all the encouragement she needed to offer to sing an aria from *La Boheme,* the only one she really knew.

"Oh, there she goes again," Erika winced. We felt embarrassed for her.

A group of young officers had become rowdy. Molkow was drunk. Hilde thought we should retire.

We stayed in a stone house with many small-paned windows all around and a huge fireplace in the center. While it was still light outside we decided to wash up, curl our hair and then go to bed early for a change to save the only candle we had left. A pounding on the door and men's voices begging to let them in disrupted our plans. After checking that windows and the door were locked, we tried for awhile to ignore them and went on with what we were doing. Suddenly we heard footsteps on the roof. "What the heck is going on," we asked ourselves. Pebbles bounced down the chimney and landed in the ashes of the fireplace. Outside we heard men laughing. Next we heard a scraping and knocking coming from the chimney flue. Soon we saw a boot, then two legs kicking, then a soot-covered man came crashing down into the fireplace. He yelled up to his cronies to feed him down a bottle on a string. The guy was stone drunk. We figured that together we could boot him out, but at the door were others waiting to come in.

"I think we have a problem," Emmy laughed. There was no point trying to reason with these crazed men. To get rid of them we needed help.

"What if you kept them at the door, pretending to open it, while I climb out of a window on the other side," I suggested. Since nobody came up with a better idea, we took the chance. It worked. Unseen by them I ran next door but found only a bare-chested corporal. "Can you help us," I asked and explained the situation briefly. "Heck! They are officers. What can I do," he replied.

240

"You have just been promoted to General. Go out there and order them away," I proposed jokingly. The corporal's face twisted into a sheepish grin. He grabbed a towel off a hook, draped it over his shoulder, stretched to his full, impressive height and strode out. "*Famoos!* Anyone still here 30 seconds from now will report to me personally tomorrow," he bellowed.

"Thank you Herr General," I said loudly so the men could hear me. I heard heels click and, "Jawohl, Herr General," and then they were gone. Even in their stupor they still followed orders.

Meanwhile, the drunk who had dropped in on us through the chimney had passed out. The corporal lifted him over his shoulder and carried him off. Before he left he made us swear not to divulge his identity. He would be in deep trouble for impersonating a general.

Next morning Hilde came knocking on our door. "Pack up. Hurry. The place is being evacuated." Her face spelled alarm. Eyes wide with fear she added, "The Russians are coming. They are only a kilometer from here. Hurry!"

We threw our clothes on, stuffed things in bags and suitcases, did not even bother to comb our hair, just covered curlers with a scarf and stood outside ready to go in less time than it usually took us just to get out of bed. The bus arrived, we piled in and sputtered off in a northwesterly direction.

A few miles down the road the driver stopped, released a deep sigh and wiped his brow. Behind us the sky darkened with smoke. We heard explosions. It could have come from Russian artillery or from our retreating, bridge-burning troops. We could not tell which. This was another close call. We wondered how long our luck would hold, and if we would ever get out of Russia.

XVI

Nightmares

Orders finally caught up with us to head northwest to Chatalovka, an air force base many miles from the front. We remembered well the horrible night spent at the Chatalovka station house while en route to Smolensk. How scared we had been over every little noise the wind made, thinking that any minute the Russians would break in and slaughter us. Looking back on it, we could laugh about it now, even Ilse, the only casualty that night when one of the rickety, flea-infested bunks collapsed over her head.

Our arrival at the base drew an instant crowd of cheering men. They lifted us onto their shoulders and carried us to the officers' clubhouse where the base commander had an official welcome planned. Ten hands volunteered to do the job of two to carry our personal baggage.

"That sure beats the last time, when you, Inge and I had to haul everything," I said to Erika, quite pleased.

"Over ice and snow, and the wind whipping coal dust in our faces," Erika recalled.

Erika, Inge, Ilse, Emmy and I moved into a room directly above the officers' mess hall. Everything was squeaky clean from the white linen on the beds to the neatly folded towels next to white enamel washbowls. A far cry, from the old gunnysacks at the station and the other awful dumps we had stayed in lately. The room itself was plain, had white washed walls, a single undressed window, and a rustic door held shut by a wooden latch. The only thing missing was indoor plumbing. Two large buckets and plenty of water substituted for it. We cleaned up, changed clothes, and headed downstairs to the reception.

The stairs descended into a large lobby with a wooden wainscot, a few plants, pictures on the walls, a table with a lamp, and an upholstered bench. An Oriental carpet over the tile floor added warmth and a casual elegance. In one corner of it, a small group of musicians set up their instruments, then began to play selections from Strauss and Lehar. We mingled with the officers that drifted in, and waited for the arrival of the commandant and the rest of our group. Open French doors offered a view into a dining room with meticulously set tables and a bar along one side. The aroma of roasting meat made me salivate. These civilized, tasteful surroundings suddenly made me aware again of my appearance and my shabby clothes. "Do I look all right?" I asked Erika. I wore the same black velvet dress I had worn in Warsaw that evening with Dieter. It was in need of cleaning, puckered at the seams, and had crush marks everywhere. She looked at me, back and front, wrinkled her nose and said, "What can you do about it? If that's the best you have, it's the best you have. Guess, it's got to do." I wished I could make myself invisible. "What about me?" Erika asked and turned around slowly. "At least you have a clean blouse," I said. She wore a navy blue, pleated skirt with it, with a few extra creases where none should have been.

The rest of our group straggled in. Hilde wore a black skirt with a white, swallowtail lace jacket. She looked elegant. So did Hannimusch, in a dark lavender silk dress with a stand-up collar and a deep V line front.

The commandant arrived and we followed him into the dining room. Waiters, wearing dark trousers and white shirts, with towels draped over one arm, lit candles and handed out hand-printed menus. Next, they filled glasses, offering a choice of wines or aperitifs.

"This does not seem real, " I told my table partner, a pudgy captain. "It's like a dream. Whatever it is, I am thoroughly enjoying it."

"We are a little more civilized here than on the front, perhaps." He smiled at me patronizingly.

"Have you been there?" I asked innocently. "Yes! This is quite a change from the front. What a way to sit out the war," I marveled. It just slipped out before I realized what I had said.

The smile shrank from his face. He stiffened and turned to the officer sitting next to him, asking how he liked the wine. Well, I thought, I must have touched a raw spot.

The four-course dinner from soup to desserts, prepared and served with flair, matched nothing I could remember. When it came to the food, even the night with Dieter in Warsaw paled. My vocabulary dwindled to "Ummmm..." and "Uhhhh...and Ahhh." The chef, we were told, came from one of Austria's best hotels.

After dinner, the musicians changed the beat from semi classical pieces to popular songs and even some American jazz.

"You boys must have been listening again," the commander smirked and jokingly shook his finger at them. Jazz was strictly forbidden in the Third Reich, as was listening to any foreign radio stations.

"Would you like to hear the latest, *Herr Kommandant?*" the leader of the quartet asked sheepishly.

"You are determined to get me into trouble. Well, what is it?"

"It's called 'Lullaby of Broadway'. We took the liberty to translate the lyrics."

It went like this:

> "I saw a pretty girl stand
> At midnight on Broadway
> In a negligee
> At midnight on Broadway
> I asked her for a date
> At midnight on Broadway
> She smiled at me
> At midnight on Broadway
> Then she said
> I cannot go with you
> At midnight on Broadway
> I have to model underwear
> At midnight on Broadway

244

The song was an instant hit. Hannimusch immediately copied it down to add to her informal repertoire. Because it poked fun at the American lifestyle, it was also quite safe.

The agenda for the next day included a horse-and-buggy ride to a still operating Russian collective farm for coffee, strawberries and whipped cream. Some of the officers accompanied us on horseback. Leaving the base behind, we rode over seemingly endless prairie. The terrain was uneven and rough. Eventually, we saw a group of small buildings in the distance. As we came closer, we recognized the typical layout of a co-op farm--small cabins around a square, with the stables or barns at one end. In the center of this square stood an unusual contraption. At first we thought it was a well. Close up it looked like some medieval torture instrument. Two flat, large round stones the size of at least three manholes lay on top of one another, and from their center rose a tall iron pole with chains and leather straps attached to it. "It's a mill," our escorts explained. "That's where they grind the grain into flour."

"Out in the open? What did they do when it rained?" I asked. We wanted to know how it worked. "Sometimes they use oxen, horses or people, hitch them to the iron, and make them walk round and round to turn the grinding stones," we were told. I still did not understand how the grain got between the stones and where the flour came out. I wanted to know more but was herded with the others into the 'cookhouse'.

This large building had served as a community kitchen, as a washing, eating, and meeting place for the peasants before it was occupied by our troops. A huge cooking stove dominated the center of one half of the building. Shelves along the walls held dishes, bowls and kettles. Tables with benches furnished the other half. Continuous windows along one side looked out on once planted fields and flooded the room with light. Outside, curious Russian peasants gathered, looking in at us. The women wore ankle-length dark skirts with printed blouses and aprons and the traditional white cotton scarves tied around their heads. The few old men among them wore rags tied around their feet, and dark trousers knickerbocker-style with dingy, gray shirts cinched at the waist. I thought it was odd that they wore fur caps with earflaps on a hot summer day. Slowly and cautiously, they inched up to the windows, encouraged because we waved and smiled at them.

Meanwhile our hosts placed bowls full of wild strawberries, whipped cream, cruets full of fresh milk and pots with coffee on the tables and bade us to sit down and serve ourselves. I felt uncomfortable indulging myself while the peasants looked on, hoping we were not taking this food out of their mouths. My cravings, however, overcame any twinges of guilt. Fresh milk, fresh fruit, whipped cream--I could not even remember the last time I had any of it. I ate slowly, savoring every spoonful, while I listened to the incredible stories told by one of our hosts about the first German troops that came upon this isolated farm. "These peasants knew nothing about electricity. When we wired the place and switched on the lights, they fell to their knees, awed and frightened, thinking we had supernatural powers. The telephone, they thought, was a communication from the grave, a voice from the dead. Same with the radio. This is 1943, for heaven's sake, and Russia isn't some remote island in the South Seas." Perhaps, they had never seen Western women either, and that could explain their intense interest in us.

While we were at the farm, Molkow courted the quartermaster in charge of provisions back at the base. It paid off royally. Erika, Inge and I hauled boxes full of goods to Molkow's room, from canned butter, meat, liquor, to cigars and cigarettes, all goods diverted from our fighting men on the front. It made me angry.

That night we performed on a large stage accompanied by the band from the base. It felt great to be able to move, leap, and swing our arms and legs without hitting or running into each other. Dancing to music played by a competent orchestra further boosted our spirits. We moved with zest and abandon, and played the audience for all it was worth. One of our numbers was the 'Wooden Shoe Dance' from the opera *Zar und Zimmermann*, a folksy, robust dance for which we wore Dutch costumes and real wooden shoes. It ended with what we called the 'windmill,' when we linked arms in a circle, then chassed around faster and faster until, under centrifugal force, every other girl could let go of the floor and swing her legs out. Somehow, in our abandon, Emmy's shoe flew off, right into the audience. The audience loved it and roared with laughter except, maybe, the fellow who got hit with the shoe. Emmy wanted to die.

After the show, exhilarated and bubbly, we gathered in the officers' club for a drink. Erika and I did not care for most of these men, especially the fat, slobbering quartermaster who did not know where his fat hands belonged. We thought it obscene how they wallowed in luxuries, getting rounder and more overbearing, while our troops up front often went hungry. Then, during the course of the evening, they bragged about orgies they had engaged in with people from other shows. They joked about how drunk they all got, and how available the women were. I considered their talk vulgar and insulting. I much preferred the cook, the waiters and the musicians. Not only did they treat us with respect, they were also more fun.

The five of us who roomed together, vowed to be on our guard that evening. We asked the waiters to dilute or substitute our drinks with water, which they did. Nevertheless, Emmy and Ilse suddenly acted very giddy, giggly, making faces and complete fools of themselves. Erika, Inge and I became alarmed and coaxed them outside.

"Remember...you weren't going to drink tonight," I chided Ilse. "You are acting like an idiot. At least put your finger down your throat and try to heave up before you go upstairs and do it there."

"Why? I feel fine. Never felt better," she sputtered and staggered back inside. Emmy was equally defensive. Erika and I had never seen them like this. "You don't suppose that somebody put something into their drinks?" Erika worried.

It was no use talking to them. They were too drunk to understand.

Molkow, who had been drinking since morning, fell off his chair and Hilde needed help to carry him to their room in another building.

Annoyed and disgusted, Erika, Inge and I talked about what to do. We knew it was time to leave and we wanted to go upstairs, but not without Emmy and Ilse.

"Sit down. You can't go yet," my table partner protested. He tried to pull me back into my chair. While I was involved in a wrestling match with him, Erika turned to the waiters for help. "Leave it to us," they assured her. A few minutes later, a cloud of black smoke boiled out from the kitchen and someone yelled "Fire!" It was the diversion we needed. A nod from the waiters told us that it was staged. Erika, hanging on to Emmy and Ilse, signaled Inge and me to help them upstairs. We lifted Ilse onto her bed. She was out the instant her head hit the pillow. Emmy hung her head over the 'pee bucket' and puked. Meanwhile, I made sure the door was secure. I did not trust the latch and jammed the iron frame of my bed against it. The crisis downstairs had ebbed; the party was breaking up. Men stomped up the stairs past our room and down the hall. Finally we heard only a few slurred voices downstairs and an occasional boot hitting the wall from an adjoining room. Emmy had emptied her stomach and was asleep. We covered the bucket, opened the window, undressed and went to bed ourselves. I lay there, staring out at a large, bright full moon, the tension in my body eased and my mind started to drift.

A sudden commotion, a stomping of boots, grunts, laughter, then a drumming on our door, startled me out of bed.

"Open up, little kitties, the party is just starting," I heard a high-pitched man's voice croon.

Erika and Inge sat up in bed. Inge's face was white as the sheet. Her eyes looked round and dark like two coals on a snowman. We held our breath, saying nothing, hoping they would go away.

"Come on, you kittens, the wolves have come to play." Whoever the spokesman was, the other men must have thought he was being real funny, because they laughed uproariously. Suddenly, somebody threw himself against the door. I saw the latch give. Only my bed still held the door shut now, but that, too, gave inch by inch.

"Go away. Leave us alone now," I finally yelled at them.

"Oh, come now, don't play hard to get. We don't want to break down the door." The tone of the voice was now belligerent and impatient. I was afraid.

Ilse and Emmy did not stir. Inge cowered in the farthest corner on the floor covered to her eyes with a blanket. "Please, let us go to sleep. We are tired," Erika pleaded. Both of us, side by side, braced our entire body weight against the bed.

"We can't hold them. They're coming in. What are we going to do?" Erika grunted and stared at me for answers. In spite of our utmost effort, the door opened wider with each thrust.

"The bucket! I'll douse them with the bucket," I said.

"Go away!" Erika tried one more time.

One fellow tried to squeeze through the opening. Erika still pushed with all her might, though we both knew that this was a lost battle. My knees were shaking. I grabbed the bucket.

"Hold it," I warned the men, "you take one step in here and you'll get it with this bucket full of pee and vomit."

"Ha...ha...ha," the men mocked. "You would not dare." One was already all the way in, pushing the bed back, and the others crowded in behind him. There were four or five of them. I recognized my table partner and behind him the quartermaster. Erika and I backed up to the window. The door stood wide open now. I had not a split second left to think. I swung the bucket and 'swoosh' sloshed its entire contents at them. I got them good, everyone of them. Stunned, with 'sauce' dripping from their hair, their faces, and down their uniforms, they gagged, coughed, spat, and cursed and...they left. Erika and I wasted no time barricading the door again. This time we wedged parts of the broken latch underneath and jammed two beds against it, but first cleaned up the stinking mess that had spilled over my bed and on the floor. We ripped the sheet on my bed and used it and most of our water to clean up. Inge emerged from the corner shaking like a leaf. Ilse and Emmy never even moved a muscle during the entire incident. Because my bed was soiled, Erika let me share hers. It took awhile before we could calm down, but as everything remained quiet in the building, we finally did fall asleep.

Next morning we hesitated about going downstairs for breakfast, not sure what sort of trouble we were in, but no one was around except the waiters and the cook. They greeted us with laughter and cheers. "We heard what happened last night. Those slobs had it coming. Good for you." We begged them not to tell anybody, but wondered how they found out.

Drawing us into the kitchen, doubled over with glee, they told us. "The quartermaster woke up his aide in the middle of the night, ranting and raving that you girls doused him with shit. He demanded hot water to take a bath and handed his aide the uniform with puke all over it. Oh, was the quartermaster mad! But he was still so drunk that he spilled his guts, not realizing that this story would be all over the base by morning. He won't show his face for awhile. That you can be sure of."

"Our boss'll kill us if he finds out," Erika fretted.

"Hell! Where was he? What were you girls supposed to do?"

Every time the cook and waiters saw us, they started laughing anew. And all day long, soldiers asked to meet and shake the hands of the girls from the 'pee-bucket brigade'. Of course, Molkow learned what happened that night but did not say a word. The quartermaster and his cronies never came to see us off when we departed a day later.

Meanwhile, the story had been broadcast over field telephones, with embellishments, no doubt. Every unit we visited thereafter had heard and laughed about it.

From Chatalovka we headed northeast into densely wooded terrain. "Partisan country," our driver warned, keeping his helmet on and his rifle ready. It could have been the forest where the partisan got shot en route to Smolensk. For many miles we sat between the seats on the floor of the bus, afraid of snipers, especially after we heard intermittent machine gun fire and explosions.

A SS outpost deep inside the forest had requested our show. We traveled there in a convoy of armored cars with heavy machine guns mounted on top of the first and last car. The woods had been cut back on both sides of the road. Carcasses of burnt out, rusted vehicles served as a warning that this was no place to linger. We were told to keep our heads down because snipers often lurked high up in trees.

This white-knuckle experience did not end even after we arrived at the SS compound, which was fortified with guard towers and walls of barbed wire. Men from the armored car escort helped us unload and get settled in barracks. Boardwalks connected various buildings on the compound, which included an old medieval church. It reminded me very much of the one in Orel that Rauff and I had visited. Except for a few guards, the place seemed deserted. The SS unit, we were told, had gone on a mission hunting down partisans, and was expected back that evening. Meanwhile, we were advised to remain inside the buildings.

For most of my life, I had lived near a forest. The woods were my favorite playground, where I could spend hours by myself, track and watch little animals and birds, pick mushrooms, or gather bouquets of wild flowers. I was never afraid. However, looking into these woods gave me goosebumps. Danger seemed to lurk behind every tree.

It was still early in the day. My colleagues were busy with their own projects. I wanted very much to look inside that little church and I saw no harm in walking over there. Also, I had a real need to be alone and to get in touch with myself again. The everyday grind of going from place to place, the unpacking, performing, packing, sleeping and going on to the next place, almost daily facing new dangers, new challenges, pushed feelings into the background. I wanted to get in touch again with my brother, whose image threatened to fade like an old photograph beneath the faces of Rauff and Alex, and so many others who had since come and gone. I needed to acknowledge my heartaches, hidden deep and private beneath a smiling face.

Alert and cautious, I walked the short distance to the chapel. It was smaller than the one in Orel, but built in the same style except for a deeply recessed, arched portal. I walked up the few steps, opened the door and stepped from bright sunlight into the dark interior. A sickening sweet odor hung in the air. Suddenly, I felt a strong urge to turn around and run, sensing that I had trespassed into some dark, forbidden zone. Momentarily blinded by the brightness outside, I could see nothing.

Gradually, my eyes adjusted. In the dim, defused light coming from long, narrow, windows, I began to see shapes; the arches of the ceiling, the pews, the alcove of the altar, and in front of the altar..."No...no!" Horror turned me to stone. I screamed, but had no voice. In front of the altar, not more than ten feet away from me, I saw a mound of corpses, stacked like firewood. Heads and limbs of women and children dangled from the heap, some of them mutilated beyond recognition, awash in blood. The chill of death shivered through my body. I could not move and was afraid to breathe. Absolute terror held me paralyzed.

When I came to my senses, I was staggering through the woods, disoriented, panting for breath and bathed in sweat, not sure if I was awake or dreaming, back home in Munich or somewhere else. My knees buckled; I fell to the ground. Sitting there, I slowly remembered. My skin crawled when I looked through the trees and saw the church. Renewed panic gave me the strength to get up and run back to my quarters.

"Where have you been?" Erika asked, following up with, "You look terrible. Are you sick?"

"Erika...Erika..." my mouth and throat was so dry that I could not talk. "Water...please...water..." I rasped.

"Are you sick?" she asked again. I nodded.

She handed me my canteen. "Hilde was just here. Tonight's show is canceled. The troops have not come back yet. That means we have to stay an extra day. This place gives me the creeps." She looked at me, scrutinizingly. "You were gone a long time. Where were you?"

I wanted to tell her, but when I opened my mouth, nothing came out. She felt my forehead. "You better lie down."

The girls' chitchat flowed over and past me like the wind rippling through trees. In a way it was comforting. I took out paper and pencil and pretended to write a letter. Before my eyes floated the mutilated faces. Who did that? I was afraid I to learn the truth. No. It could not have been us. Not even the SS. The partisans? I remembered stories about what they did to captured Germans. I thought of the mass graves at the Katyn forest. Could the Russians have done this? Would they massacre their own people? What other explanation was there? Then I thought of the village I saw being torched by our German troops with everybody in it. "This is war. It's them or us." That excused everything. It seemed to make everything acceptable. Soldiers on either side got medals for it.

My heart, my mind was in torment. I wanted to pray, but to what God? If He did not hear even the cries of innocent children, why would He listen to my prayer?

"Oh, Rauff," I thought, "if only I could talk to you now."

"Without experiencing darkness, you can't appreciate the light," he said to me once when I told him of my heartaches.

Exhausted, I drifted off to a restless sleep.

After sundown the compound came alive. Trucks pulled in, men jumped off, unloaded equipment and hauled it away. Others walked wearily to their barracks. An hour later we got word to join the commandant and his officers at their quarters for dinner. I had to come along, though I did not feel like eating.

The officers occupied a lodge-type building among a scattering of barracks. When we arrived there, men were already seated at a narrow long table in a narrow long room, and rose briefly to greet us, clicking their heels and introducing themselves. When the commandant, a colonel, arrived, he welcomed us and apologized for having been detained. Stewards added more chairs and place settings for us. There was hardly room between chairs and walls for them to serve the food. On the menu that night was baked liver with canned vegetables and roasted potatoes. Serving and eating took place in silence. Molkow, Hannimusch and others from our group tried to start a conversation, but it died on short one-word responses from the men. I became aware of the clinking and scraping of forks and knives against the porcelain, the squeaking and scooting of chairs, and men clearing their throats a lot. I was not hungry but picked up knife and fork and poked at the food on my plate. The liver had curled up on all sides like a piece of old shoe leather and was just as tough. My fork could not pierce it. Suddenly, a piece of liver shot across the table and landed next to Ulla's plate. A few snickers escaped from our group but died in the gloomy silence. An obviously embarrassed young officer mumbled a brief apology. Any other time, in any other place this would have started a barrage of witty remarks and rounds of laughter.

Everybody concentrated again on their plates and labored to cut the pieces of meat. Suddenly Hannimusch put down knife and fork and blurted out, "I can't cut this, much less chew it. What the heck did the cook want us to do with this? Play tiddlywinks?"

With a sense of relief, others put down their utensils, also, looking toward the commandant. "Steward," he ordered, "bring the cook out here." Looking at Hannimusch he said, "You are right. It is tough as leather." The cook appeared, wiping his hands on his apron before saluting. "What did you do to this liver?" the colonel asked.

"Sorry, Herr Oberst," the cook replied snapping to attention, "I baked it an awful long time but it would not get soft. It got tougher."

Hannimusch snorted and covered her face with her hand. She shook her head. "A little longer and you could have shod a horse with it," she said. "Don't you know that this is what happens when you overcook liver?" The ice was cut. Polite chuckles swelled to hearty laughter here and there and loosened the men's tongues.

The colonel apologized for the meal and for the somber mood. "We've had a few very rough days," he explained. In individual conversations, which we rehashed later in our rooms, the men told of a raid by the partisans on the nearby village in which they killed every living creature in it. Only the Russians working inside the SS compound that night had survived. They said that the partisans wanted the villagers to poison the German food and water supply. When they did not comply, they were seen as traitors. The partisans took revenge. Then, in retaliation, the SS raided and burned their camps in the forest. From all reports, these had been bloody, gruesome and exhausting days. I still had not told Erika what I had seen in that church. I was afraid to. It was dangerous to know, to see and hear too much.

Before we retired for the night, the colonel invited Hilde and us to an early morning buggy ride around the compound. Hilde only accepted to be polite. Erika came along because I wanted to go. I thought it would help to get the horrible pictures out of my mind. Hannimush and the rest were either too scared to venture out into the woods, or did not want to get up that early.

Next morning an aide took us by car to a barn and stable in the forest. Two horses hitched to an uncovered, leather-upholstered buggy stood waitng. The colonel petted the animals as we walked up and invited us to climb aboard.

The compound was enormous with watchtowers every few hundred yards. For a while we followed a small stream that meandered through a meadow with wildflowers. Many I knew from home--forget-me-nots, daisies and buttercups. The horses seemed to know where to go. At a sunny clearing we stopped, got off and picked wild strawberries the size of my thumb--at least twice as big as back home. Everything was bigger in Russia, the land, the trees, the flowers. In the peace, majesty and fairy-tale beauty of this forest a door sprang open inside of me. Suddenly, sobs shook my body and tears started streaming down my face. Hilde, Erika, and the colonel looked bewildered on. "What is wrong?" they asked. I could give them no reason. "Leave her be," the colonel advised. "She may have things to unload." Somehow, he seemed to understand.

That evening we gave a show. The colonel thanked us afterwards and said he would see us off the following morning. Everybody was glad to leave.

The convoy to take us out of this dangerous area was late. Packed and ready to go, some of us stood out in front of the barracks and watched men hurry back and forth with expressed urgency. We waited--and waited. Molkow approached one of the SS men and asked where the colonel might be.

"He...umm...umm..." the fellow stammered, "I don't know if I'm supposed to tell you...he is dead. The commandant is dead." He said and walked off.

"Dead? What happened?" We could not believe what we heard.

255

Hilde turned white. With a blank stare and trembling voice she recalled, "He said he would be here to see us off."

I had to sit down.

The armored cars assembled. A young captain reported that everything was ready, that our baggage could be loaded and we could take off. He evaded any and all questions about the colonel's death, saying he did not know the circumstances. But as we stood waiting to climb into the cars, a man from the convoy told us. "We found him this morning in the stable. He had hung himself."

"Just last night," Hilde told the informant, "he promised to see us off."

"Never know what's going on inside a person. Don't know if I could stomach what he had to the last few days, first the killings in the village, then the raid...it must have been gruesome.

This explained the somber and strange behavior of the men at dinner after they came back from their mission. Erika threw me a concerned glance. After the buggy ride I finally had shared my secret with her.

The convoy left us where they had picked us up and we continued on through the woods by bus. Every few hundred yards we passed a log tower with armed guards. Suddenly there were towers but no more guards. The dirt road narrowed to a trail with deep, water-filled ruts. It was stop and go. Tall, dense evergreens filtered out the light. The driver scanned the tops of trees and we sat in our seats like statues. Suddenly the engine made a strange noise. "Damn it! That's all I need," the driver growled. He kept on going. "If we just make it out of these damn woods, I'd feel a lot safer." The engine roared, the wheels stopped turning. We were stuck. He killed the engine, jumped out and looked under the hood. With a helpless gesture he said, "I can't fix this. Guess I have to go for help." He figured that we had traveled about ten kilometers since the last manned watchtower. It would take him about two hours to get back there on foot. He had no choice. Not quite sure if this was even the right road, he wanted to go back rather than venture ahead. He took his rifle and handed Molkow a revolver. "Just in case a Russkie sneaks up on you," he said and marched off. That did not make us feel safer; if anything, it scared us even more.

"What a spot to be in," Hilde muttered low, her large green eyes widening with panic. We jerked at every shadow or crackle of a branch. Hannimusch usually helped us through many tense moments with her dry wit, but even she finally broke down and cried. Only Hilde never cried, at least not in front of us. She nipped on her medicine instead. Erika, Inge and I held hands. "We'll make it. We'll make it," I whispered to them, trying to reassure myself as much as them. I no longer had the same faith in my intuition. Fear ruled now. My legs chattered like a jackhammer. I could not make them stop. When we spoke, we spoke in whispers.

Two hours passed. Some of us had to relieve ourselves but were too scared to step outside. We waited until we could hold it no longer. As quietly as we could we got off the bus and went behind bushes.

Another hour passed. Still no sign of the driver. "What if something happened to him?"

Four hours passed. "Shhhh...I hear something," Emmy whispered. "Duck," Molkow warned with hand motions. I could hear nothing other than my heartbeat. Molkow stuck his head out the door. "It's an engine. It sounds like a truck. Stay down everybody, just in case."

Before long, we saw a truck bounce toward us, one of ours, thank God. On the back a soldier manned a machine gun on a stand. Our driver and the driver of the truck jumped out. Relieved, we stepped off the bus and stood around while the men debated how best to proceed to hitch the bus to the truck. First, they had to clear away shrubs and small trees so the truck could pass. The men worked themselves into a sweat.

The bus was hooked up. We climbed on the back of the truck to add traction. It started to move, slowly. I think, the driver never got out of first gear. Molkow became impatient. "How far is this place to which you are taking us?" he asked. "Couldn't you have taken us there first and then got the bus?"

"It would be dark by the time we got back," the soldier on the machine gun answered.

We reached another outpost--three small cottages that once housed Russian woodsmen. It was deserted. Its last occupants seemed to have left recently and in a hurry, leaving behind a half-empty cup and a deck of dealt-out cards for four players.

Concerned that we might get stuck again if the truck's engine overheated, the men decided we should spend the night there. Besides, once the sun set, night came quickly to the forest.

So, there we were, still deep in the woods, in partisan territory, with three men, one machine gun, two rifles and a revolver to protect us. We had to lay low, could not build a fire nor light candles for fear of drawing attention to our presence. We did not feel any safer here than on the bus.

"I wish the guys would stay under the same roof with us. How would they know if somebody broke into our hut?" Hannimusch asked Molkow.

"They'll stand watch," Molkow replied.

Huddled together on bunks in the front room of this three-room house, we shared rations, cigarettes, and our fears, hoping the night would pass quickly. Nerves stretched to their limits. Remaining fully dressed, we sat up into the wee hours until our eyes kept falling shut. One after another, our troupe slowly surrendered to sleep, retreating to one of the cots. Soon everything was quiet.

As tired as I was, I could not fall asleep and stared out of the window across from me and listened to the night. I heard the deep, regular breathing coming from Erika and Emmy's bunk. My heart raced at the slightest, irregular sound like the rustling of trees, something dropping on the roof, or the creaking of a bunk. I tried every trick I knew to ban recurring images of the mutilated bodies, forcing myself to think of happy events. It did not work.

A loud, bone-chilling scream, followed by muffled sounds of a struggle jerked me up. It came from the front room and sounded like Hannimusch. I listened. Silence. Nobody moved. Had they not heard it?

"Psst... Erika?" I whispered.

"Yes."

Another scream and a desperate cry, "Help...! Help...!" In panic, Emmy tried to climb out of the window. Erika and I rolled under our cots. I could not see her in the dark but found her hand.

"Where are the men? Where is Molkow? Maybe they are all dead, that's why we don't hear anybody stir." We whispered back and forth. Seconds, maybe minutes raced by. Another scream, this time muffled. "It is Hannimusch. We can't just lie here and do nothing." I was caught between terror and guilt. "What the hell difference does it make if we die now or later?" I whispered to Erika.

"I'm crawling out there to check, Erika whispered." I did not care anymore either. My brother was dead, Rauff was gone, a whole village was dead. Living from fear to fear, from death to death was no life. If it was my turn, so be it. With sudden resolve, I crawled on all four into the other room behind Erika toward Hannimusch's bunk, stopping and listening every few seconds. I could hear her breathing and softly whimpering. Suddenly I bumped into Uschi, the gutsiest of all of us, who was already by her side, shaking her. "Hannimusch...Hannimusch...!" Once more she screamed and kicked, and flailed her arms. "Hannimusch...wake up...wake up."

"Huh? Huh?" She sat up.

"God, you scared the life out of us," I told her. She appeared confused. "It's us, Uschi and Elfi."

"Oh..." she sighed. "I just had the worst nightmare. I dreamt that a tiger jumped out of the woods and attacked me."

I did not know whether to be angry, relieved, whether to laugh or cry.

Hearing us talk, the rest of our crew appeared on the scene, including the Molkows. I turned to Betty and Ulla who slept just a few feet from her. "Why didn't you wake her up?" They were too scared, they said.

The Molkows went back to bed, but the rest of us were now wide-awake. We rehashed the terror and the relief.

The first sunrays fingered through the branches of the forest. And I had thought I would never see another day. "Death is the end of pain; also the end of joy," I remembered Rauff saying to me.

Dancing Outdoors on Makeshift Stages
Audience Includes Military Elite

Tap Dance

German Officers

Pas de Deux

Parody of Military Drill

Pepi

Dancing

Waltz — Bavarian Dance

Graves of Fallen Soldiers

Townhall in Minsk

Russian Prisoners

XVII

Pepi and the Prince

Leaving the menacing darkness of the forest behind us, we now traveled through wide-open country with sun-drenched wheat fields. Gentle breezes rolled over the swollen spikes of grasses and wheat like easy waves over a placid sea. The air was sweet and warm. For a short time we rediscovered our youth, bathed and frolicked in sparkling ponds and streams along the way, lazed in the sun until it browned our skin, and picked bouquets of daisies, poppies and cornflowers to weave into our hair. When the sun touched the horizon, splashing heaven and earth with its gold, the world fell into a silent calm. No wind, no bird, no buzzing of insects could be heard, not even distant guns. We stopped what we were doing to soak in the silence, and to draw strength from the infinitude of land and sky. When night took over with cooling gentleness, crickets strummed a lullaby under the watch of a gigantic moon and a profusion of stars.

One such night we spent in the camp of a Russian Cossack unit which was fighting on the side of the Germans. Amidst a scattering of small, odd, onion-shaped tents, men wearing red-trimmed uniforms and tartan hats sat on the ground around a campfire, singing. Their voices rang out like cathedral bells, deep and rich. Fast-paced ballads told about conquests and bravery, interchanged with melancholy songs about their homeland and the loves they had left behind. It was unnecessary to understand the words to grasp their meaning. Intermittently, one or the other bounded to his feet to dance, kicking and twirling low to the ground only to leap suddenly high into the air as if jet-propelled. We watched in awe, admiring their virility, their strength and spirit, as primeval and untamed as much of the Russian landscape.

Breathing free and easy, we grew young again. We joked, giggled, and teased so much that even Hannimusch cut in on occasion with a call to order. Her hands over her ears she cried, "Children...Children...! Your prattle is wearing on my nerves." Molkow was more direct. "Shut up. Enough of this silly goose chatter."

I was still captain of the ballet. The girls had accepted me back into the fold, gradually realizing the advantage of using me as their voice to complain to Molkow. Only Betty and Ulla remained cold and aloof, especially Ulla. She never forgave me for taking over her solos, yet I had no say in this matter. That was Molkow's decision. Hilde told Ulla that it was because of his concern for her health. But Molkow also liked the compliments he received about my dancing. Ulla expressed her resentments in ridiculing me for my lack of polish and social etiquette, and by her refusal to cooperate when I had to conduct a rehearsal or workout. This led to some nasty spats, which usually ended in her calling me an ill-mannered brat, a boor, and me calling her 'schwuel'(a lesbian). I knew only vaguely what that meant, but it carried a punch.

Days went by without anything dreadful happening. We traveled on the back of an open truck over miles and miles of dirt roads, eating dust until we choked. Fresh water was in short supply. A swallow now and then from a canteen was not enough to flush the grit from our mouths and keep our parched lips from cracking. Quite often a Fieseler Storch plane saw and buzzed us, wiggling its wings and once, even a Russian 'coffee grinder' dove down and waved. We wondered how we had endeared ourselves to him.

Hopping from unit to unit, we finally came to a larger village again with a headquarters and some of the amenities that came with it. We got mail, rations, clean and bug-free housing, and occasional warm meals. At the bottom of a grassy slope, troops had built an outdoor amphitheater where army bands regularly entertained large audiences. One of these orchestras was assigned to accompany us.

A wooden, double-walled shell with a partial roof hugged the stage. The space between the walls served as a place to change between numbers, and to spy on our audiences through cracks and knotholes. Before our first performance, I scanned the hundreds of men sitting on the grass and thought I saw a familiar face. I could not place it at first but soon it came to me, It was Alfons, the son of a neighborhood storeowner. My parents had been shopping there for years. Though we knew each other only by sight, so far away from home, this was a special event. I sent him a note and we met after the show to reminisce about familiar haunts and childhood friends.

He was with a couple of friends, handsome, polite and pleasant, who made such an impression on Ilse, Emmy and even on Erika that, by mutual consent, we invited them to our place after the show. Since the Molkows were housed in a different building a distance away, it was unlikely they would check on us. We figured we were safe. Uschi and Hannimusch were interested in members from the orchestra, so we also invited some of the musicians. It promised to be fun and far more innocent than the drinking parties Molkow forced us to attend. The only problem was that all of us, including Hannimusch, shared a one-room house, and Betty and Ulla had a fit when we told them of our party plans. However, majority ruled.

We spread a blanket over a small table at the end of a row of beds, decorated it with weeds and wildflowers, placed goodies from our rations on it, then lit and placed a few candles around the room. Hannimusch kept her accordion ready. What the atmosphere lacked we made up for in enthusiasm. For once, this was a party of our own choosing with fellows we liked.

While I happily reminisced with the boy from home, I could not help noticing that one of the musicians had his eyes on me practically the whole time. When our glances met, he quickly looked away and I pretended not to no-

267

tice. Hannimusch started playing and singing and this fellow joined her in duets and arias from operettas. A pleasant Vienna accent added a special lilt and warmth to his mellow tenor voice. She delighted in the way their voices blended and so did the rest of us.

"You are truly a son of Vienna," Hannimusch complimented him. "Music seems to run through your veins." She wanted to know all about him, where he had studied, in what theaters he had performed before he was drafted, and what his plans were for after the war. The fellow--Pepi was his name--laughed. He admitted to being only a music student, but added, "I do get a lot of practice out here, maybe that shows."

The party was in full swing. We laughed and sang, and reminisced about home and better times when Emmy and Uschi, who had left to go to the privy, came running back, shouting, "Molkow...Molkow's coming!" Conditioned by his often brutal reprimands, we panicked. "Quick, hide! Get under the beds," we urged the fellows. "If he finds you here, he'll skin us alive...and you, too."

"Why? What's wrong?" they protested. We had no time to think. Panic-stricken, we pleaded and pushed our reluctant guests into hiding. I scrambled to empty ashtrays, blow out candles, pull blankets, pillows, and suitcases over and in front of incriminating boots and body parts. At the very last second, before Molkow burst in, I struck a relaxed pose on my bed. He took one look around the room and demanded to know "What's going on in here?" His eyes searched the room and switched back and forth from the table with the food, the still smoking candles and to us.

"We were just having a little party," Hannimusch answered him calmly. One of the fellows lay behind her on the cot, against the wall, covered to look like a blanket roll. I was too scared right then to see the hilarity of it. Any second I expected Molkow to spy a boot or head sticking out somewhere. Then Molkow noticed the wide-open window. He lunged for it and leaned out as far as he could. "Where are the men? Where are they?"

"Good luck, Egon. If you find any, send them in. The more the merrier," Hannimusch joked. She never lied.

She just rearranged the truth a little.

I held my breath. Molkow usually checked every-where, in wardrobes, under tables, behind chairs and, of course, always under the beds. But for some reason, he was stuck on the idea that the men had jumped out the window. "If I catch any of them," he threatened, "I'll report them. I'll deal with you later." I thought I saw steam pouring from his nostrils as he stomped out of the room.

"Why don't you stay awhile and join the party?" Hannimusch called after him.

We heard him stomp around outside of the house.

Oh, God! I felt so embarrassed, embarrassed for myself, for us and for the men. Molkow could make us feel so cheap as if we had done something terribly immoral or criminal. Ulla sat on her bed grinning and gloating.

"If you guys had a star or two on your lapels, or were in charge of supplies, then it would be all right. Then, Molkow would just look the other way," I explained. We waited until Molkow was out of sight before we let the men come out.

The party was ruined. Had he caught them he would have turned the heat on every one of them. However, they were not concerned about what Molkow might do to them. They were just plain angry at the way he treated us.

The next day, as we readied for the show, we could see the musicians do the same in a partially open tent beside the stage. Looking through a split in the wood, I watched this Pepi from Vienna.

Not bad looking, I noticed. He finished shaving in front of a mirror hung on the tent's center post, toweled his face and felt for spots he may have missed. I noticed his long-fingered, slender hands. Hands of an artist, I thought. He then combed his thick dark-brown, slightly wavy hair back from his forehead, donned his uniform jacket, and walked out. It was minutes to showtime.

The orchestra consisted of about twelve musicians, and many played several instruments. Pepi played the violin and also conducted, dividing his attention between directing and watching us. When I came on stage, I could feel his eyes following my every move.

"What's going on here," Erika remarked back stage.

"This Pepi has his eyes glued on you ever since last night." The other girls noticed it, too, and snickered and teased.

After the show, headquarters invited us to what they called their 'summer place', a two-story wooden house with intricate latticework and a wide, wrap-around porch. Built-in benches, made for cozy corners, invited us to sit and linger. Down a short slope along one side of the house a lazy little stream flowed into a shimmering pond. This unique house stood alone amidst fields of ripening wheat and rye. It was one of the loveliest places I had seen in Russia, from the setting to the artful architecture of the building. "What a shame," I thought, "if this place were destroyed or left to rot." Already it showed signs of disrepair--broken slats and cracking boards. I hoped it would survive the war.

A soft breeze fanned the warm, earth-scented air, carrying sounds of a violin from inside the house. Headquarters had engaged a few members from the orchestra to play for the evening. Leading them was Pepi.

Inside this enchanting place, by candlelight, we sipped river-cooled Russian champagne and listened to Pepi play and sing our favorite folk songs and hits from movies. He wandered from girl to girl, playing into her ears and making each feel very special. At certain parts in the lyrics he turned and looked at me as if the words were meant for me alone. He made me blush. The more I watched him, the more I liked him. He seemed to charm everyone, including Hilde, with his musical gifts and his personable ways.

Everything about this evening was perfect. I thought my heart would burst with happiness. Feeling giddy and lightheaded, I stepped outside, filled my lungs with the cool evening air, gazed at the stars, and thanked God for being alive.

"What are you thinking?"

I felt a hand on my shoulder. It was Pepi. He was on a break. Without turning around I told him how beautiful I thought the world was and life could be if...I did not finish. I did not want to remind myself of the war and its gruesome realities. Remaining silent, Pepi joined me in staring out into the star-studded universe. Finally he said, "I like to watch you dance, you must have noticed. You do more than please the eye. You make me want to jump up and dance with you."

A little embarrassed, I thanked him for the compliment and said, "And I love to hear you sing and play. I could listen to you forever."

After a short silence Pepi said quietly, as if thinking to himself, "Forever...I can almost imagine it."

As dawn crept over the horizon the band packed up, the party ended, and a bunch of starry-eyed kids, Hannimusch included, fell into bed hugging their pillows, dreaming sweet dreams.

We spent about a week in the same area, around the same people and the same orchestra. Under the spell of bewitching summer nights, romance flourished in the most unexpected places. Hannimusch swooned over a silver-haired major who kissed her hand, all the way to her elbow, and when he thought no one was looking, went on from there. Cupid's arrow also pierced Erika's armor, finally. I had never seen her become so unraveled as in the presence of a certain young lieutenant. Molkow diagnosed our condition as an epidemic of heat strokes. Poor Hilde! We felt sorry for her, being married to him. I had never seen Hilde and Molkow exchange any kind of affection.

I saw much of Pepi during these few days. The more I got to know him, the more I liked, respected and admired him. On long walks through wheat fields, we talked about everything under the sun and discovered that we thought alike about many things. We shared a deep reverence for nature and all its living creatures. We liked the same music, the same authors. We talked about our lives, our ambitions, our hopes and dreams. He told me about his family, especially his mother whom he idolized, and about his love for romantic Vienna. He wanted to know all about me, my life, my family, and made me promise to show him Munich when, and if he got a furlough.

Being with Pepi was like being with a best friend. We romped and teased and laughed, just being young together. And, yes, we kissed. His approach was tender, almost reverent, caring and affectionate. Besides making

271

me feel wanted, he made me feel loved and cherished.

I watched for warning signs, for a red flag to pop up, but everything seemed so right. We dreamed about the future, visualizing ourselves at the Vienna opera, he conducting the orchestra, me dancing Giselle. When I was with him I felt complete. He was that missing something I had longed for. During the hours we spent apart, I wrote him long letters only to find he had done the same with almost identical wording. Throughout the day, I found little love-notes tucked in among my things, in my pockets, suitcase, makeup-kit and under my pillow. At times, it seemed as if we could read each other's mind.

"Oh, Erika, I think I am really in love this time," I said to her.

"Again?" She furled her brows.

"This is different. Pepi...well...he is everything I dreamed of. We have so much in common."

"We'll see."

"What about you? I asked.

"We'll see." That's all she said. She was superstitious about being happy too early.

I could understand her doubts about me. My track record was certainly not very good. But I had changed. Pepi did not sweep me off my feet like Karlemann and the chaplain. I looked for inner qualities, remembering the talks with Rauff about love. He compared love to a house. "If it does not sit on a good foundation, the first storm can blow it down. Love is a place where you can feel secure."

On about the fourth day Pepi presented me with a song he composed and dedicated to me. After the show that day, he sang and the band played it for me. The melody and lyrics were as catchy as any of the many popular songs I knew. And it was written for me, only for me. Hannimusch immediately wanted to know who wrote it, where it was from, and wanted a copy.

"Sorry," Pepi said. "This song belongs to someone special."

During these few blissful days the war had been put on hold for us. Then came the hour of parting and reality struck. "When do you think we will see each other again?" I asked Pepi, holding back tears. "How much longer can this war last? Please, don't be a hero, just try to come home again."

"I'll try my best," he said. "Just promise that you'll think of me, that you will write to me. I have no right to ask more just yet."

"I will, Pepi, I will."

We exchanged pictures and our home addresses. "If you come to Vienna, look up my mother. She already knows about you," he said.

"Oh, Pepi, couldn't you just hide some place until this awful war is over?" I begged. "We both know the war is lost already. Why keep on fighting?"

"You can't be serious." He looked at me surprised.

"I've lost my brother. I've lost so many friends. I can't bear to think that I might be losing you, too."

"You would not want me to become a deserter. I'll die with honor rather than live in shame."

I knew I was grasping at straws. "But don't we have a right to a future?"

"The war has got to end some day. I'll see you in Munich when all this over," he said.

Hannimusch, Erika, and Emmy had an equally hard time saying good-bye to their friends.

"You think you finally found Mr. Right?" I asked Erika. Her face twitched, her lips quivered. She shrugged her shoulders and uttered an almost inaudible "Could be."

Ilse stood arm in arm between Alfons and his friend, flirting with both, unable to make up her mind between the two. Hannimusch sang the praises of the major, how wonderful it felt to be romanced by a 'real' man.

During our last hour together, Ivan and his coffee grinder paid us a visit. We stood in the village square and watched him circle above, looking for a target. Some soldiers scrambled to lay out a large X with rocks then yelled up to him "See if you can hit it." The pilot looked over the side of his plane, grinned, saluted, made another sweep then dropped his bomb. He missed the X by about hundred feet. The men on the ground laughed and waved him off.

Before we left, our friends wanted us to pose for pictures with them, promising to send us copies. Then, as we climbed onto the truck, the band started to play, "*In der Heimat, in der Heimat, da gibt's ein Wiederseh'n.*" (In the homeland, in the homeland, we'll see each other again.) As the truck pulled away we waved to them, and kept on waving until they were just little specks in a cloud of dust and finally vanished from view altogether.

We now counted the days when our tour in Russia would come to an end. I dared not to imagine myself back in Berlin or at home in Munich just yet. In the weeks we had left, much could happen. Every day that we survived was a gift.

These months in Russia had hardened us. They taught us to endure and to carry on in spite of the hardships, the terror and the brutalities of war. Strangely, the thought of leaving now made us sad. We felt as close to the men on the front as we did to family. It was a comradeship not found in civilian life. Under fire, in the foxholes, one quickly saw what a man was made of. In most cases, they would have given their lives for us.

While having enjoyed this short reprieve away from the war, it raged on at all fronts. It caught up with us first in letters from home. Reports from there were frightening. Hamburg had been obliterated. In the latest and one of the worst air attacks on this city, a firestorm killed thousands of its citizens in a matter of minutes. Cologne, Frankfurt, Schweinfurt, Bremen, Berlin, even cities deep in the heart of Germany had suffered a similar fate. According to the descriptions, every major city in Germany had become a graveyard.

"We'll be trading one war zone for another, when we get home." Hilde assessed the situation gloomily, adding, "IF we get home."

"Inge and I have no home left," Hannimusch sighed. Her place had been bombed out some time ago.

We headed northeast again to a place called Shisdra. Endless columns of weary Russian refugees, Russian prisoners and retreating troops clogged the roads leading west.

"Do you remember those cocky young faces in the train station in Poznan?" I said to Erika. She nodded. "Well, look at them now." The men looked tired and gaunt. Mechanically and expressionless, they set one foot in front of the other. The war had already taken most of their strength and hope.

Not having been directly on the front for a while, we did not realize how chaotic the situation had become. Troops could not retreat fast enough to escape the advancing Russians, much less get into some kind of a defensive position. Again, the earth trembled under the thunder of guns and explosions.

"From heaven to hell."

We pulled into Shisdra, a little town that had been well behind the lines not long ago. Now it dug into Russian flanks like a spike. A narrow corridor along a railroad track was the only way in and out of it.

"A good place to get trapped." Hannimusch said, looking worried. That was my fear, too.

First we unloaded our show trunks at the performance hall. Next, we checked in at the command center housed in an elaborate underground bunker. It looked like moving day in there. To the right of the cave-like entrance stood a counter stacked with boxes packed and ready for shipping. Behind it, soldiers cleared a few remaining files and papers off shelves that reached from floor to ceiling. To the left was a door marked with the Red Cross sign. Straight ahead, past an archway, we could see an area with picnic tables and benches, evidently the staff's mess hall. Along a timbered wall between counter and archway stood a few small round tables with chairs where we sat down while Mokow reported to the commandant for a briefing. When he reappeared, he seemed agitated and nervous. As always, Hilde and Hannimusch had to pry the information out of him. We learned that Shisdra had come under heavy artillery fire of late, signaling a major thrust by the Russians. Headquarters was in a hurry to move out and appropriated our truck. We would have to get out by rail as soon as an engine arrived to hook on to a string of empty cars that stood idle on the tracks. Meanwhile, we were to give one last show, to boost the morale of the troops who had been looking forward to it for so long.

Our personal luggage was still on the truck. We followed an officer out, who climbed in the cab to direct the driver to our quarters. Small houses behind stick fences lined the village street. It had been raining off and on, turning potholes into puddles and small ponds. Grass and shrubs were caked with mud and as gray as the weathered wood of the fence posts. Fresh craters, parts of trees, debris and the charred remains of a still smoldering house presented alarming evidence of recent attacks. We had to split up in pairs, sharing a house here and there with troops. Erika and I were assigned a room resembling a dark attic closet, just big enough for a double bunk. We did not bother to unpack, even if we could have. Urged on by loud rumblings--partly thunder, partly artillery--we hurried back to the bunker only a short walk away.

Erika and I took a seat at a table in front of the archway and chatted with a middle-aged major who asked if he could join us. He introduced himself as Baron von Wagner from Austria. Our conversation started over our mutual concern about the urgency to evacuate Shisdra, then led to a discussion of what we were doing in Russia in the first place.

"I can't imagine how a country as big and primitive as Russia can ever be conquered. In all of Germany, there aren't enough people to occupy, much less control it. People here can survive on nothing. Every conqueror who tried to defeat this country got a licking. When will we learn?" My comment coaxed a smile onto Major Wagner's face. He nodded in agreement.

"You are right. History should have taught us a lesson," he said and leaned back in his chair. We bemoaned the senseless killing and the destruction everywhere. Millions of lives had already been lost on both sides, and there was no hope in sight that this slaughter would end soon. "Not as long as we have this madman at the helm," the major said.

I nodded. "But what about Stalin? He is no better, if not worse?" I asked.

The major leaned forward and lowered his voice. "We could take care of that," he said. "Right now, negotiations are going on with the Western Allies that once we remove Hitler from power, to join forces with them and march on to Moscow to take care of Stalin."

Erika's eyes grew shifty and big. Holy Mary! I felt my

276

blood run cold. This man talked treason. More than treason. He talked about a conspiracy to overthrow the government. Merely by listening to it, Erika and I became co-conspirators. Oh, my God! I did not want to be part of a conspiracy. Erika and I exchanged worried glances.

The Major continued talking, giving us more details of the plan, when Hannimusch and Uschi stopped at our table, accompanied by a couple of officers who introduced themselves. I was too flustered to catch the men's names, ranks or titles. I saw us already hanging from a scaffold in front of the *Reichskanzlei* in Berlin (seat of the Nazi government). Was the major just talking to get a reaction? Or did we fall into the trap of an informer? In my mind, I went over our conversation with the Major, preceding his revelations. What did we say that would encourage him to confide in us? This man had just met us. Maybe, he is just a blowhard. Even so, my God, he must know what terrible consequences this may have for him and for us? Filled with dark anxiety, I could not help to secretly wish that there were some truth in what he said. Toward the end of our stay in Smolensk, I had overheard officers at headquarters discuss similar proposals. I long wondered why the Allies did not concentrate on getting after Hitler instead of bombing our cities and killing innocent civilians.

The two officers in the group that had joined us seemed to be friends of Major Wagner's. The one standing next to five-foot Uschi was of tremendous stature. He towered over her, and even over Hannimusch. They did not bothered to sit down with us, because it was already time to leave and get ready for the show.

On the way to the performance hall, Hannimusch and Uschi told us excitedly that the tall officer with them was Prince Burghard of Prussia. "I've never met so many blue-bloods in all my life as gathered here in one spot," Hannimusch said. "Every other one who introduced himself is either a baron, a count, or a prince." She was clearly in awe of it.

Erika and I could not talk. We only locked eyes now and then.

Original plans called for us to give one show, then move on the next morning, but headquarters had confiscated our truck and we were temporarily stuck. The hall was packed beyond its limits and a large crowd of soldiers had to be turned away. When we saw that, Molkow decided to schedule another show for the following day, since we were forced to stay anyway. We girls had no objections. It was a most gratifying experience to bring a few hours of cheer to these men.

That evening and night it rained strings accompanied by lightning and thunder, indistinguishable sometimes from the steady bark of canons. It kept us awake for most of the night. When I opened my eyes the next morning, a grayish haze from a tiny window fooled me into thinking that it was only early dawn. I turned over to go back to sleep, when Erika suddenly exclaimed with alarm, "Oh, my God! It is almost noon." I had no watch. Erika did. We both jumped instantly out of bed. Molkow expected us at the bunker for lunch.

Drenched and covered with mud to our ankles, one after another straggled into the bunker. We cleaned up in the first-aid room, then sat down at the picnic tables to a bowl of soup with rye bread dished up by the kitchen crew. Thereafter, the Molkows disappeared into someone's office, Ulla and Betty retreated into a corner to write letters, some played cards, and Erika and I sat again at one of the small tables out in front. Major Wagner was already looking for us and wanted us to join the Prince and a few other officers with Hannimusch and Uschi. The men stood gathered in a tight circle off to the side and were involved in a low-voiced, serious discussion. From their somber faces we could tell that something was amiss.

"What's wrong? Or can't you tell us," Hannimusch asked. "We are not cut off by the Russians, are we?"

"No, no! Not yet, anyway," they reassured us with a shallow smile. The conversation remained light, centered mostly around our show, but I could feel a tension in the air.

Our group dispersed. First, Uschi left with the Prince, then Hannimusch and the other officers left also, leaving Major Wagner, Erika and me.

The major then told us that the Prince had just been ordered back to Berlin. The aristocracy had come under suspicion for plotting to overthrow Hitler and his Nazi regime, and restore the monarchy in Germany. The Nazis also feared that this move would have the support of the German people. Hence, anyone with a royal connection was now in jeopardy. Many had already been arrested and charged with treason. The Prince feared the worst.

We listened to Major Wagner expound on the intrigues and conspiracies between and within political and military factions. It boggled my mind. Scared, yet fascinated, I listened. He told us of plots to assassinate Hitler that had failed. Why did he divulge so much dangerous information to us, I asked again. Either we seemed to him too innocent, too insignificant to matter, or he considered us part of this subversive brotherhood. I wanted so much to ask him, but I was just too scared. This was bigger than me; bigger than anything within my experience. I was just a little fish in the ocean.

Around three-thirty that afternoon we left for the theater. It was an hour before show time and the place was already full to capacity. When Hannimusch stepped out on the stage in her long, blue satin gown to sit down at the piano, the crowd went wild. The building shook under the stomping feet, applause and shouts of hundreds of men, drowning out crashing sounds of explosions that had grown dangerously loud and close during the day. Between the second or third number a deafening clash of thunder rattled the building, followed by several more. We could not hear the music anymore. A rumble surged through the audience, men shifted in their seats, looking around, checking the walls, the rafters and the roof. Then we realized that it was not thunder but hits from Russian artillery. The shelling increased. Molkow stopped the show and debated what to do. We looked out at the audience. Not one man rose from his seat to leave. They started to applaud.

"Well, if they aren't scared and stay put, we'll go on with the show." It was an unanimous decision and foolish heroics. When we resumed the program, the men went berserk. They clapped, shouted and stomped their feet. Before we could finish the next number a blast shattered a window; another blast blew off part of the roof. Driving rain now forced us off the stage. Water leaked into the dressing room, threatening to soak our costumes. In haste we gathered and stuffed everything into the trunks and got dressed. The shelling never ceased. Except for a few men who stayed behind to give us a hand, the theater had emptied and everybody disappeared. We did not know what to do. There was no shelter, the bunker was some miles away and we were left without transportation. We cowered into dry corners and away from flying debris, hoping that somebody would come and rescue us. It seemed like an eternity before we heard a voice.

"Hello...hello...? Is anybody still in there?"

"Here...yes...we are here," we shouted and ran toward that voice. I saw the Prince and behind him another fellow.

"Get in the cars!" they yelled. It was dark outside. I jammed with others into a commando car driven by the Prince. He jumped in, gunned the engine and roared off. Sitting on top of one another, we hung on for dear life as the car bounced and swerved around craters, fallen trees, over branches and other debris, and fishtailed through the sloppy, slippery ground. Shells exploded close enough to hit us with rocks and splash us with mud. They actually lifted and moved the car sideways. The Prince drove with his head stuck out the side in order to see where he was going. Suddenly, we hit something. It threw us from the back seat to the front seat. I hit my knee, my arm, my head. We had rammed a light post. The car was stuck. Ignoring our injuries, we frantically helped the Prince free the car. Soaking wet, covered with mud and blood, we made it to the bunker. Nobody complained about pain until we were safely inside. We saw with horror blood streaming from Betty's head and Ulla's face. Emmy limped and complained about her ankle and knee. I had a bloody elbow and knee, and a big knot on my head. Everyone else had minor bruises.

"I am so sorry...so sorry," the Prince apologized to us over and over. I knew he felt bad. He brought us tea, and blankets, trying to make us as comfortable as he could, while a medic treated our wounds. We assured him that he was not to blame. On the contrary, he deserved our gratitude for risking his life to save ours.

We spent the night in the bunker. Betty had a long gash over one eye. Ulla bled from her scalp. Also, both had signs of a concussion. My knee ballooned to twice its size. I could hardly walk.

The shelling continued through the night and part of the next day. When it stopped, Molkow's first concern focused on our costumes, Hannimusch worried about her accordion. Of course, we all worried about our suitcases with our clothes. All of it was irreplaceble.

At first glance, the street looked like the epicenter of an earthquake and seemed impassable. Soldiers with picks and shovels filled in craters and cleared away debris. Most of the houses remained standing but none had escaped damage. At least we could retrieve our personal things. Later we learned that the walls of the theater had caved in but miraculously no harm came to our equipment. All we wanted now was to get out of Shisdra while we still could. Molkow spent the day on the phone, ranting and raving. Finally, he was told that a locomotive was on its way to gather up the empty, idle cars standing on the tracks. We got permission to get on, but no promises how far we would be able to go. At that point, we just wanted to get out of Shisdra and out of the line of fire.

Meantime, the Prince tended us with much compassion, as did some of the other officers, including Major Wagner. Betty and Ulla rested on cots in the first aid room. The rest of us lounged around on picnic benches and in chairs, putting cold compresses on our bruises. Only a skeleton staff still occupied the bunker. Everyone else had left. The remaining officers were in charge of a general retreat from the area, buzzing back and forth between the bunker and the front lines. Though the Prince had orders to leave, he stayed behind because of us. We noticed that Uschi was always where he was, and *vice versa*, which made her the subject of merciless teasing. "You could, at least, pick someone your own size," we needled and laughed, not without a twinge of envy. To see them side by side was pretty funny--this stub of a girl with this giant of a man.

When we got word that the locomotive had arrived, we said good-bye to our hosts and once again thanked our hero, the Prince, for his unselfish bravery in rescuing and guarding us. Betty was still not feeling well and was told to stay off her feet. The rest of us mended slowly but steadily.

The men loaded our baggage. Once more we shook hands, hugged, and wished each other well. Ready to climb aboard, we turned and waved one last good-bye, and there was Uschi standing on her tiptoes on the running board of the Prince's car, stretching up to him while he bent down for one last kiss. Funny as it looked, we minded our manners and saved our laughter for later.

XVIII

A Long Way Home

The war had turned into a scramble to the rear. Thinned-out, under-equipped German units fought bitterly to stem the Russian tide and suffered heavy losses. We saw columns of Russian prisoners trudge west, accompanied by just a few armed guards. They shared the roads to the west with even longer columns of fleeing civilians.

Our tour in Russia was over. We had to get out while we still could. On our schedule was one last performance at the Minsk opera house, but because of our injuries, that seemed unlikely now.

Less than an hour out of Shisdra, our train stopped at a switchyard and we had to get off, baggage and all. The engine that pulled us was needed elsewhere. We watched it being hooked to another train and pull out. "What about us?" Molkow asked the man who seemed to be in charge of the switchyard. He shrugged his shoulder, too busy to answer.

The only building in sight was an engine repair shop. We hauled and stacked our baggage there. At least we got out of the rain. Molkow spent most of that day on a field phone, trying to get through to someone with the authority to get us another ride. Nobody knew what to do with us. Without travel orders we were stuck. We saw no other trains come or leave. The only engine there was a small locomotive that dismantled and then reassembled strings of idle cars. That went on for hours. We breathed steam and coal dust all day. When I blew my nose, my handkerchief turned black. Night came. Molkow was unsuccessful in his quest to find transportation. We spent the night sitting and dozing amidst our luggage, trying our best to make Betty and Ulla as comfortable as we could.

This was the first time I saw Molkow acting scared. He actually talked to us about his fears that we might not make it home. It was the first time that he dropped his armor. Maybe, behind it there was a human being after all. Though he was frustrated, he became very quiet. When the clatter of switching cars subsided, we heard the firing of heavy guns in the distance.

"They are getting closer," Molkow said. Even the tone of his voice had changed. It was no longer belligerent. We all have our limits, I thought.

Around dawn the next morning, the switchman took pity on us and, orders or no orders, put us in an empty boxcar and hooked us up to a freight train bound for Minsk, the only train to go there, he said, possibly for days to come. He threw in a couple of bales of straw for us to sit or bed on and wished us luck.

Sleep-deprived, tense and irritable, we finally arrived in Minsk. Molkow reclaimed his bulldog personality, immediately phoned headquarters and shouted into the receiver so loudly that, I think, they could hear him all the way to Moscow. A short while later, a truck picked us up and drove us to a hotel next to a plaza.

Minsk was the largest Russian city on our tour, and the least damaged, as far as I could tell. Buildings from the tsarist past with ledges and balconies stood broad and boastfully between newer, narrower, plainer ones. Like in Polish cities, monotonous shades of gray left the eye to wander in search of a patch of color, a focal point.

Molkow assigned Erika, Inge, Ilse and me to a room on the fourth floor of the five-story building. The Molkows occupied a suite on the second floor. Compared to our room, theirs looked palatial. It had a large bed, a settee, a huge, mirrored wardrobe, a dresser, plus an alcove with a round table and three upholstered chairs. Oriental carpets covered the floors. The ultimate luxury, however, was a large marble bathroom, shared with occupants of an adjoining suite. Walls, floor and furniture showed decades of wear, but after living like rats so much of the time, all this seemed extravagant to us.

Our room was nothing like theirs. It held four beds and nothing else. The ceiling was almost as high as the room was wide. Even with two windows it made me think of a box car or cage. But it did not matter anymore. We had spent many nights in worse places. Besides, we were so tired that we could have slept standing up.

We went downstairs to the lobby to get our suitcases. Across the hall from the lobby was a restaurant, the first we had seen in six months. It was closed for business, with tables and chairs stacked on top of one another. Still, the mere sight of it brought us closer to home.

As usual, Erika, Inge, Ilse and I had to carry up Molkow's bags, then help Betty and Ulla with theirs before we could ascend with ours. On the fourth floor, the stairs ended in a dark hallway extending left and right. Directly opposite the stairs hung a large, cast-iron sink, deep enough to set a pail under its dripping faucet. A few doors to the right was a single, smelly toilet. That, too, did not matter anymore. We had seen worse, and soon we would be home.

One of two windows in our room looked out at the wall of another building, the other on the street below and across to a small city park, not bigger than a large corner lot, where a few vendors had set up shop to sell vegetables and fruit. Tired as we were, that caught our interest. Our mouths watered at the mere thought of a fresh cucumber, carrot, apple or plum. At once, all four of us ran downstairs and across the street to see what they had.

The first vendor offered mostly spinach, cabbage and a few large white radishes. The next had tomatoes, cucumbers, and green apples--all items we had craved for so long. A wrinkly old woman, wearing a white scarf and a toothless smile, sat on a wooden crate behind a makeshift table and sized us up. She rose as we approached and pointed with a gnarled finger at the different baskets and bowls saying, *"dvah khleb, dvah... dvah...."* She held up two fingers. Erika pulled a wallet from her purse and took out some money.

"Nyet... nyet...!" The woman shook her head. *"Khleb... dvah khleb,"* she repeated.

"I think she means bread... two bread," I interpreted.

She lifted a basket from under the table filled with small, not quite ripe peaches. "*Tree khleb*," she said, holding up three fingers. But all we had at the moment was 'scrip' money the military used in occupied territories. "*Nyet khleb*," I told her and shrugged my shoulders. As we started to walk away, she called us back and renegotiated marks for a cucumber and a few carrots. We wound up paying a ransom for them and decided to go back to the hotel to see how much bread we could scrounge up between us. We still wanted some fruit.

"Now I understand why there is no line to buy their produce. Who can afford it?" Erika grumbled.

Back in the hotel lobby we ran into Hannimusch. We showed her our purchase and told her what we had to pay for it. "We are going back to get more but can cut a better deal if we have bread to bargain with," we told her. Her mouth dropped open, her eyes rounded. "Can you get me something, too?" she asked. "I don't care what it costs." She pulled a wad of bills from her purse. "Here," she said, "get what you can for it. I want fruit, maybe some tomatoes and a cucumber, too."

After consolidating our rations, the four of us came up with three partial loaves of bread and a can of blood sausage. With that we went back and bartered again, this time for apples, peaches, tomatoes and more cucumbers. The clerk at the counter in the hotel warned us not to eat anything without washing it first, or we would get the Russian trot. We heeded his advice and held everything under the faucet in the hallway. So eager were we to take a bite, it did not occur to us that the water from the tap might be contaminated also. Excited and momentarily revitalized, we joined Hannimusch in her room and gorged on our purchases, exchanging stories about how our cravings for certain foods had invaded our dreams.

"I dreamt the same dream over and over," Hannimusch told us, munching on a carrot, "I bought myself an apple, and every time I was about to bite into it, I woke up. Never got to taste it. It drove me crazy." We laughed because we all had had similar experiences. I had cravings for fresh, green salads and *Bretzen*, the big pretzels in Munich.

A knock at the door. Hilde came in, looking upset. Egon had just returned from headquarters with bad news. "There is absolutely no train or truck available to get us out of Russia right now, nothing at all. Egon tried everything," she told us.

"Well, how long did they say we would be stuck here?" Hannimusch asked, worried. Every day the Russians advanced by ten, twenty miles. Minsk was still far in the rear but that could change quickly. Meanwhile Russian bombers and heavy artillery pounded all support and transportation systems, making organized withdrawals impossible.

The door opened and Molkow stuck his head in. "So, there you are," he said to his wife, then announced. "We have to give a show at the opera house tomorrow."

"Egon," Hilde acted surprised. "I thought you would decline."

"Changed my mind. Why not? We can't go anywhere anyway," he answered.

"What about the girls?" Hannimusch reminded him. "Should Betty and Ulla be jumping around yet? They still get dizzy just walking and their wounds have barely healed shut."

"Ahh... in another day they'll be all right. Betty can stay out of some numbers." He dismissed her concerns with a wave of his hand and left. Hilde followed him with questions, "What made you change your mind? Isn't it kind of risky for the girls?"

"Wonder what bribe made him agree to that?" I muttered.

"Bet you, he struck a deal with somebody to get us out. The man is a strategist. He calculates everything he does," Hannimusch concluded.

Exhaustion took over. We went to bed while it was still daylight and slept straight through until the next morning.

That afternoon we went to the theater to unpack, rehearse and get ready for the show. The house was dark except for a single light in the orchestra pit. Voices and piano music drifted through the closed curtain. Back stage, an older woman with a bamboo stick conducted a ballet class. Stocky young girls wearing woolen, hand-knitted tights and socks, held on to a pipe in front of the ropes that raised and lowered scenery. We watched for awhile and shared every grunt, every stretch and strain as they sweated through rigorous *barre* work. The aging but tough ballet mistress gave them no slack. She did not hesitate to use the stick to whack somebody's behind, or a leg when she felt it was not straight or high enough. I observed with envy how clean and tight these dancers fifth positions were. Toes met heel and heel met toes. That had taken me years to accomplish and now I had lost it. The same with *developes*. These dancers could extend their legs with ease out front and side to above shoulder level. I strained to hold mine just above the hip. Feelings of frustration, anger, inferiority and self-pity churned up bitter, resentful tears. I knew I could have been as good, or better than any of them, if I had been able to keep up my training. Would I ever get back what I had lost?

When they finished with a series of *changements*--on-the-spot jumps, changing feet in the air--we broke into spontaneous applause. Molkow walked by, sneering at us, saying, "Now that is what I call elevation!" I could have spat in his face I was so mad. "They've got a ballet master. What have we got?" I snapped.

The Russian dancers curtsied and left the stage. Molkow talked to the ballet mistress for awhile. They conversed in French.

During our rehearsal, some house lights and stage lights had been switched on, revealing a magnificent theater done in brocade and velvet, with romantic, gold-leafed reliefs framing balconies and private loges. The inside of the opera house had escaped major damage, but suffered from neglect and disrepair. As so many other beautiful things, this was another treasure going to waste.

Our less than spectacular performance that night was followed by a morning of gorging on wild strawberries and cream, traded at the market for a new ration of bread. Later that day, Hilde brought us a pail full of freshly made wieners. They came from a unit that saw us perform.

After wolfing down the wieners on top of the strawberries, we felt sick. Actually, some of us had stomach cramps already the night before and blamed it on not being used to fresh vegetables and fruit. We felt miserable for most of the day, and spent the evening, then the night running to the toilet. There was no toilet paper, no paper at all. Short of ripping apart our journals, we used a washrag, soaping and rinsing it after each use.

On the fourth day we received one last delivery of mail. Our families were frantic, fearing we would fall into Russian hands unless we got back to Germany soon. But when we read about the nightly air raids at home and the destruction, we worried more about their survival than our own.

In my mail were five letters from Pepi. I read them first. They were the longest, most wonderful love letters I had ever hoped to receive. When I closed my eyes I could almost hear his voice, could feel his kiss and his touch. At long last, I also heard from Hugo, the Todt engineer from Roslavl, who now served in Italy. But there was still not a word from Dr. von Rauffer, nor had we heard from any of our friends in Orel.

Before we had a chance to finish reading the rest of our mail, Molkow barged in. "Pack up. Want you downstairs in twenty minutes. We are leaving." He was in and out before we could ask questions.

An hour later, a truck took us, baggage and all, to a train yard. Molkow and Hilde sat in front with the driver. All we knew was that a train to Brest would be leaving shortly.

"See, I told you," Hannimusch reminded us, "he was working on a deal."

The truck dropped us off at a switchman's hut where we unloaded and stacked our baggage. Single and short strings of idle boxcars cluttered acres of tracks as if someone had left and forgotten about them. Nothing moved. Molkow set out to find the stationmaster. We found out now that he had acted mostly on a tip that if we waited here where trains got assembled, it would be our best and, perhaps, only chance to get on one.

Doubled over with stomach cramps, suffering from diarrhea and having no place to go, it was sheer torture to stand around waiting...and waiting. We had no choice but to hide and squat between box cars, then use whatever paper we could find--letters, pages out of our diaries, anything. Hilde was concerned and inquired about a first aid station, but she would not share her 'special' medicine.

Molkow returned, then left again, checking here and checking there without success. Hours dragged by. It threatened to rain again. Once in a while a switchman stopped by to chat. He empathized with us. "I'd be getting out of here, too, if I could. The way the war is going, the Russians might break through any day."

I could not have cared less about the Russians right then. I was nauseated, my stomach hurt, my head pounded and all I wanted was a place to curl up.

Evening approached. "I hope we don't have to sit through another night waiting for a train?" Hannimusch groaned. Hilde looked at her, helplessly shrugging her shoulders. Finally, Egon appeared again, this time with the stationmaster. "He said we can have a box car. He'll hitch us to the next train west and mark us down for Berlin.

"All the way to Berlin in a cattle car?" Hannimusch gasped.

"Well, we may not get another chance. It's that or nothing," Molkow replied.

I believed him. He would not subject himself to such humiliation and degradation were it not a matter of life or death.

The station master lifted his cap and scratched the back of his head and said, "Sorry. I wish I could offer you something better." He then led us across a dozen or more tracks to a boxcar. Blowing a whistle, he summoned a few fellows to help with our baggage. Erika, bless her common sense, took charge of our housekeeping and asked for a few bales of straw and buckets with water and newspaper, "lots of paper," she emphasized. We stacked the trunks and suitcases on one side of the car and created a private corner for the unavoidable. When we got the straw, we spread it on the floor of the other half of the car, with blankets over it. This would be our bed as well as our living space. Molkow immediately objected to this arrangement. He was his old self again, insisting to be separated from us. However, he soon saw that it was impossible. Next, Erika sorted the buckets-- actually just large and small tin cans--the cleanest for drinking water and for washing, and the biggest for use as a toilet. The fellows gave us tablets to purify the drinking water.

Darkness descended with thunder, lightning and pounding rain. Water dripped from the ceiling and seeped in through splintered sideboards. We repositioned the buckets to catch the drips and sealed cracks with paper. We spent a hellish first night. All of us, except Molkow and Hilde had the trots so badly that we had to run in and out all night long, getting soaked, then sitting around freezing. Molkow, who insisted on bedding down nearest the door, cursed us every time we had to slide it open. Not only did it make a racket, but it also let the rain blow in. We offered to trade places with him but he refused.

Sometime in the wee morning hours, we heard the puffing of an engine, whistles, and a lot of clatter like cars slamming into one another. When it got light, we watched the activity and realized that our car was about to be hitched onto a train. "Hallelujah!"

A violent jolt knocked us over and spilled water all over the floor. We scrambled to save what was left in the cans. Since we could no longer leave our car, intestinal emergencies forced us now to use the buckets. It was embarrassing and retchingly awful. Aside from our physical misery, we had to endure Molkow's derisive comments about how he would rather share a pigsty than share this car with us.

The stationmaster said good-bye and wished us good luck. "I've put you between the middle and the end of the train. That's the safest spot if there is trouble ahead," he mentioned. He meant to reassure us. However, it only reminded us of all the things that still could go wrong. We thanked him. He blew his whistle and the train labored into motion.

"I can't believe it. We are actually rolling out of here!" Hannimusch exclaimed. Erika, Inge and I hugged and cried. At that point we had seen all we wanted to see of Russia. We closed the door part way and laid down--six of us on one side, five, including the Molkows, on the other, heads to the wall, like sardines in a can.

Tension drained away and exhaustion took over. I fell asleep.

Hours later when I woke up, I realized we had stopped. Molkow snored loudly. Everybody was asleep. I shook Erika. "We are not moving anymore," I said. Quietly and carefully we got up and climbed over Inge and Ilse to look out the door. Someone had shut it to just a few inches and secured it there with a piece of rope. I stuck my head out. "Can you see the engine?" Erika asked. "No. Can't see that far up the train," I told her. While the others slept, we thought this would be a good time to use the bucket. It was pretty full. We wanted to dump it out, but would wake up everybody in the process, so we decided to wait. Erika and I lingered by the door, peeking out, talking quietly. "What's the first thing you want to do when we get to Berlin?" I asked her. "Take a long, hot bath," she answered without hesitation. Those were my exact sentiments, too. The closest we had come to taking a bath was at the village where I met Pepi. We bathed in a little stream or under a makeshift shower soldiers had rigged up--a perforated pail filled with sun-warmed water from the creek.

The two of us stood there for the longest time. Then we heard a distant train whistle. As we had guessed, our train had stalled at a turnout to let another pass. When it did, it rattled everybody awake. Oddly, it was heading in the same direction as ours. "Matter of priorities," I sneered.

I started to feel better because I had not eaten anything for a day,. At least the griping, horrible cramps subsided, but most of us still had dysentery. The bucket smelled awful and needed to be emptied. When the train moved again, Molkow told Erika and me to pour it out. We carried it carefully to the door. Molkow moved back, watching us with apprehension. "Don't open the door too far," he warned. Erika and I grabbed the bucket, one hand on the rim, the other on the bottom and, counting "one--two--three," sloshed the contents out. Neither one of us figured what the airflow from the moving train could do. A spray of the stinky mess back-washed and covered half of our sleeping space. Molkow caught the worst of it. I expected him to throw us out with the bucket. He cursed, ranted and raved, and made Erika and me clean it up. We dared not to look at each other or we would have burst out laughing. This incident put us on everybody's shit list for a while.

During the second night, a sudden impact tossed us out of our sleep, toppling suitcases and water containers. It was pitch dark outside. We could not tell what had happened, why or where we stopped, only that we were not moving anymore. As everything remained quiet, Molkow opened the door and looked out. Erika and I lit a few candles to straighten out the mess. When Molkow saw the candles, he went berserk. "What the hell are you trying to do? Set the straw on fire? How dumb can you get?" Muttering to himself, he put his shoes on, grabbed his flash light and jumped out.

"Egon...Egon...stay in here. What if we start moving again?" Hilde called after him, but he was already gone. About ten minutes later he came back. "The engine and most of the train is gone," he reported. Only a few cars, including ours, stood on a track all by themselves. It was after midnight. The jolt had scared us wide-awake. We sat at the edge of the open door letting our feet dangle down, and enjoyed the fresh air. Moonlight outlined drifting clouds against the night sky. The air was mellow and still. Thoughts turned inward.

"Children," Hannimusch broke the silence with a deep sigh and said, "All I can say is, that anyone who survives a tour like this without losing his or her mind can survive anything." We relived some of the worst moments, when death had missed us by a hair, when we had performed in front of the wounded and dying, when bugs had eaten us alive, and when rats had shared our beds at night. We could already laugh at some of it. Soon, this would be behind us. We were heading home.

We also remembered the happy times. I thought of pleasant evenings when I had sat with Russian peasants on the steps to their homes, listening to them sing and play the balalaika, watching the setting sun spill its gold over the land and the onion-shaped spires of a Russian cathedrals. I fondly remembered the Cossack camp, the flowing wheat fields, the starry skies. I remembered the rides into the country with Rauff, and his wise and gentle guidance. Never far from my mind, of course, was Pepi. He filled my heart with dreams, with promise and longing for a tomorrow.

Into all my happy thoughts and memories, however, crept ghostly faces, faces I could never forget. Faces of young men laughing, faces of young men dying, frightened faces, mutilated faces. A deep and profound sadness attached itself to even my happiest thoughts.

Our group had fallen silent again and one after another we returned to our spot on the straw. Inge cried softly beside me. It was not hard to guess what was going through her mind. While the rest of us looked forward to going home, she had no home left to return to. I stroked her back, quite aware that any of us could soon find ourselves in the same situation.

Toward morning, when I woke up, we were moving again. I did not hear or feel our car being hooked to another train. Around noon, the train stopped again, this time at a water tower. "Hurrah!" We discovered a spigot, refilled our cans and washed up, spraying each other until we were sopping wet. It felt wonderful. Afterwards, I slipped into the last set of clean underwear and felt refreshed. A few farmhouses in the distance hinted that we might have crossed into Poland already. Soon we would be taking baths, sleeping in clean beds, and eating off clean dishes. Maybe we would even get a week off to see our families. It sounded almost too good to be true.

The landscape became more populated. Signs on houses changed from polish to German. Names now had a familiar ring. The closer we came to Berlin, the more excited we got. Ilse, Hilde, Hannimusch...everybody started to primp for our arrival.

When we reached the first suburbs of Berlin, the scene suddenly darkened. Entire streets, entire neighborhoods lay in ashes and ruin. The destruction was as bad as what we had seen in Poland and in Russia.

The train slowed to a crawl. We heard sirens. Then flak started barking at the sky. A strange hum vibrated in the air, growing louder and louder. We looked up. Between broken clouds we saw planes--hundreds, thousands maybe--like swarms of migrating birds. The earth trembled under the roar of their engines. Bombs started falling like driving rain during a thunder squall. Explosions shook the ground, though we were still miles away from the action. If the bombers held their course, we figured they would miss us. Just when we thought we were safe, the squadrons divided, banking right and left, some heading directly toward us. By now the train had stopped. We scrambled out and under it.

"Here we go again," Erika nudged our memory to when soldiers were laughing at the Russian 'rust-bucket.' Nobody laughed this time.

The deafening noise gradually subsided and shortly after, the 'all clear' sirens sounded. Shock and disbelief robbed us of words. We climbed back into the boxcar and rode the last few miles to our destination, staring out at bombed-out buildings and twisted wreckage. Dark smoke from the burning city blackened the sky.

"From the frying pan into the fire." Hannimusch summed it up.

She was right again. The worst was yet to come.

****

The war raged on for almost two more years. Finally, when the guns fell silent, Germany and Europe lay in ruins, millions had lost their lives, millions more were homeless, and millions bled and suffered on behind the iron curtain. One tyrant was dead, another rose to even greater power.

Dark secrets of the Third Reich came to light and shocked a confused, disbelieving public. What I had seen and experienced in Auschwitz, in Warsaw and in Russia took on a new and sinister meaning. I chastised myself for being so naïve and stupid, for not having realized what was going on.

As reward for the Russian tour, the military sent us to southern France, a beautiful place, untouched by war. France was a place where, for a price, one could still buy anything. Money had suddenly new meaning. Molkow still refused to pay us our combat bonuses and I did what my friend Rauff had suggested. During a lengthy illness stay in a French hospital, I had time to file formal charges against him. I was discharged and sent home with a heart murmur, never to return to the Molkow ballet. When Molkow found out about my lawsuit, he intercepted and confiscated all mail between my colleagues and me, and forbade any and all contact between them and me. Only Erika defied his orders and wrote to me. In the last of the only two letters I had received from her from Berlin, the city was under siege. She mentioned only how grateful and obligated she felt to Molkow for taking her and some of the other girls in who had nowhere else to go. Molkow, as it turned out, not only stole our money; more tragically, he stole our friendships as well. He never had to answer for his crimes. When the Third Reich collapsed, so did my case against him.

I lost all contact with Molkow and my colleagues until almost a year after the war, when I bumped into Ulla. Both of us worked for the American Special Service and met, performing in a show for the American troops. I was a featured soloist, she the assistant to a famous, incredible caoutchouc act (a contortionist whose body seemed to be made of rubber). Between Ulla and me had always been some kind of tension, and our feelings for one another had not changed. She did tell me briefly what she knew. According to her, Molkow's villa, she and everybody else in it, narrowly escaped the pillaging, plundering, raping Russians. Luckily, the division of Berlin placed them in the American zone. Hilde Molkow totally succumbed to drugs. She and Molkow divorced and, according to Ulla, Hilde walked the streets. Betty married Kurt, the doctor from Smolensk. Erika became caregiver to five children who lost their mother in an air raid. What became of Hannimusch, Inge and the others, Ulla did not know. My many attempts to contact them failed due to the chaos of the after-war years.

Six weeks before the war ended, Pepi wrote me a heart-rending letter of good-bye. Surrounded by Russians, with no way to escape, he was resigned to being killed or taken prisoner. I never heard from him again. Dr. von Rauffer also vanished from my life, as did so many of my friends. But wherever they are, they live on in my memory and in my heart.

**Order form
For an autographed
copy**

Please ship _____ copies of book

𝔇ancing to 𝔚ar

to

Name ....

Address ....

State .... Zip ....

Phone ....

Retail price $16.95

Please include $ 2.50 for shipping

Mail to:

Elfi Hornby, P.O.Box 25477

Federal Way, WA 98093 - 2377

Visit web page
http://hometown.aol.com/rauna